"I began my Zen practice in 1967 in Mel's living room, and he has been my good friend, mentor, and teacher ever since. He was an extraordinary man, but you had to look closely to see it; he didn't advertise it. What he did do was encourage people, whatever he did and wherever he went. One time in 2001 when I had become angry and discouraged about Zen, I came to his Berkeley Zen Center for meditation, and afterwards watched while Mel made his bows to Buddha. Suddenly something clicked, and tears came to my eyes. He was so completely himself, a no-nonsense, just-this American, not trying to be holy or wise, bowing just to bow. His bows brought me back and made me whole again. That morning I saw his inner light. Read this book and I think you will see it too."

—Lewis Richmond, author of *Aging as a Spiritual Practice*

"I hear my old teacher talking as if he's sitting right in front of me in the zendo. His presence is warm and breathing in these pages, kind and encouraging. In reading all the material gathered here, both the autobiographical section and the dharma talks, I was struck as never before by Sojun's genuine lack of personal ambition and his self-less dedication to sharing the dharma with his students, or rather, with whoever wanted to practice with him as a student. He didn't see them as 'his' students, although many people saw him as their teacher. He knew that nothing belonged to him. This book inspires me anew to follow Sojun's example and 'cooperate with the universal activity,' even in challenging circumstances. He practiced what he taught. His words are helpful to me in my daily life, whether I'm doing what's simple or what's difficult."

—Susan Moon, author of *Alive Until You're Dead*

"Sojun's is a voice of American Zen, inflected with a ferocious wisdom, unafraid to address our weaknesses, our foolishness, and always with gentleness. Intimate memories of Suzuki Roshi blend with the real everyday problems of today's Zen practitioners and Zen Centers. His teachings of classic Zen stories are made relevant to our lives today. Do read it!"

—Enkyo Pat O'Hara, author of *A Little Bit of Zen*

"Mel Weitsman is the pure blood running through the entire artery of Buddhism, from the Buddha to himself. When his teacher, Shunryu Suzuki, founded San Francisco Zen Center, there was little pomp and ceremony other than meditation because Suzuki Roshi wanted to leave room for Americans to reinvigorate the spirit of Zen practice he felt had weakened in modern Japan. Early on, Suzuki Roshi asked Mel Weitsman to open a zendo in Berkeley, California, which he did. For fifty-odd years Mel personified the 'nothing-special,' everyday clarity and intention of his teacher in a secular Zen practice. I know of no more trustworthy, dependable, and inspiring collection of dharma talks than *Seeing One Thing Through*, and recommend it without reservation."

—Hosho Peter Coyote, Zen priest and
author of *Sleeping Where I Fall*

Seeing One Thing Through

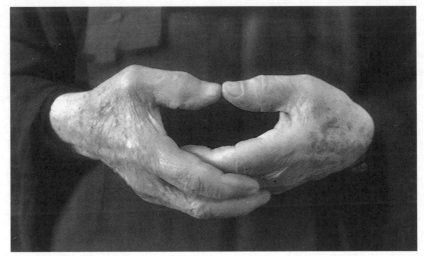

Credit: Hozan Alan Senauke

Seeing One Thing Through

The Zen Life and Teachings of Sojun Mel Weitsman

Sojun Mel Weitsman

COUNTERPOINT
Berkeley, California

First Counterpoint edition: 2023

Edited by Ron Nestor and Kika Susan Hellein, with Hozan Alan Senauke. Editorial support from Raghav Bandla and Ryushin Andrea Thach.

Library of Congress Cataloging-in-Publication Data
Names: Weitsman, Mel, author.
Title: Seeing one thing through : the Zen life and teachings of Sojun Mel Weitsman / Sojun Mel Weitsman.
Description: Berkeley : Counterpoint, 2023.
Identifiers: LCCN 2023034736 | ISBN 9781640096196 (trade paperback) | ISBN 9781640096202 (ebook)
Subjects: LCSH: Weitsman, Mel. | Buddhist converts—Biography. | Weitsman, Mel—Teachings. | Buddhism—Doctrines.
Classification: LCC BQ996.E583 A3 2023 | DDC 294.3/927092 [B]—dc23/eng/20230807
LC record available at https://lccn.loc.gov/2023034736

Cover design by Lexi Earle
Cover photograph of Mel Weitsman's ordination ceremony with Shunryu Suzuki, Berkeley Zen Center, 1969, courtesy of San Francisco Zen Center
Book design by Jordan Koluch

COUNTERPOINT
2560 Ninth Street, Suite 318
Berkeley, CA 94710
www.counterpointpress.com

Printed in the United States of America

10 9 8 7 6 5 4 3 2 1

Contents

Lectures

Section 1: Practice

Section 2: Insight/Wisdom

Section 3: Daily Life

Foreword

By Norman Fischer

IT IS WITH GREAT PLEASURE THAT I INTRODUCE THE READER to my teacher and friend of many years, Sojun Mel Weitsman.

I met Mel (I still call him that, though most people refer to him as Sojun Roshi) at the beginning of my Zen practice, in the spring of 1970—which was not far from the beginning of his. Mel was a recently ordained priest whose practice consisted of taking care of the grounds and building of the small Zen center he ran in an ordinary house on an ordinary Berkeley street. And, of course, sitting zazen faithfully every morning and evening.

In those days Mel was not a Zen teacher. But he was happy to practice Zen with whoever showed up. No internet, no advertising, just a phone book listing. The Berkeley Zen Center sign on the door was so small you could not see it from the street. There was a coffee can on a table for whatever small cash donations might be offered (though never asked for) by the young, lightly employed people who were in those days virtually the only audience for Zen practice.

As you will learn in these pages, Mel was a straightforward and completely unpretentious person, raised poor in Los Angeles during the Depression. This made him almost a generation older than me and most of the 1960s youth like me, who became the first generation of Americans to seriously study and commit themselves to Zen practice in large numbers. Mel had begun to practice half a decade or so before us, so on both counts—his age and his experience in Zen (in those days five years of practice was a very long time)—he was a senior person from the beginning. In these pages he describes the earliest days of Suzuki Roshi's teaching in San Francisco, as what came to be the San Francisco Zen Center was beginning to be formed. For the rest of his life, Mel carried these days with him; they formed his personality and his Zen life. Simplicity, dedication, and faith were their hallmarks.

This book is divided into two sections: a memoir, and edited versions of his Dharma talks. The memoir includes, besides vignettes from Mel's early life and memories of Suzuki Roshi and the San Francisco Zen Center, his impressions of Richard Baker, who as a very young man became the second abbot of the SF Zen Center after Suzuki Roshi's untimely death in 1971. Suzuki Roshi was only sixty-seven, and had been in America for twelve years.

A little-explored dimension of the sociology of American Zen is its relation to social class. Most Zen students, then as now, come from the white middle class—they are college graduates, and in most cases so were their parents. But some Zen students—Mel was one—did not attend college (he attended art school, which was more like a trade school in those days) and did not come from middle-class parentage. Though it was never mentioned, or perhaps even consciously noticed, there was a distinct class division within the Zen Center community. Mel and Richard Baker were on opposite sides of that division. This gave them oppositional views of Zen practice—and of Suzuki Roshi.

Richard Baker's father was a college professor, and Richard himself, a brilliant intellectual, had attended Harvard (though he did not graduate). In Suzuki Roshi, Mel saw himself—a plain and simple

Zen priest, solid and devoted. Richard Baker, an impressive person well connected to many of the intellectual and cultural leaders of the time, must have seen something else in Suzuki Roshi—a radical and quietly courageous foil for normative American culture. Mel's Suzuki Roshi was just doing the practice. Richard's Suzuki Roshi was remaking the world.

This difference between the two Suzuki Roshis, and the two versions of Zen that went with it—which were identical in practice and doctrine but divergent in tone and presentation—was the difference between Mel's and Richard's conditioning. So although Mel's views about Richard as he states them here may strike the reader as surprisingly critical and personal, they represent an important division not only within American Zen at that time, but throughout Zen's history: simple Zen practice for ordinary people on the one hand; Zen as a cultural vanguard on the other.

(I should mention here that Richard Baker, with whom I still enjoy a warm relationship, ordained my wife, Kathie, and me together as priests in 1980, though Mel was our first and last—our Dharma Transmission—teacher.)

Mel's rather strong remarks about Richard in this book illustrate another aspect of his character that might seem at odds with his modest approach to practice: he could be fiercely indignant when he considered something to be incorrect.

The talks section of this book represents many years of editorial work by Mel and many of his disciples to select and polish some of the many thousands of lectures he gave over the five decades of his Zen teaching career. He was still working on them with great pleasure weeks before his passing. They express in straightforward and often passionately eloquent language his basic understanding of Zen as a way of life and practice. Mel's understanding, as you will see, comes almost entirely from Suzuki Roshi. Just sit. Just let go of complications. Just live your life as it is, beyond your ideas of it. Pay attention to the world around you, but don't get caught up in it. This is the unadorned and authentic Zen message, never needed more than now, and never expressed with more integrity and stead-fastness than Mel expressed it. He was my friend and teacher for fifty years, always reliable, always kind, always patient. It is hard for me to believe he is not still here—and yet here he is, in and between the lines of this book.

Norman Fischer is a poet, essayist, and Zen priest. He began practicing with Sojun Mel Weitsman in 1970 at the Berkeley Zen Center and received Dharma Transmission from Sojun in 1988. Norman practiced for many years at the San Francisco Zen Center, where he served as co-abbot from 1995 to 2000. In that year he founded the Everyday Zen Foundation, where he now practices. His recent poetry titles include Nature, There Was a Clattering As . . . , *and* Selected Poems 1980–2013. *His most recent dharma book is* When You Greet Me I Bow: Notes and Reflections from a Life in Zen. *He lives in Muir Beach, California, with his wife, Kathie, who is also a Zen priest. For information see www.everydayzen.org and www.normanfischer.org.*

Preface

By Sojun Mel Weitsman

I HAVE BEEN WRITING A BOOK FOR ABOUT TWENTY FIVE years. A publisher asked me to write this book. He said, "Will you write a book?" And I said, "Well, there are so many Zen books. Why write another one?" And I still believe that. He said, "I'd like you to do it." So I said, "Okay." And little by little I've been doing that, and I do have some part of it done.

I said to him recently, "I'm getting old, so I'm going to give you some lectures." He said, "No." He didn't want it just to be lectures. He wanted it to be a book about my history. Some people say, "Oh, you don't have to do a book of talks, later your students will collect your talks and put together a book." And then other people say, "Oh, you don't have to do a memoir, someone else can write your biography." So, I've collected a number of talks and I continue to do that. And as I do that, it stimulates me to write my autobiography. I'm in that kind of stage.

Introduction

By Hozan Alan Senauke

HAKURYU SOJUN MEL WEITSMAN—WHITE DRAGON/ESSENCE of Purity—entered Parinirvana peacefully at home on January 7, 2021, at the age of ninety-one. Sojun once asked his teacher Shunryu Suzuki Roshi, "What is nirvana?" Suzuki Roshi said, "Seeing one thing through to the end." This is just the way Sojun Roshi lived and died.

Mel Weitsman met Suzuki Roshi at Sokoji Zen temple in San Francisco in 1964. Three years later Suzuki Roshi encouraged Mel to find a place for people to do zazen in Berkeley. Mel soon found a suitable house on Dwight Way, which he fixed up and opened for daily zazen in February 1967. In the spring of 1969, Suzuki Roshi ordained Mel in the attic zendo (meditation hall) on Dwight Way, and gave him the Dharma name Sojun (White Dragon). In December 1971, Suzuki Roshi died during the first period of zazen at San Francisco Zen Center's Rohatsu *sesshin*.

For fifty-three years Sojun Mel Weitsman quietly cultivated the fields of Zen in Berkeley. He also taught at SFZC's three practice places—City Center, Green Gulch Farm, and Tassajara. To those of us who knew and practiced with him, Sojun was a Dharma jewel hidden in plain sight. His light shines through the personal sketches and the

selection of lectures in this book. But the light of Sojun's Dharma—
what Zen Master Dogen referred to as self-fulfilling samadhi/*jijuyu
zanmai*—shone most brightly in the Berkeley Zen Center community
he led for so long.

BZC has been my home since 1985—living here, practicing, and
raising a family. After Sojun's death I inherited the temple's abbacy.
For nearly forty years Sojun and I were in almost daily contact, except
when he was away serving as co-abbot of San Francisco Zen Center,
or when my engaged Buddhist travels took me far from home. Here
at BZC, Sojun's door was always open to me and to anyone in the
community. As a matter of principle, he allowed himself to be interrupted. When someone knocked on his door, Sojun answered, "Hai!"
and turned his full attention to that person.

Trusting the Practice

Sojun completely trusted zazen and Zen practice. I think this grew
from completely trusting his teacher, Shunryu Suzuki Roshi, who
himself had the deepest faith in zazen as the manifestation of "no
gaining idea." Sojun's practice was an expression of enlightenment,
not an excursion to get there. Suzuki Roshi spoke of this kind of
practice in his book *Zen Mind, Beginner's Mind*:

> When you give up, when you no longer want something, or when
> you do not try to do anything special, then you do something.
> When there is no gaining idea in what you do, then you do some-
> thing. In zazen what you are doing is not for the sake of anything.

Each of Suzuki Roshi's students found him open, free, responsive,
and unassuming. He was as aimless as an ancient patch-robed monk,

wandering through the marketplace with "gift-bestowing hands." Suzuki Roshi's extraordinary ordinariness and ability to meet each person and thing with respect was an inspiration for Sojun and many others. Sojun moved, physically, with the same kind of ease and comfort in his own body, which itself was an expression of practice. In these lectures and throughout his life Sojun guarded this flame of inspiration. He passed it on to his students at every opportunity—with his words and with the simplest of his actions.

This is not just a matter of Sojun's or Suzuki Roshi's unique character, but of the Soto Zen school's "wind of the house"—complete trust in a practice that, as one contemporary Zen master put it, is "good for nothing."

Community

Reading this book, I am surprised to find little mention of the central presence of community or the Berkeley Zen Center sangha in Sojun's life. Whether this was by intention or oversight, I cannot say. I wish we'd had an opportunity to discuss this before he was gone. But as Master Dogen wrote: "A fish swims in the ocean, and no matter how far it swims there is no end to the water." A fish does not necessarily see the water it swims in. A Zen teacher practices completely in the sangha. I think this was so naturally Sojun's environment that it went without saying for him. Nevertheless, Sojun was completely attuned to the community he led.

When I came to Berkeley Zen Center in the fall of 1984, Sojun was in Japan receiving Dharma Transmission—authorization as a full Zen priest—from Hoitsu Suzuki Roshi, Shunryu Suzuki's son. So, my first encounter with BZC was with the sangha. There were no BZC priests other than Sojun at that time. But the sangha included mature lay Zen students, many of whom had already been practicing for ten years or more. I bow to Ron Nestor, Maylie Scott, Fran Tribe, Bill and Connie Milligan, and others. They were roughly the same age as me, but they all seemed so much more settled in the zendo and in their lives. These were my spiritual elders and mentors, ordinary (in the best sense of the word) Zen students. They all spoke highly of Sojun. His years of training guided them in his absence, and together they gracefully managed the day-to-day activities of a busy Zen center.

Sojun returned from Japan with his new brown robes in the late fall of 1984. Several months later he was installed as BZC's first abbot. My vision of BZC as a practice place and sangha clicked into focus with Sojun's return. I still looked toward the mature students for guidance, but now I could see the whole BZC mandala—a Zen circle with Sojun at the axis. He was a Buddha at the center of things: steady, patient, (generally) unruffled, and present. Sojun sat with us every day, officiated at every service, led all our *sesshins*, labored alongside us during work periods, and—like Suzuki Roshi—bowed to each person at the zendo door as we left. (A zendo is a place for zazen—seated Zen meditation. A *sesshin* is an all-day or multiday zazen retreat.)

The mysterious thing was how smoothly it all ran, seemingly without much effort on Sojun's part. This became even clearer in the years he served as co-abbot of San Francisco Zen Center, from 1988 to 1997. During those years he was gone from Berkeley quite a bit, leading practice periods at all three SFZC practice places. Without explicit instructions, we students took good care of the Berkeley practice in the ways we had been taught. Though Sojun was away, it seemed that he was always present with us. We felt taken care of.

This is a rare quality of presence that I have met in only a few others. Such people are always hard workers, of course, but they also have a mysterious ability to catalyze the activity of others, without any special exhortation or expression of need. Suzuki Roshi surely had this quality. Just by being himself, people around him felt seen and at ease. In this way Zen communities were created, and great deeds were done. Sojun also had this gift, but I don't think it was actualized until he planted the dharma flag in Berkeley.

Sojun was not a saint. He had flaws that I needn't speak of. There were students who did not always feel seen by him. But I think of him as at once a very ordinary and a very unusual person. By character and by cultivation he was remarkably even-tempered. Sojun's life and activity were marked by balance and great determination. Seeing each thing through to the end, Sojun Roshi, the White Dragon, lowered his head, strengthened his back, and forged ahead.

Like his teacher, Sojun emphasized daily zazen practice together. At BZC we have always had zazen six days a week. While Sojun recognized that lay people, with their complex lives, would sometimes sit at home, he always encouraged us to come to the zendo for our practice.

When he rented that big house on Dwight Way and set up a zendo, Sojun's expectation was that people would come for a time, learn how to do zazen, fold the practice into their everyday lives, then leave. Things turned out differently. Living with his partner Liz Horowitz and a handful of residents, Sojun created a dharma family where there was always room around the kitchen table. At first, Suzuki Roshi or one of the other Japanese teachers came over weekly for a Monday morning talk and breakfast. An informal community took shape, very "Berkeley" in its openness and inclusivity. Sojun has written, "I always envisioned BZC as a kind of grassroots endeavor supported by our members—a kind of neighborhood zendo." While some students did move on, Sojun was surprised that so many stayed for years. The "neighborhood zendo" included members with families, jobs, bad backs, and everyday joys and sorrows. In the circle of sangha, babies were born, members matured and aged. Some moved away, some came back, some died. Sojun's teaching, absorbed from his teachers, was that zazen and Zen practice includes everything—every thought and feeling, and every circumstance.

It all boils down to zazen. That was Sojun's great faith, a faith reinforced by the very shape of his life. He came to Zen as a talented and creative young man. He left this world as an old man, a Zen master, who had charted a steady course through all the storms of life, even that final storm. He was a true man of no rank, seeing things through to the end.

This Book

This book consists of two sections. The first part is a kind of memoir, a collection of autobiographical sketches and reflections on Mel Weitsman's early life—youth, being an artist in 1950s San Francisco, his coming to Zen and his early teachers there, practice at San Francisco Zen Center, and the creation of Berkeley Zen Center. Not truly a chronological autobiography, these pages offer glimpses of Sojun's life at key moments and points of departure. Reading about Mel's Depression-era childhood in Southern California, his bohemian days as a student, artist, and worker, and his encounter and immersion in Zen, we see that he was clearly in harmony with his times. Of course, there is much more about his life that we would like to know. That will come with other books.

The larger part of this work is a collection of lectures. Most of these were given at Berkeley Zen Center, and many were edited down for publication in the BZC newsletter. This considerable collection is just the tip of the iceberg. BZC has been archiving all of Sojun's lectures at BZC and elsewhere. From our earliest tapes in 1980, there are more than 2,200 individual lectures. Charlie Wilson of Engage Wisdom has worked with BZC to digitize all of these recordings, and the audio versions can be found at berkeleyZen.engagewisdom.com.

The scope of Sojun's lectures is astonishing: how to practice Zen, basic Buddhism, Zen koans, the teachings of Dogen, lessons from Suzuki Roshi, living a life of practice. Throughout his life, Sojun was deeply immersed in Dharma study. Many of the books in his personal library are bookmarked and extensively notated in his carefully penciled hand. But how he lectured week after week for years, staying fresh and engaged and encouraging—that is beyond me.

Sojun's talks underscore three principles. First, zazen is always available to us, wherever and whenever we are willing to take it up. Second, as I mentioned above, zazen is free from any goal or gaining idea, it is the practice of embracing "things as they are." Third, daily life and Zen practice are one essence that merge in zazen. He constantly taught us how to meet, include, and transform the difficulties we inevitably encounter. As Suzuki Roshi said and Sojun echoed: "If you sit in this way, you will find that your problems are valuable treasures that are indispensable for you."

Sojun tested these principles in his own life and found them reliable. These pages are a kind of transmission. Some of us were fortunate to see and know him. Readers here have Sojun's living words. May they settle deeply with you.

Hozan Alan Senauke is abbot of Berkeley Zen Center, successor to Sojun Mel Weitsman Roshi. He is former director of Buddhist Peace Fellowship, and founder of Clear View Project. Hozan serves on the advisory board of the International Network of Engaged Buddhists. In other realms, he's a musician, writer, activist, and father—not necessarily in that order. His most recent book is Turning Words: Transformative Encounters with Buddhist Teachers (Shambhala, 2023).

Like a Grinding Stone

Monks ought to behave like a grinding stone.

Chang-san comes to sharpen his knife.

Li-tsu comes to grind his ax.

Everybody who wants to have their metals improved in any way
makes use of the stone.

Each time the stone is rubbed

it wears out, but it makes no complaint nor does it boast of its
usefulness.

Those who come, go home benefited; some of them may not be quite
appreciative of the stone, but the stone remains ever content.

—from *A Mirror for Zen Students* by Master T'ui-yin
(fifteenth century)

Note: This poem was found on Sojun's bulletin board. It seems to perfectly express his life of steady practice and accessibility—always being there to guide his diverse and numerous students. It is found in *The Training of the Zen Buddhist Monk* by D. T. Suzuki.

~ ~ ~

Memories

Childhood

When I was ordained as a Zen priest on May 19, 1969, I asked my teacher, Shunryu Suzuki Roshi, "Now that I am a priest, what should I do?" He looked at me and said, "I don't know." I then asked his assistant, Katagiri Sensei, the same question. He looked at me and said, "I don't know." That answer has been the keynote, the koan, if you will, of my life ever since.

Whether one is a religious Jew, an agnostic Jew, a secular Jew, an atheistic Jew, or a happenstance Jew, there seems to be an ancient religious seed embedded in the collective unconscious that sprouts upon encountering certain conditions. My parents and my brother were inclined toward secular happenstance, while I seem to have been born, for better or worse, with a religious seed fairly close to the surface.

I was a quiet child on the one hand, and an obnoxious and noisy one on the other. I would sit in the rocking chair, sucking my finger, for hours, possibly preparing for my then unknown destiny as a meditator. When I grew a little older my friends and I played cops and robbers, cowboys and Indians, and a variety of gun-related activities. Guns and cap pistols. Bang, bang! The high point of the drama was to get shot and fall as realistically as possible. It was even more dramatic if one could find a low cliff to fall over, or a hill to roll down.

We also built forts in the soft ground of vacant lots, pulling up handfuls of grass attached to a dirt clod and slinging them at each other. Nevertheless, I was at heart a kind child. I remember finding a penny on the sidewalk and giving it to my brother, who found it curious that I would do such a thing.

In the religious realm there seems to be faith types and doubt types. I consider myself a faith type. The other members of my family seem to have been doubt types, except for my mother, who kept her spiritual feelings to herself. From an early age I respected all cultures and nationalities, as well as the equality of women and men. When I was twelve, I announced to my mother and my blind aunt Clara that I had no prejudice against any race or nationality. Aunt Clara turned her head toward my mother and in her very dignified way said, "Melvin is very broad minded." I thought she meant that I had a big head and asked for an explanation because I felt puzzled by her remark.

Even though my parents were poor, we were always well taken care of. There was always food on the table, and a certain kind of order that held things together. My family didn't complain much; they were able to take things in stride. They had a certain cultural dignity that wasn't pushed around by events. That was how my parents expressed their love for us.

I was born in Los Angeles on July 9, 1929, the year of the Great Depression. My father worked for the WPA, the Works Progress Administration, which was started by President Franklin D. Roosevelt. He was the only president I knew up until junior high. My parents loved Roosevelt because he was the hero who saved the country by ushering in Social Security, the eight-hour workday, and many other reforms.

Later my father worked as a clothing salesman in a store with a permanent sign in the window that said GOING OUT OF BUSINESS.

My mother stayed home and took care of the house and family. Sewing was her talent.

My father's family were kind of intellectual peasants. My mother's family lived in New York, and they were sophisticated and artistic. Her nephew was Zachary Solov, who was a famous ballet dancer in the 1930s and '40s. His parents could neither speak nor hear, and he always used to seat them in the front at his performances, and they would use sign language when he was taking his bows.

My mother, Leah, came to California from Brooklyn to work for my aunt Clara, who had a small business in Hollywood sewing fancy handmade underwear for the movie industry, and who eventually went blind. That's how my mother came to meet my father. After they were married she spent her time at home making beautiful afghans, quilts, and doilies. When I think of my mother, I can see her sitting on the sofa with her knitting needles in her hands, the single thread wrapped around her uplifted finger. When I think of my father, he is in his chair reading the paper.

My father, Eddie, was a hard person to know. He was opinionated, critical of almost everyone, and somewhat unapproachable. He was intelligent, but he was suspicious of educated people and would point out those he thought were phonies, especially psychologists. Although he quit school around the tenth grade, he could add up long, broad columns of numbers in his head quickly and apparently without effort. People often felt intimidated by his abrupt and critical manner. He was not ordinarily mean to us, but when we didn't obey him, he could be terrifying.

One incident that really affected my relationship with my father was when I was about sixteen. The man on the corner who had a gas station had this old car, I think it was an Essex or something, a 1920s car. He said he would sell it to me for fifteen bucks. I asked my dad if I could have it, and he said I could if I earned the money. So I mowed lawns and other odd jobs and I earned the fifteen bucks. I told him that I had the money, so could I get the car? He said, "No, I can't let you get the car." Now I understand why he wouldn't do it, but I didn't understand it then. I felt like it was a kind of betrayal. I just never respected my father after that. If he had let me buy the car, he would have had to buy the insurance. So I thought my father would never take responsibility for anything that I wanted to do, for anything that he needed to sign for. My parents wouldn't let me play football because he would have had to accept responsibility. I was just a little guy anyway, but playing football in my league was what I wanted to do.

The subject of money was never discussed in our family. This was not uncommon in the Depression days. People felt ashamed to be so poor. Our finances were no one else's business. I remember one time my mother sent me to the butcher to get a bone for the dog, and when I brought it home she put it in the soup for us. When I was in high school my mother gave me twenty-five cents a day for bus fare, and I would keep the money and hitchhike to school. That was the only spending money I ever had, except for a period when I did the family laundry once a week for a dollar. As a young boy living in Los Angeles, I had played with boys from wealthy families who lived in the Hollywood Hills. So at the time I felt underprivileged. But later I saw it as a blessing and was grateful for the education I received in not depending on money to make my life meaningful.

One time, a friend and I decided to ride our bikes down the side of the Los Angeles River after school. It was a rainy day, and since we were wet and tired, he invited me to come to his house and dry off. His family lived in a big house in the Hills. When we got there his parents were not home. He said, "Let's have dinner." We sat at this long table in the dining room, he at one end of the table and I at the other. He asked me if I wanted some buns. I told him yes. Right away a butler appeared asking what we wanted. I couldn't figure out how the butler always knew when we wanted him until my friend showed me the floor buzzer. In the meantime, my parents, worried about having missed me after school, contacted the police. The police, looking for clues, were told that someone had seen us heading toward the river. Putting the pieces together, they called my friend's house, and there we were having a great time playing tag with the butler.

Up until the 1950s kids were free to roam all over town. At that time in Hollywood there were a lot of vacant lots and empty spaces kids could roam in. Once in a while, we would scale the fence of an abandoned movie lot. There was an old sailing vessel, possibly used in a pirate movie. It was a ship above deck and a collection of timbers below holding it up. There was a Venetian canal with a few gondolas lying about on its dry concrete floor. Around the corner was the Western movie set, a street with its hotel and bar, the façades tattered and torn, leaning against their props.

I remember one time our family was riding in a car. We used to take what we called joy rides in those days. We'd get in the car and take a ride out to the San Fernando Valley, which was all orchards at that time. I was sitting in the back of the car with our dog, his face out the window—I always had a dog—and with a magazine, I think it was *Life* magazine. On the cover of the magazine was a picture of these rabbis with long beards. I didn't know who they were exactly, but I just felt this terrific affinity with them. It awakened something in me. My parents were not religious at all. The whole family was not religious. I think I went to Sunday school once, and that was it. But I had this kind of longing in me that was never fulfilled anywhere. And Sunday school wasn't it either. Then when I saw this picture, it awakened something in me, some kind of feeling which I didn't understand exactly, but I kind of knew what it was.

School Days

Until the end of junior high school, social status didn't mean so much. My peers and playmates were from the entire spectrum of the social and societal network. There was not much concern among them about who your family was or their social or economic status. I had a wide circle of friends, both boys and girls. We used to play spin the bottle and had a lot of fun kissing each other. But when I entered high school for the first time after the summer vacation, everything changed. I was shocked, rudely awakened to the fact that there were such things as social status, economic status, and dress status. The society boys had a dress code: shoes called brogues, which were dyed cordovan leather and highly polished, and starched dress shirts, pants pegged at the ankle, and maybe a key chain disappearing into the pocket. And to top it off, a crew cut. There was sports status, fraternity/sorority status (no Jews, blacks, or whatever allowed), car-ownership status, and wealth status. I missed my old group of friends. As a Jewish boy from a totally nonsocial, nonreligious, no-status family, subsisting on twenty-five cents a day of spending money, I was pretty much shut out of the social activities that I had taken for granted in junior high. I was a pretty good runner and got a letter in track. I was not interested in my academic classes, but compensated by taking as many art classes as I could. The sexual repression I was suffering also made me depressed and somewhat melancholy. We didn't have a phonograph at home in those days, or a telephone, so I sometimes went to the public library after school and listened to classical music. I also had a crush on the young librarian who sat at the music desk.

Once when I was walking someplace, I had a feeling that this was not my real life. There was a life I knew that was my life, but what I was doing was not my life, it was just my assignments. I had my assignments, but they were not my life. That was a very strong feeling I had, and I kind of had it all through school. I felt that there was something significantly missing.

Ever since kindergarten I had never seriously thought of being anything other than an artist. Throughout my twelve years of public school I was always drawing on my school papers. In junior high I won a poster contest for the cover of *The Roundup*, the annual school publication. It was a picture of a rider on his horse, with the horse rearing up. I still have a photo of it. When I got to high school, hot rods and dream cars were exciting to draw. This was a creative and imaginative side of teen society, and it was free of social status. Private autos were not manufactured in the U.S. from 1942 until 1945, so there were a lot of old Fords and Chevys, which served as raw material to modify, chop down, and create new styles that often were an improvement over the original. Besides style, there were also under-the-hood advancements. Then there were the midnight drag races. But that is another story.

So I spent a lot of time drawing pictures of cars during my classes and creating new imaginative styles. Pretty soon kids started paying me to draw pictures of their cars. That was gratifying and gave me some money to boot.

When I think about it now, while I was in high school in Long Beach, two of my best friends had physical deformities. These disparities from the norm had an effect on their personalities. Jack, who had a cleft lip, also had a fertile imagination and was always drawing. He was a wonderful and imaginative artist. We had our art as a common bond. His father was the manager of the Buick agency. Jack would drive me around in the new Buicks his dad would bring home.

Charles, who had what we then called a club foot, was a gentle and thoughtful boy. He had an older sister, and his father sold P-41 fighter planes to the Chinese government during the Sino-Japanese war. They must have been flown by General Chenault's Flying Tigers in Manchuria around the time Suzuki Roshi was there as a Japanese Buddhist priest. Charles's parents were always away. They had a nice old house and a beautiful young nanny who cared for their children.

These two friends were societal bystanders, as was I. With them I could have deep and intimate conversations about anything and everything. So, what was my disability that allowed me to have this intimacy with these two? For one thing, my being Jewish meant nothing to them. Being Jewish at that time had a stigma attached to it. Some Jews were obvious, while others could pass as "other than." I think that many Jews, as with other immigrants, gave up or hid their identity so they could move freely in society without burdening their children. Instead of yarmulkes, Jewish men wore snap-brim hats in the street. It was the time when Hitler was coming to power, and there was anti-Semitism in the air. So there was a question: Should you say you are not Jewish and be accepted, or say you are and accept the consequences? When faced with this dilemma, I felt that I could not betray my roots. In grammar school, a gang of Christian kids harassed me: "Hey kid, you Jewish? Don't you know the Jews killed Christ?" I thought that maybe they wanted to kill me in retaliation. Jews often have this kind of problem. That is one reason I didn't think of myself as being white.

Being out of the mainstream allowed us to consider the more profound aspects of life, free from peer pressure to conform. Nevertheless, it was painful to be marginalized.

Active Duty

While still in high school I joined the Marine Corps Reserve, and in 1947, after graduating from high school in Long Beach, I went on active duty with the Marines. I ended up as a maintenance mechanic on a navy airfield, checking out two F4U Corsair fighter planes every day, making sure they were ready to fly, and occasionally doing guard duty. It was a new and exciting time for me as an eighteen-year-old, joining the company of men from diverse backgrounds and living and sharing our lives together on a daily basis.

There was Captain Colby, the squadron commander. He was a tall, very handsome, and extremely kind man in his forties, well educated and upper class. His face was totally smooth, without a single wrinkle. He had the appearance of a movie actor. He would show up once in a while to check us out. But our real leader was Master Sergeant Randall. Randall was the archetypical career marine. Not tall, but always ramrod straight. He was probably in his sixties. He had a thick neck and a weather-beaten face with character creases in all the right places, along with a slightly meaty nose and ears to match. He was strict without being mean, and serious but with a sense of humor. He didn't have to do much because his presence and his integrity were enough to hold us all together. Then there was my best buddy, Pecarraro. Pec and I were the same age and the youngest of our group. It was between wars and the men were mostly older regulars. Pec was about five feet tall, with a handsome (enormous) nose, a real character. Sergeant Goshen said that Pec was the only man who could smoke a cigar in the rain without it getting wet. Goshen could also have held that title. Pec was Sergeant Randall's favorite. One day the three of us were together and Sergeant Randall said to me, "You are just an ordinary kind of guy, but Pec is unusual, something special." Although that was a little painful, I had to acknowledge that he was right. Then there was big Sergeant Roper from South Carolina. We had heated arguments about race. He once called me a "n____-lover." I thought for a moment and said, "Yes, I am." I took it as a fact as well as a compliment. He could hardly contain himself.

One day both airplanes I worked on took off and only one came back. The pilot's helmet was returned to me. It was something I had never experienced before, and it made me aware of the great responsibility of taking care of someone's life.

Art School

I wanted to be a soldier and I wanted to be an artist. I got the soldier thing out of the way and was discharged from the Marines in 1949. All through high school I spent my time drawing, and that's all I ever wanted to do. So I just continued doing that. Through the GI Bill I started at a new art school in Los Angeles called the California School of Art. But two friends told me that the real art school was up in San Francisco. I was persuaded to go with them to study at the California School of Fine Arts (now known as the San Francisco Art Institute).

So my friends and I moved up to San Francisco. This was in 1950. I wasn't even twenty-one. I remember walking around the streets of San Francisco, which were totally different from Long Beach. Long Beach had all these houses with spaces in between and green lawns, whereas in San Francisco all the buildings were up against each other, and the streets were all dirty and stained. It was cold and windy, a totally different feeling. But once I got used to San Francisco, I couldn't go back to Los Angeles.

I studied painting with Elmer Bischoff, David Park, Hassel Smith, and Ed Corbett. I also studied commercial art and design. But it was Clyfford Still who opened a path for me. As a new student I went to the opening of his show at the Metart Gallery in San Francisco, which was arranged by his older students. It was an eye-opener. I had no interest in academic art and always drew from imagination. Clyfford Still went beyond that to nonrepresentation. We called the style non-objective painting. There were other painters doing this, but Still's paintings were different, especially his more mature ones. Where Pollock was more into making effects, Still was making profound statements. Each painting stood out as an individual statement that, if you were open, would resonate in a powerful way. I studied with him for about two years until he went to the East Coast.

Under the influence of Clyfford Still, I felt a great creative freedom. Still's way was a nonteaching teaching. With this nonteaching, you as a student had to rely on your own intuitive perceptions. His way of teaching had that quality that we often associate with a mature Zen master. The students would be painting in the studio, and he would visit each one and start talking about something. He would never say a word about your painting, no criticism, no good or bad. But somehow he would communicate something that would encourage and inspire. Our style of painting was on the edge, and there we had to discover our own guidelines. Every painting was an adventure in form and color, dynamics, and mood. Being only twenty at that time, I felt an obligation to study commercial art in order to have a career. But when I tapped into my own creative impulse, all I wanted to do was paint. I remember making a major decision to drop commercial art, which I couldn't bear, and to devote myself to painting, even if I didn't know how I would be supported and with absolutely no concern for the future.

Making that decision, I felt totally liberated. At that time, I also felt that my effort was to express a deep spirituality in my painting. I was inspired as much by music as by painting and wanted to express that in my work. The music I was listening to at that time was Bartók, Stravinsky, Vivaldi, Bach, and Giovanni Gabrieli. Gabrieli's canzona for antiphonal brass choirs inspired my religious consciousness (even though music historians feel that this is secular music, probably because it is purely instrumental). I had the sense of great spiritual beings calling and responding to one another over the vast reaches of the universe.

I lived my life in the 1950s as an artist, and married a wonderful poet named Ruth Weiss. Suffice it to say that the fourteen years between 1950 and 1964, when I first encountered Zen, were rich and eventful in shaping my destiny as a priest.

Jobs

One of my painter friends said, "You know, I've got a job as a journeyman painter." Normally you have to be an apprentice painter for four years before you can become a journeyman. But he had only spent two years as an apprentice, washing brushes. He said, "I've got a job in a housing project in Marin. Big housing project. They're hiring anybody as a journeyman because they need painters to stain carports and stuff like that. You don't have to know anything." I signed on, and I joined the union—you had to join the union. I made $2.40 an hour. In those days, $2.40 an hour was like $30 now. It was incredible pay. We would drive to Marin County every day. That was really a good job. That was my beginning.

I learned how to be a house painter. And then after that I would go to the union and get jobs, and learn on the job. I supported myself as a house painter, but I didn't like it very much. It's very hard work. In a housing project you have to paint so many doors a day, so many windowsills a day, and you're working all the time. The roller had not been invented. It was all brush painting, brush artistry. There were wonderful paint brushes which are no longer made. Chinese pig bristle, and there was a brush called the 47, I think it was. It was about six inches wide, and the bristles were about ten inches long. It was just this beautiful paintbrush. And the wall brushes were ten inches wide. There's a technique to painting a wall. When you paint woodwork you go with the grain; you make the lines go with the grain, and you don't leave any brush marks. But when you paint a wall, there is no grain. You just slap it on in an artful way and then you brush it out. You have to know these techniques. My right arm got very strong. Also, you learn how to wash brushes, and you learn how to wash buckets, so there's no paint left in the brush when you're done, and there's no paint left in the bucket when you're done. You can eat out of the bucket. These are all wonderful techniques. When I look around at how we take care of our paint stuff, it kind of upsets me, but I've learned to not let it upset me. I've learned to just ignore it, let it go. But there was a time when it really upset me.

Anyway, then I got a job in a boat shop. There were a lot of boat shops along the bay and one of these shops was in Sausalito, owned by the Nunes brothers. They built Errol Flynn's yacht, the *Zaca*. The brothers were Portuguese yacht builders, and I worked there off and on. I was actually their only painter. When they needed a boat painted, they would call me up and I'd come in and paint it. Then I'd go back to working on my own paintings. So I had this great part-time job at the boat shop. They paid twenty cents less an hour than house painting, so no self-respecting house painter would ever do that. But I found the work far more interesting than painting houses.

I learned how to paint boats, and all that goes along with that. That sort of painting is difficult because the paint is very heavy with oils, and if you don't spread the paint evenly, it sags. I enjoyed doing that. I did that for about six years, and I was always covered in paint. I was always covered in acetone and dust and fiberglass particles. This is when fiberglass first came out, so we were fiberglassing the bottoms of boats and sanding it all. I was enveloped in fiberglass dust, and paint dust, and copper dust, but as far as I know it never hurt me.

When I later moved to San Francisco, I was a taxi driver. That was really the job I wanted: to drive a cab. I did that for six years. I did many things for six-year periods. I started out with Yellow Cab. The company was owned by a man named Rothschild, who was one of the famous Rothschilds, and the taxi drivers called him "the rabbi." The wonderful thing about taxi driving is that you get so much money every night, and then you turn in your money, and they give you half of it back in cash, so it's all cash. Fifty-fifty. It was really nice, every night you'd get paid half of what you earned. And you kept your tips. Then I got to driving for DeSoto Cab. I told them that I was an artist and I didn't want to drive every day. I wanted to work part-time. The nice guy said, "Okay, you can do that." I did that for four years. I'd just go in whenever I wanted to. Whenever I needed some money, I'd just go in and work. It was great, and cash on the line.

One time a young customer pulled me over and said, "What would you do if I pulled a gun on you?" I said, "If that's what you want to do, go ahead." I did not want to get down on my knees and plead for my life. He didn't say, "Your money or your life." I just felt that I didn't believe him. He wasn't really convincing. He was just testing me, playing with power.

The same thing happened again. The second time, it was "What would you do if a guy put a gun to your head?" I said, "Well, if that's what you want to do, go ahead." He put the gun down and said, "I'm sorry. Please forgive me. I'm really ashamed of myself."

North Beach

San Francisco was where I met my first wife, Ruth Weiss. She lived in a room that was painted black. She had green hair, she wore her dresses inside out, and she was a wonderful poet who had been a refugee from Berlin with her parents. She came to the U.S. in 1939, narrowly escaping across farmers' fields with machine gun fire overhead. Later, we shared our space with a wonderful and powerful shepherd-collie whom I named Zimzum, son of Thunder and Lady (his parents' names). He would sometimes intervene on behalf of young children who were being mistreated by their parents.

Ruth and I really connected. She was a poet and I was a painter. This was in maybe 1955; I was around twenty-five or twenty-six and I wasn't going to school anymore. We moved into a little room in North Beach—a couple of artists struggling to get along in that environment, with a lot of friends, including many other painters and poets.

Those were the days of bebop—Charlie Parker, Miles Davis, Dizzy Gillespie, Thelonious Monk. It was the beginning of the sexual revolution. Bohemian culture was giving way to beatniks, pot, heroin, peyote (a natural psychedelic), and LSD. It was the time of Allen Ginsberg, a young Jewish poet whom I occasionally saw walking around North Beach. Gary Snyder had gone to Japan to study Zen. I didn't get to know either of them until much later, in a Buddhist context. There were the Beat poets, and poetry and jazz. Ruth was, to my knowledge, the first to perform poetry and jazz on stage. She collaborated with a tenor sax player named Bruce Lippincott in a club on Green Street called The Place, where local and visiting musicians jammed every night. It was a creative time and the arts overlapped and mingled and influenced one another.

Between Nineteenth Street and Cumberland Street, off Dolores, there was a former orphanage, Hill Haven, that was owned by a woman, perhaps a former schoolteacher. At some point, Hill Haven became a kind of a haven for visiting musicians and some other folks—temporary residents who came to check out the San Francisco music scene. A guy named Johnny, from New Orleans, a very good piano player, married the Hill Haven owner. It was a wild scene.

Although it was a creative time, there was the other side, the degenerative underbelly. Many people have a creative impulse, but it is only the self-disciplined who can maintain a creative life in the arts. The arts created a vortex, a "scene." North Beach was the scene—large and small parties with jazz combos, downtown clubs like the Blackhawk, and places like Bop City in the Fillmore District where jazz musicians would jam after hours. Many people were strung out on heroin, not realizing they were hooked until it was too late. If they couldn't find a way out, many of them died. I had friends and acquaintances who were victims of this kind of life. I remember my late friend George taking an overdose of heroin and turning blue. His wife and I stayed up all night with him, not knowing whether he was going to live or die.

I was smoking pot during those early years. On the one hand I was feeling high, and on the other hand I was feeling depressed. I felt like I was under water, like the sky was up there but I could never get above the water line to breathe the fresh air. When I finally did break through to fresh air, it was the most valuable thing in the world. After beginning my Zen practice, I realized that the most wonderful thing is my pure, natural mind without any modifications, which I had always had faith in before I started smoking pot.

After living in North Beach for a while, Ruth and I moved to the Mission on South Van Ness and Twenty-Third Street. We knew a lot of the poets and painters and musicians. We were at that Six Gallery event where Ginsberg first read his famous poem "Howl." When he finished, everyone was howling. Gary Snyder was also there, and Philip Whalen and Philip Lamantia and Michael McClure.

Before it was the Six Gallery, it was called the King Ubu Gallery. Robert Duncan, a well-known poet of North Beach, and Jess Collins, a painter and his partner, formed a new painting gallery and invited Ed Corbett and me to have the opening show there. And that's where they had that famous poetry reading.

Ruth and I knew Philip Lamantia very well. Yesterday I took his obituary out of the paper. The person who wrote the obituary, I think it was some art critic, said that Philip was the most creative surrealist poet of the twentieth century in America. So many of these people we hung out with later became famous. But to us they were just who they were. Michael McClure popped up in my life periodically. The last time was in about 2010, when he wanted to do a recording of people chanting the Heart Sutra with him. We got some people together at Berkeley Zen Center to be the accompaniment and we went down to the Fantasy Studios in Berkeley. I was playing the *mokugyo*, the wooden fish, in a kind of jazzy way. And other members were playing other Buddhist instruments. So these things continue.

Judaism and Religion

During this same period I was looking for a spiritual teacher and community. I was inspired by Martin Buber's *Tales of the Hasidim*. I was completely swept away by the deep mysticism, the simplicity, the power of faith, the idea of the person as the pillar connecting heaven and earth, and the insightful logic of the *tsadik*, the holy man. I liked the way that disciples gathered together around the teachers in small communities, studying and practicing together. I also liked the concept of the hidden *tsadik*, the one who appears as an ordinary person, a fool or an idiot, but who is in reality a great sage. In Zen I later found some of these same parallel qualities.

At that time, I had key words and phrases that I used like mantras, though I didn't think of them as mantras. I would get into an ecstatic state repeating the holy name *Yahweh*, and other Biblical phrases like "*The angels call to each other from one end of the firmament to the other*," as exemplified by Gabrieli's antiphonal choirs. It was not until many years later that I discovered Bach's wonderful cantatas, so full of this same kind of spiritual ecstasy.

I imagined myself, by myself, following that kind of path. I went through a lot of changes, and I was totally supported by my wife, Ruth, in doing that. I studied a little bit of Kabbalah, a little bit of the Kabbalistic Inner Mysteries, and I realized at that time that the great meaning of all this mysticism was just to be a true person. A *mensch*. That's all you have to do. That's what the whole thing means. When I later met Suzuki Roshi and he talked about "beginner's mind," I knew right away what that was, and totally connected with it.

Inspired by Buber's writings, at first I wanted to connect with a Hasidic rabbi, but I couldn't find one. I did locate a nice rabbi, a refugee from Germany who married Ruth and me, and I attended his congregation. But there was something missing for me. Jewish mysticism was frowned upon and ignored at that time in favor of materialistic prosperity. This attitude had always turned me off. I also felt that the Jewish view of themselves as an exclusive people tainted their relations toward the rest of the world. My understanding was that the Jewish people had a mandate to bring peace and harmony to the world. I had grown up free to explore any spiritual avenue, and that made it hard to fit into the narrow world of Judaism as a socialized tribal religion. I had been outside of it all my life, and my idealized view didn't correspond to what I experienced. Present-day Hasidism still preserves the old dress and the old forms, but in my view it seems to lack the ancient spirit. In my heart I longed for a universal practice that would embrace everyone through choice rather than through birth.

I also studied the story of Jesus and felt an affinity, but I couldn't reconcile Jesus with Christianity.

When I think about the successes and failures of religion, I can't help feeling that religion is a necessary evil. When our intuitive consciousness is awakened, we have an opportunity to experience the fullness of our all-inclusive, universal existence, which stimulates both wisdom and compassion, creating unity rather than divisiveness. On the other hand, due to our instability, religion becomes perverted by greed, ill will, and delusion. The original message becomes misunderstood and yields to factionalism and exclusivism. The result is division, which plays into the hands of corrupt governments, allowing manipulation and creating horrendous massacres of innocent people. So the question comes up: Do we need religion?

I don't think we have a choice. Even though there are many people who say that they have given up on or abandoned "religion," the reason it has been around for so long and has permeated every culture and won't go away is our yearning to understand and live in harmony with our universe, beginning with where we stand and our immediate surroundings.

There are many people who will not admit to being religious, or who are critical of religion, who actually live their lives in a truly religious way. I once told my late father-in-law, who was a scientist and a confirmed atheist, that I felt (because of his dedication to discovering what he felt was fundamental truth) he was a truly religious man. He was not happy with that. It is a commonly held view that a religion needs a deity and is associated with the supernatural and the miraculous.

One of the major problems facing religion is the roadblock of revelation. The founder's words (or what they are reported to be) are thought to be inviolable. This puts much of religion in conflict with evolution, and ignores the fact that religion itself is always evolving and adapting to the transformations within society. When we cling to a founder's words as dogma, we lose the vitality of the message.

When religion is not allowed to evolve, it becomes fossilized, defensive, intolerant, and often mean-spirited.

As an established religion continues over time, it becomes weighted down with accretions such as rules, dogmas, superstitions, miracles, prejudices, self-righteousness, exclusivity, power, and hypocrisy. The original message becomes so watered down over time that religion can become a façade for corruption. It is hijacked for political reasons.

What made our teacher, Shunryu Suzuki Roshi, so happy and optimistic when he came to San Francisco was that his students had no Buddhist cultural baggage and could respond to the practice from a pure and open perspective. The other side, of course, was that we didn't have the support of a Buddhist culture or any of the positive aspects which that would have provided.

I believe that religion must serve as a unifying factor for the world. Modern science and psychology have become anchors that people find reliable and that can no longer be ignored by religion. Religions should set an example of tolerance and acceptance of the diversity of systems and work together, letting go of their ego-centered chauvinism. They should provide an example and a direction for society, free of greed, ill will, and delusion. Regardless of any otherworldly beliefs they may have, religions should be able to show people how to sanctify the ordinary activity of their daily lives right here and now.

Introduction to Zen

My wife, Ruth, had a very close friend, a painter named Sutter Marin. Sutter was one of a kind. He had his ear to the ground, so to speak, and would pick up on what was current in art, religion, and politics. One day in the late fifties or early sixties he handed me a small, thin book with a brown cover called *The Sutra of Wei Lang (or Hui Neng)*, translated by Wong Mou-Lam, commonly known as the Platform Sutra. Hui Neng was the sixth Zen Ancestor in China (known as Daikan Eno in Japan), and this is still my favorite translation of this key Zen text. It turned out to be an important text for me. I still have this old copy and often teach from it.

Sutter then introduced me to Mr. Williams, a self-taught philosopher, who spent a lot of time at the George Fields Bookstore on Polk Street in San Francisco, which was one of the few bookstores that carried volumes on Eastern religion and practices. Mr. Williams was a calm, well-read man with a long white beard. His interest in religion and spirituality was wide and inclusive, but he didn't adhere to any particular system. Although he didn't have much experience in meditation, he showed me various methods, such as sitting in a chair and following the breath or gazing at a candle flame to reach one-pointed concentration. From an early age I had been curious about "meditation." I think I had an instinctive feeling for it, without exactly knowing anything. So I was grateful for Mr. Williams's introduction. He also told me he had heard there was a Zen teacher at Sokoji, though he himself had not been there.

Sokoji is the building where San Francisco Zen Center started. It was at 1881 Bush Street, and was originally a synagogue, and it had been built in a Moorish Revival-Venetian style. It was founded as Sokoji Soto Zen Mission in 1936. When Japanese Americans were interned in concentration camps in America during World War II, they saved their money, and when they were released they reopened the temple. The Japanese practice there was called Soto Zen, but the practice was modeled after that of an American Protestant church.

The congregation needed a priest. Shunryu Suzuki was offered the job, and on May 23, 1959, he arrived. Every morning Reverend Suzuki, as he was called, would sit zazen in the pews with the few people who were around him. Gradually some people who had heard about him and were interested in Zen sought him out. He invited them to come and sit with him every morning at 5:45.

I had also heard about Sokoji from a friend named Stan White. Stan had been visiting Sokoji to play Go in the basement. I told him, "Stan, there's a zendo upstairs and you might like that better." He became a member. Phil Wilson, a former Stanford football lineman, who was one of Shunryu Suzuki Roshi's early disciples, told me about the temple on Bush Street with a Zen priest, where he went to do meditation.

I had also heard about Suzuki Roshi from my friend Daniel Moore. He was a poet and was the founding director of a sponta-neous acting group called the Floating Lotus Theater. He eventually became a Muslim. Early one cool San Francisco morning in 1964, Dan brought me to Sokoji.

I had read some of D. T. Suzuki's books on Zen, but didn't get a picture of Soto Zen's meditation practice from his writing. D. T. Su-zuki almost never mentioned zazen or meditation in his books. There was plenty of philosophy, and talk about koans, but no clear pic-ture of Zen practice. In those days there was very little literature on Zen and Buddhism. You had to go to either the Field Book Store or the Metaphysical Bookstore on Powell Street. So when I arrived at Sokoji Temple for the first time, I found myself stepping into an entirely new world.

Suzuki Roshi at the Sokoji Zendo

There was this bare room with tatamis around the edges, along the walls, and an altar on one side. We went in and sat down and faced the wall. Somebody came up behind me and adjusted my posture and showed me how to hold my hands, not saying a word, just all feeling, all touch. It was Suzuki Roshi, of course. I was sitting there, and it was just wonderful. I thought, "Here I am just sitting here all by myself, with nothing else but this wall, this seat, and this place." It felt like I had come home. Phew! Right there! That was my first time at Sokoji.

Later, another morning zazen was added at 5:00 a.m. and there was also evening zazen at 5:30 p.m., Monday through Friday. Saturday morning there were two forty-minute periods of zazen, followed by chanting and bowing, breakfast, a short rest period, a work period, zazen, and a lecture by Suzuki Roshi. Once a month there was a one-day sitting, and periodically a five- or seven-day *sesshin*. Wednesday night there was zazen followed by a talk and a discussion. We would place the chairs in a circle for the discussion while tea was served by Mrs. Suzuki.

Suzuki Roshi would ask for questions. One time I asked, "What is nirvana?" He looked at me and said, "Seeing one thing through to the end." All the teaching I had absorbed from him up to then came together and became a confirmation or turning point for my practice. Master Dogen said, "Our practice is like one long rod of iron." Suzuki Roshi once said that Soto Zen practice is like sucking up one endless Zen noodle. I think of it as the long-distance runner who forgets about the finish line, rather than the sprinter who runs as fast as possible in order to receive a medal at the end.

Although Suzuki Roshi had been asked to lead the Japanese American congregation, whose temple it was, he had been "discovered" by Westerners who began to sit with him. We were the congregation's guests. In those early days he sat with his students in the pews in a room at the top of the stairs. In time the pews were moved out and replaced with tatami mats and *zafu*. The Japanese American congregation did not sit zazen at Sokoji. Their practice was more like a Sunday Protestant service. So Suzuki Roshi took care of their needs as a priest or pastor, while at the same time practicing with his own students in an entirely different way as a Zen master. When someone would call him inquiring about Zen practice, he would tell them that he sat in the morning at 5:00 and that they were welcome to join him.

At that time we didn't call him Suzuki Roshi, we just called him Reverend Suzuki or Suzuki Sensei. In 1966 Alan Watts wrote a letter that said we should call him Suzuki Roshi.

As I got to know Suzuki Roshi, I came to like him a lot. After I'd sat at Sokoji for a little while, I had a certain kind of feeling that I can't describe, but I thought, "This is samadhi"—an aspect of Buddhist concentration. It was just my idea; Suzuki Roshi talked about samadhi. But that's what I thought, and I thought, "I'm going to keep coming back and do this."

I found out that every time I did zazen my legs hurt. Finally, I said to Mike Dixon (Mike's wife, Trudy, edited *Zen Mind, Beginner's Mind*), "Mike, this always hurts." And he said, "Yes, it will always hurt." I said, "Ohhhh." Mike always sat in full lotus, and so little by little I started sitting in full lotus. I didn't think I could do it. It took me maybe a couple of years until I could.

This was 1964. I started coming to zazen every day. I would come to zazen in the morning, and I'd come to zazen in the evening. I was very regular, and I realized that this was the most important part of my life. I was thirty-five. I said to myself, "I know that this is exactly what I've been looking for, and if I don't do this now, it'll just pass me by and I'll be lost again." I really devoted myself to sitting. Suzuki Roshi seemed to like me, and his way of teaching was very subtle. Every day he would adjust posture; he would never let anybody sit slumped. He would adjust your posture, over and over and over again. He talked about zazen a lot. During zazen he would talk. He'd say, "You're like loaves cooking in the oven. Just keep cooking."

You got the idea that you should not move. Don't move. I went through excruciatingly painful zazen periods for a long time. But he was always very encouraging, never criticizing. He never criticized.

I was just in there, just doing the best I could, and his attitude was "Just don't ever give up. Put your energy in it and don't ever give up." I realized that this is the essence of the practice, that you put your whole body and mind into what you're doing and you never give up. That's what it's all about. Everything comes out of that. Whatever it is that you've "gained" (which is nothing) comes out of that.

Little by little there grew to be enough students to form a Zen center. The Japanese congregation allowed this to happen, and were tolerant and generous, but they had their reservations for various reasons. There were a lot of strangers coming and going, many of them hippie types in unwashed, unconventional, or occasionally outlandish attire, which was sometimes offensive to the Japanese congregants. Some were barefoot and some had long matted hair, which was seldom washed. They sometimes didn't smell so good either. Suzuki Roshi loved them and was never critical about their attire or their lifestyle, but he was also sensitive to the concerns of the Japanese congregation. Once, after evening service while everyone was waiting to leave, he said something like "We should be careful about the effect we have on our neighbors when we sit. Before you come to zazen, you should bathe or wash your feet. A little deodorant is okay. I sometimes use it myself." He said this in a sweet, diplomatic manner, trying hard not to hurt anyone's feelings. Another time, he placed a mirror in the hallway outside the door so people could reflect on their appearance.

At the same time, it should be understood that not all of the students were hippies. They represented a cross-section of American society.

The Japanese American congregation pretty much left us alone and didn't interfere with what we were doing. Suzuki Roshi wanted them to accept us. He asked me one time to get together with the president of Sokoji, who lived in Berkeley, which I did. We had pretty good communication, and I think that helped a bit. Most of Suzuki's students were sensitive to the feelings of the Japanese Americans and were careful not to offend them. But for the most part we maintained a respectful distance from each other.

Everybody knows about Suzuki Roshi now, about how plain and simple his practice was. I feel that one of the most important things is that he never saw himself as apart from us—he always treated everyone as himself. I felt that he always looked for the light in each person; he was always interested in the treasure that each person embodies. That's why everyone loved him so much.

He once said, "When our practice is neither Japanese nor American, then we will have our true practice." Although he introduced Japanese practices to us, he never expected us to be Japanese. He was always trying to bring forth the best qualities of our culture and our own inherent nature. He said, "When you are you completely and thoroughly, then Zen is Zen." He didn't say "when you are like me." He said, "When you are completely you."

We always felt this great trust, and it was very easy to put ourselves in his hands, because we felt there was no gap between us. He was willing to work with anyone as long as they were sincerely making an effort. He worked with students without regard to their race, social standing, place in society, or appearance. He was always ready to acknowledge his mistakes and humble enough to apologize when he was wrong. He taught not just through his words, but through his actions.

We tend to think of a mantra as a phrase that we repeat over and over in order to evoke or to maintain a certain concentrated or pure state. But when I observed Suzuki Roshi, it seemed to me that the way he lived his life was as a mantra. His life had a very obvious form: every day at Sokoji Temple, doing zazen and services. Every day he did the same thing, which was amazing to me. I had never seen anyone do that kind of an activity before. His life was devoted to sitting zazen, bowing, lighting incense, and the various other things that he did. When there were so many other things to do in the world, here was this person simply doing these things over and over again, every day. And he had been doing them over and over every day for most of his life. I never thought of myself doing anything like that in what seemed like such a narrowly disciplined way of life. I was impressed by this. After a while, it occurred to me that his life was a mantra. Every day he had these tasks that he would do. He was always concentrated and went about his activity in a light and easy manner.

The Challenge of Zazen

Suzuki Roshi would say that for most people, it takes about six months to a year to find confidence in your posture. During that time the student usually experiences some pain and discomfort. This is the time when one learns how to accept thoughts and feelings as they arise, and how to harmonize with the breath. As new students we usually fight or resist the pain until we come to a dead end and realize that the only way to deal with it is to let go and "be one" with what we experience, to just let it be. Pain was a big problem for me. I started out sitting campfire style with my ankles crossed, which is not a stable position because one's knees are not touching the floor. We didn't put support cushions under our knees but allowed them to slowly settle during the forty-minute period. With persistence the body stretches out, and little by little, one finds the legs comfortable in the position. The full lotus position is the most comfortable, but the hardest to achieve and maintain. I always encourage people to take a position that they can easily manage over a long period of time, and not compete with others to see who can be the most extreme. If one continues to sit consistently for some time, the legs will naturally want to incline toward the lotus positions, but this is not necessary.

For the first two or three years, zazen had been excruciatingly painful and a great challenge for me, as it was for most of us. When I took a friend to the zendo at Sokoji for the first time, he couldn't stand up right away after zazen and crawled out on his hands and knees. But hard as it was, I took to it like a duck to water, struggling like hell, until I finally gave up and realized that it was not the pain that was causing me a problem. It was my mind that was creating a problem around pain.

Suzuki Roshi once said, half-jokingly, that this practice is for those of us who are not smart enough to do it any other way. And I remember Katagiri Sensei saying that in order to do Soto Zen practice, one must be a little stupid.

Suzuki Roshi always encouraged us to sit without moving. He would say things like "Don't chicken out," which would crack everybody up.

After sitting for some months at Sokoji, I attempted my first all-day *sesshin*. By late morning I had had enough and walked out. It was a sunny day and I went down to the marina. I walked around a little, but there was nothing for me to do. I was still in *sesshin* and was totally unconnected to this other world. It was as if there were a thin gauze curtain between me and the world outside the zendo. I realized that although I had left the zendo, I couldn't leave *sesshin*, and there was nothing for me to do but see it through. So I went back. When he saw me return, I thought I heard Suzuki Roshi say something like "Oh, he comes back."*

At one of my first *sesshins* at Sokoji, I sat all the way through in full lotus without moving except for the last period. I felt like a failure—all that effort, and then moving at the last minute. I felt ashamed of myself. When we filed past Suzuki Roshi to make our departing bows, I went last and asked him if he thought I should continue to practice. His face lit up and he smiled and said, "Isn't it difficult enough for you? If you can find something more difficult, maybe you should do that." That was a significant moment for me.

One time after another *sesshin* he said to me, "You represent all the students." I think what he meant was that I was a good representation of everybody, lots of dimensions. I thought I understood what he meant, but when I thought about it, I realized that maybe I didn't, and I'm still not sure.

In the early 1960s there were not so many seasoned students. Almost everyone had a hard time sitting. There was a lot of struggle and many silent internal dramas going on in the meditation room. The zazen periods were forty minutes, but sometimes Suzuki Roshi would ring the bell to begin zazen and then walk out. As the period went on, everyone would wonder if he remembered they were sitting. Maybe he was so involved in something that it slipped his mind. After all, he was known to be absent-minded. No one knew what to expect or how long they would be there. Pain becomes intense when you are attached to relief. Could we hold out? At that point one has to settle with no expectations and simply exist fully on each moment, on each inhalation and exhalation. After a while he would come back, sometimes after forty minutes and sometimes longer. Sometimes just before the period was coming to an end, he would say in a very polite way, "We will sit ten minutes longer," which would throw everyone's expectations out the window. Not being sure of what to expect, we had to be ready for anything. Suzuki Roshi expected us to sit without moving, which was excruciatingly difficult for me. It took what seemed like a very long time for me to let go of fighting and resisting the pain in my legs. The expectation was that when you sat down and took the position, there was a commitment to see it through. This is how I learned the value and the power of commitment—to stay in my position and maintain my composure, literally from moment to moment, and finally one breath at a time. At such a time, one breath, inhaling and exhaling, is your whole world, inspiration and expiration, birth and death alternating in one moment of time. Breathing in and arising with the life of the present; breathing out and letting go—the great lesson of maintaining composure within the duality of birth and death.

Most people are restless. It's hard to be still. When I perform a wedding I ask people to sit still for five minutes, sitting in their chairs before we begin. One time a woman told me that that was the longest she had ever sat still in her entire life. A good portion of our attention is devoted to shifting positions in order to get comfortable. Nowadays, convenience is a major motivator for human behavior. It seems like the desire for comfort and convenience is taking over our creative abilities and our very lives. What we actually need can easily be obscured by what we want. Suzuki Roshi once said that it is impossible to obtain true comfort or satisfaction when all we are doing is changing our equipment over and over. During zazen he would sometimes say, "Don't change your position for your own convenience." When we don't move, we come face to face with the great wall of ourself. Then we have the opportunity to realize that true comfort or satisfaction comes through the ability to make an internal adjustment which frees us from the domination of the variables of circumstance. It's like riding the waves of the great ocean without being inundated by them.

It is interesting, the motivation that brings us to practice. We hear or read about Zen, Buddhism, enlightenment, nirvana, and all the benefits that go with it. When we arrive at the gate of practice, it's usually because we want something. This is quite normal. Our desire, our ego, leads us to practice. What motivates us may be the desire for enlightenment or the desire for some more modest kind of physical or mental benefit. When we engage in zazen for the first time it is an enlightened act. But not everyone is aware of the ultimate object of their desire, and fewer still are ready to turn toward that path. Practice begins from an awakening, no matter how subtle. For a long time we may not even realize why we practice. It's not unusual to alternate between faith and doubt.

Suzuki Roshi liked to say that we are Buddha on the one hand, and an ordinary human on the other. We are like two siblings under one roof. Sometimes one leads and sometimes the other. Often when one is dominant, the other is in the shadow. In some people the Buddha-nature is dominant from the beginning, and in others, the self-centered nature. Our human nature, often driven by egoistic desires, tends to willingly allow itself to be captivated and to take dead-end pathways which ultimately lead to disillusionment and suffering. The thought of enlightenment may be completely forgotten for a long time. But, driven by suffering and looking for a true path, human nature seeks out the forgotten sibling, who now seems so much more familiar and has a strange magnetism. The ego wants something that the sibling seems to have. Then the ego enters the gate and lets the sibling lead. The practice gets difficult because the self-serving ego seems to be always getting in the way. Then at some point the student gives up and makes an offering of the ego to Buddha, letting the Buddha lead. The two become one, the ego is purified, and serving others is no longer in servitude to the self.

According to Buddha Dharma, ego arises through desire, attachment, and self-clinging. When we live a life of selfless practice, we are offering up our ego, and desire is directed toward—and becomes—way-seeking mind. Ego becomes "transformed" rather than "cut off," and performs its proper function of service.

Zazen is like a crucible. In the *Buddhist I-Ching* it says: "To transform things, nothing compares to the cauldron; this is the vessel used to refine the wise, forge sages, cook Buddhas, and purify adepts. How could it not be very auspicious and developmental?"

When we engage in sitting, all of our ideas get turned around and sooner or later we realize that we have to let go of our previous notions and opinions. Zazen strips us bare. There is nothing in our inventory of dependencies to rely on. None of the supports that we habitually rely on will work, and we are forced to go more deeply into ourselves than we ever have. This is especially true of a *sesshin*: a period of one to seven days of zazen. For most practitioners there comes a time, usually during a *sesshin*, when it seems like you can't stay seated and can't leave. At this point there is an opportunity to let go.

Suzuki always emphasized "no gaining mind" as the fundamental foundation of zazen. Dogen Zenji says, "Let go and it fills your hands." I remember running across a passage in one of Edward Conze's books where he quoted a sutra that said, "A monk delights in giving up." That statement has stayed with me and seems to epitomize the essence of Buddhist practice. Zazen is not a stepping-stone to something else, or a means to get something. It's rather a letting go of dependencies. It's how we make ourself an offering to the entire universe, and how we find our fundamental position in the universe moment by moment. It's a way to allow ourself to fully and dynamically function—every fiber of our body and mind totally present in harmonious communion. It is like a spinning top that looks like it's standing still until you touch it and it goes careening away. It's like Adam saying, "Here am I."

---

* A source from San Francisco Zen Center relates the following story. After leaving midway into his first all-day *sesshin*, Sojun went to Chinatown on his way back and bought Chinese finger traps, which are braided tubes. One puts an index finger from each hand in each end. When trying to pull one's fingers free, the tube tightens, preventing withdrawal. Only by counterintuitively moving the two fingers closer together inside the tube will it loosen. When Sojun returned, he placed a finger trap at each participant's seat.

Katagiri Roshi and Chino Roshi

Our second Japanese teacher was Dainin Katagiri. We called Suzuki Roshi "Reverend Suzuki" and Katagiri, who arrived a little before me, we called him "Katagiri Sensei" or "Reverend Katagiri." He had been a priest for almost twenty years and, as is the custom for all Soto Zen priests, had received Dharma Transmission. But he had met American guests at Eiheiji—one of the Soto Zen headquarter monasteries in Japan—and he wanted to help bring the practice to America. He had heard about Suzuki Roshi.

I remember that Suzuki Roshi would always be the *doshi* (officiant for service) and Katagiri did all the other roles of the services—ringing the bells, leading the chant, and sounding the percussion instrument. He performed all those positions. For years, with occasional exceptions, no one did the service except Katagiri and Suzuki Roshi, so we were able to watch how two Japanese priests related to each other. For our benefit, Katagiri put himself in the student position and Suzuki Roshi took the teacher position

Katagiri Roshi had a very difficult time with English in the beginning. I remember his first lecture at Zen Center: it was completely unintelligible. But it was wonderful. We were so happy just to support his effort. Support was mutual—our effort to support the teachers and their effort to support us. In the process the Dharma was in full swing.

Sometimes we didn't realize how difficult it was for someone from Japan to transplant themselves to the United States. For example, when Suzuki Roshi went to Tassajara, we were all eating brown rice instead of the white rice he was used to in Japan. At the same time, we had the macrobiotic people, the mucusless-dieters, and five or six other food trend advocates living there. The Japanese teachers had to go through all this with us. It was very hard on some of them to adapt to American styles and American food. Sometimes they got very sick. Eventually we developed a monastic diet that suited most people who were residing in a practice place for a long period of time without access to any other food. Little by little we refined our diet and kitchen practice.

Suzuki Roshi was like a father figure for us. Katagiri was like the mother. He was always interacting with us, helping us, worrying about us. Did we have enough soup? That kind of thing. Between the two of them, they were like our dharma parents. They brought us up. I studied with them for seven years. Then Katagiri Roshi was invited to Monterey, and eventually to Minnesota. I think he had a harder time than Suzuki Roshi in adapting. His effort was tremendous, and his devotion to the Triple Treasure—Buddha, Dharma, and Sangha—was pure and inspiring.

Kobun Chino arrived in 1967. Chino Sensei was a young monk whom Phil Wilson had known at Eiheiji. He had come at the request of Marion Derby to be the resident priest at the small Haiku Zendo in Los Altos. But on the way there, Suzuki Roshi, who had suggested Marion invite Kobun Chino, waylaid him for a while at Tassajara. So he became one of our teachers. Each of these teachers presented something unique. Chino Roshi's character was soft and poetic. And deep. The way he would speak was so slow and so deep that it was hard to follow his words.

He was trained at Eiheiji to do the most elaborate ceremonies. My understanding is that certain priests are singled out to learn these things. He had this training and when he came here I think he was expected to do something along those lines. But actually he dropped that formality—he let go of all of it eventually. He wouldn't teach anybody anything. I remember going to *sesshins* with Chino Roshi where nobody was instructed how to do anything: the servers didn't know how to serve, the people doing service didn't know what to do.

And he didn't say a word. He wanted everyone to figure it out for themselves.

At some *sesshins* the serving seemed to take forever. One day, I just got up and took over—getting everything right and getting everybody to move. Later I realized that that was just my trip, just my expectation. Chino Roshi was doing something that no one else would dare to do. I was trying to get everybody to do the form, and he was trying to get everybody to forget the form. Which was kind of wonderful.

Chino Roshi was being a bodhisattva—loving the students, always being an advocate for them. He didn't try to make students out of them. He would just be with them. Such a radical way, but very kind. In some way he reminds me of Ryokan, the Japanese Zen poet. Nobody knew what he was doing, but we all felt that he was doing something wonderful. He seemed to have the attitude that in the long run everything will turn out the way it is supposed to. We tend to want to get everything done in this lifetime, but he didn't care about that. If you don't get it done in this lifetime, it will get done in the next: no rush! This attitude helps to balance things out.

One time in 1970, Suzuki Roshi gave a talk on what he described as "The Art of Zen." What he described was a teacher putting on airs, talking tough, and wearing splendid robes in order to make an impression. In other words, acting out the stereotype of a popular conception of a Zen Master. He said that there is no special way for a Zen Master to be identified. Each one is different. One is loud and noisy, another is soft and quiet. One is stern and unyielding, another is kind and nurturing. There is Deshan with his thirty blows, and Joshu with his golden words. When we study the masters of the past, we find an infinite variety of personalities. They are all beyond compare. The point is not their personality, but whether they are truly expressing the Dharma.

Tassajara Zen Mountain Center

For a number of years Suzuki and the older members had been talking about how it would be to have a piece of country land to create a Zen monastery. It was an exciting thing to contemplate, and we were all for the idea, even though we were a small group and had no financial resources to speak of. We looked at a few properties that were offered, but nothing clicked.

Then in 1966 we found what seemed like a perfect place for us— Tassajara. The owner eventually wanted to sell it to us, and the price was sufficiently low that, with the help of some fundraising, we were able to buy it.

The Tassajara Hot Springs resort, located in the Ventana Wilderness that lies between Big Sur on the coast and Carmel Valley inland, is at the end of a winding fourteen-mile unpaved mountain road. The Tassajara road had been built by local and Chinese laborers in the late nineteenth century. We have photos and articles from the Salinas newspapers featuring the stagecoach to the Tassajara resort and hotel: "Come, enjoy and be rejuvenated by the hot sulphur baths."

Suzuki Roshi named the new practice place "Zenshinji"—Zen Mind Monastery, or Zen Heart-Mind Monastery. It consisted of twenty summer cabins, a dining room with a dorm on the second floor, some larger pine cabins, three stone rooms, a large swimming pool, two barns, a bar, and the main feature of the resort: the natural hot spring and steam baths. All this was nestled in a narrow mountain valley, with the Tassajara creek at the bottom of a tree-studded rock cliff. There was no paving anywhere, and countless rocks and stones everywhere.

The dining room with a bar, an old stone and wood building on the near side of the creek, was turned into a zendo. The altar was set up at one end, and the sitting cushions ran down the length of the building. It was wonderful to see that old bar become a beautiful sacred space, once the old furnishings were stripped out and it was lined with tatami mats and round black cushions.

The kitchen was close to the zendo, which made it convenient because the food had to be brought to the zendo for our formal meals. The kitchen was a shack, small and antiquated. In the summer of 1971 we replaced it with a sturdy stone building—a major capital project in which we all participated, bringing stones from the nearby creek and hillside and carefully putting them in place. In the beginning, before we had built the new kitchen, the cooks brought over and served the meals, and then they ate their own formal meal in the zendo after everyone else was gone.

The kitchen's interior post and beam work, which was supervised by Paul Discoe, was our first venture into Japanese-style building methods. Paul was the master builder. He was just another student, but he was really good, and he developed himself at Tassajara before he went to Japan. He was kind of in charge of building the kitchen, which was a big summer project. It took four years, and people came from all over to help build it. It generated a lot of interest, and it's beautifully built.

So there were all these kinds of projects to deal with. The place was very run-down as a resort. We had to put in a lot of time, and everybody was working. Suzuki Roshi's main idea of practice was zazen and work. Work was equal to zazen. As a matter of fact, one of his mantras was "Cleaning first, zazen second. Cleaning first, zazen second." That all changed after he died. But he really felt the necessity for work.

I'm sure a lot of us felt that we were on the frontier of doing something really vital. We were building this thing with our own hands, and we were putting all our life energy into making it work, and it was practically from scratch. It felt like a really wholesome way to do things.

This kind of work brought the sangha together in a new way. It was a pioneering effort, creating the first Zen monastery in the West, and doing it with our own labor and resources. There were a number of young people who were traveling around that summer who for one reason or another arrived at the gate and stayed to help. Many of them stayed on and became Zen students.

In the summer of 1967 we had a four-day *sesshin* at Tassajara, for those who were only staying for the first month of the two-month practice period. It was led by Suzuki Roshi and Taizan Maezumi Sensei. There were about fifteen people who participated while everyone else was working. We held it in the dining room and did *kinhin* (walking meditation) on the porch, which was not covered at that time. It was hot as blazes. It was in the middle of the summer and it was over 100 degrees. Everybody was falling all over trying to sit zazen. I kept uncrossing my legs. It was just impossible to sit. Everyone had a hard time because of the heat. Suzuki had each of us write our names on a scroll that said FIRST SESSHIN to commemorate the event. When Suzuki looked at my handwriting, he said, "You should study calligraphy sometime." I didn't know what he meant by that.

The day after the *sesshin* Suzuki Roshi called me into his cabin and said, "I would like you to join our order." I was quite surprised and overjoyed. I said, "What do you mean?" He said, "Well, you know, to be ordained as a priest. What do you think about that?" And I said, "Sounds okay to me. When do you want to do that?" He paused and said, "When you are ready and when I am ready."

Suzuki Roshi wasn't sure whether I should be ordained at Tassajara or Berkeley. He finally decided on Berkeley in order to establish my leadership there. It was two years before I was finally ordained.

He knew I wanted to do it and I knew he wanted me to. So there was not a lot to say about it. He rarely questioned me about what I was doing and I felt completely trusted.

I had been sitting for only three years when he asked me to ordain. When I think about that now, it boggles my mind that he would give us so much responsibility so soon. But the circumstances then were different than they are now. When I finally received ordination, I had been practicing for five years.

Tassajara: Winter of 1969

It was a very heavy winter at Tassajara in 1969. We were ill prepared because we were snowed in, but it was a wonderful time. There was five feet of snow on the ridge. I remember coming up on the town-trip truck: you could just see the top of it in the snow. It was like an expedition to the North Pole where you've come upon something buried in the snow. We had to dig it out and carry the food. We didn't have much food. We had wheatberries and brown rice. Wheatberries, you have to chew them in order to get to the nourishment. But you know how Zen students eat? They just chew a little and swallow. And I can prove it to you, because the toilets all backed up. Somebody said we had a cesspool down at the lower barn. The problem was that something was swelling up the pipes. We sent Reb Anderson down there with a shovel to find out what was going on. He uncovered it and discovered that it was undigested wheatberries. The whole thing, all the pipes were stuffed with undigested wheatberries that were swelling up.

Ruvane, the gardener, was very innovative, and he said, "We must eat wild vegetables." So people went out to the flats, and we harvested all these wild vegetables that grew out there all winter—dandelion leaves and roots, miner's lettuce, curly dock, pigweed, plantain—and we made these great salads, and it was all live food—wild, live food. That was the winter of 1969.

We didn't have any heat then, either. The dining room was the only place there was any heat, and the only things everyone could think about were heat and food. Every conversation ended up talking about food. We have this easy practice these days, I have to tell you.

A young man tried to walk in during that winter. He was determined to come in, but he didn't have the equipment. So he got into his sleeping bag because it was so cold, and he inched his way down the road. At that time, we didn't let anybody who just showed up stay overnight at Tassajara. But we did let this young man stay because of the conditions. The next morning, Reb and I took him out. We had just one pair of snowshoes, which went to Reb. And this guy and I, we made snowshoes out of tin cans. We cut the sides out of five-gallon tofu cans. We made holes and put ropes through them, tied them to our feet, and clanked our way from Tassajara to Jamesburg, through the virgin snow. It was wonderful. I hated putting my feet in the snow because it was so beautiful, but it worked. As we came down the road to Jamesburg we took them off and put them behind some bushes. Now every time I come to that curve in the road I'd like to see if those snowshoes are still in the bushes.

We had run out of tobacco, and that was another reason I went out. We came back up a creek from Arroyo Seco a week later. There were five or six of us, and the creek was swollen, and we had to get across it. David Chadwick walked across the creek. It was really a torrent, ice cold. David took the end of a rope with him and tied it to a tree. We took our clothes off and held our clothes above our heads and walked across the creek holding on to that rope.

Those were fun days. I just wanted to give you a little peek at our adventures of 1969.

Suzuki Roshi at Tassajara

When Suzuki Roshi arrived at Tassajara in 1970 after the winter-spring practice period, he asked me what position I wanted that summer. I said that I would like to be the *ino*, the person in charge of the zendo, as I had not done that before. Then he said that he wanted me to be his *jisha*, his attendant. It was a wonderful opportunity to be close to him in such an intimate way. He asked Alan Marlowe to be his *anja*, the one who took care of his laundry and made the bed and kept things in order. Alan and I would carry the incense behind him from his cabin to the zendo. I had the stick incense and Alan the *kogo*, the little container with the chip incense. Alan was tall, I was medium, and Suzuki was short. We provided a bit of a humorous spectacle walking to the zendo.

Suzuki Roshi wanted to make a stone retaining wall in the creek just below his cabin with our help. Other students also helped from time to time. I made a tripod out of three-inch metal bars and attached it to a winch that we used to raise the large, heavy stones, many of which we hauled out of the creek. We had an ancient Dodge "power wagon" which was outfitted with a winch devised by Paul Discoe, arranged in such a way that we could haul the big stones on to the truck bed and carry them to the site. We also had a sled cut from the top of an old car and turned upside down. It was chained to the wagon and used to haul the bigger rocks. Collecting and hauling those rocks and building that wall with Suzuki Roshi was hard and satisfying work. The average temperature during that time was 100 degrees and more. I would carry a wet washcloth and periodically soak it and put it on Suzuki Roshi's head to cool him off.

He worked at full capacity, even though he and we knew that it was draining his energy. He was also giving his *Sandokai* talks in the heat of the evening. Those twelve talks were later published under the title *Branching Streams Flow in the Darkness*.

It was amazing to watch him move heavy rocks with his frail body. For those of us who worked with him in that intimate way it was a highlight of our practice, and the last time he ever did anything like that. We might spend all day moving one or two heavy stones into place, and if one didn't fit just right, he would have us start all over again. It reminded me of the Tibetan master Milarepa being asked by his teacher to build a stone tower and then to take it down and then to build it again, over and over. Suzuki's wife Mitsu, whom we called *Okusan* ("the one who walks behind"), would occasionally come by and complain that he was working too hard. When he knew she was coming he would stop, and when she walked on he would start working again.

Tatsugami Roshi

Tatsugami Roshi was a heavy-set, medium-sized man in his sixties. He had been *ino*—head of practice—for thirteen years at Eiheiji in Japan. After Richard Baker had invited him, Suzuki Roshi made it formal with a letter. In his youth he had been an amateur sumo wrestler. He had elephant-like eyes and a good sense of humor. He smoked all day long.

Some students thought that Tassajara was a commune and they wanted to live there as if it were. Communal experience and communal thinking were popular in the sixties when Zen Center was developing. Some appreciated the fact that it had some structure, since many communes didn't have any. Tatsugami's arrival at Tassajara separated the commune-ists from the Zen students. There was considerable controversy about that. Tatsugami Roshi had his faults, but somehow he just breezed in, and since he couldn't speak English he wasn't bothered by a lot of things.

Little by little he introduced the monastic forms. He set up the *doanryo* system (practice positions in the zendo), the kitchen practice, the monastic officers' practice, etc. He had a wonderful chanting style, which he transmitted to us. During the day he walked around, and if he crossed paths with a *doan*—a student responsible for the liturgy—he invited the *doan* to chant with him. He had a tremendous voice and a beautiful style of chanting. His voice was deep and resonant, but accessible. He always chanted at a comfortable pitch that was easy for everyone to join in on.

He had a good teaching style. I asked him if he would teach me, and he said that I should learn from the shadow. I had never heard that expression before. He and I got along very well. He spoke no English, and I no Japanese, but we communicated quite well. He would look at me and speak and somehow I knew what he was saying. Dan Welch did his best to translate, but it wasn't easy. Later on, Katagiri Sensei translated, but it wasn't nearly as much fun. Katagiri didn't seem to like Tatsugami very much. I think he felt that Tatsugami was trying to take over Tassajara, which he probably was.

When Tatsugami Roshi was in Japan he drank a lot, but when he came to Tassajara he promised he wouldn't drink. And he didn't. It was amazing! But he smoked constantly. A lot of people smoked at that time. I was a smoker. Every day the officers had morning tea and a meeting with Tatsugami. These were lively and energetic, and everything was discussed. Peter Schneider always played the devil's advocate, asking challenging questions, never letting anything that was not addressed go by. During all this, Tatsugami would sit next to his hibachi and light his pipe or cigarette on the burning embers. Students would bring him exotic brands of tobacco from the town trip as presents. One showed up with a "Zen" brand. Tatsugami had a favorite pipe with a long stem and a tiny one-or-two-puff bowl. He would lift a small ember with a pair of metal chopsticks and light his pipe, which was stuffed with finely shredded tobacco.

In 1970 when I had my *shuso* (head monk) ceremony and was receiving testing questions from all the other students, Tatsugami had me turn toward the wall so I wouldn't see who was asking the questions. He characterized this as "questions coming from all sides." It was unusual and I have never seen it done that way again. I liked him and really appreciated his kindness toward me. But many people felt that he was taking advantage of Suzuki's indisposition, trying to take Tassajara away from Suzuki. After his third practice period in the spring of 1971, Tatsugami was not invited by Suzuki to return. He too passed away, but I don't remember exactly when it was. Tassajara continues to maintain the practice pretty much the way Tatsugami set it up.

Acceptance of Everyone

Among Suzuki Roshi's very first students were three middle-aged women who attended a class at the American Institute of Asian Studies led by Kazemitsu Kato, a Soto Zen priest who assisted him at Sokoji when needed. Kato had invited Suzuki to join him for the class. Both women and men came to practice with him, and he treated everyone the same. When I came to Sokoji in 1964 the men sat on one side of the zendo and the women on the other. When we stood up after zazen, we bowed to each other across the room. But that changed eventually, at Tassajara and the city, when some women thought that was sexist. At both Tassajara and City Center there were single men, single women, married couples, unmarried couples, gay men, and gay women. There were some celibates, either by choice or circumstance, but they were not considered as being more proper or traditional than anyone else. I don't remember us getting much feedback from the Buddhist world that was aware of us, but in the Japanese congregation at Sokoji there was a perception that, among other things, we were a wild bunch of sexual partners and unmarried couples living together.

Suzuki Roshi was well aware of this and did his best to soothe the congregation. If an unmarried couple wanted to live together, he wanted them to take the same last name. That idea didn't last long. If the students were going to have a relationship that was serious enough to warrant moving in with each other, he felt they should be serious enough to be moving toward marriage. He didn't want our sex lives causing a big problem for our practice, but at the same time he had a lot of tolerance for our needs and frustrations. Instead of imposing rules and regulations, he wanted to see how we could work out our relationships in a meaningful and satisfying way. How can a relationship support a couple's practice rather than inhibit it? There was one student who had no inhibitions about having multiple sex partners and he asked Suzuki Roshi if that was okay. Suzuki Roshi said, "As long as you can remember the names of each one of them." I don't remember him ever getting upset or angry at anyone over problems that arose in this area. I think he was more interested in letting us learn from our mistakes.

Suzuki Roshi and Japan

Suzuki Roshi had few formal ties with the Japanese hierarchy and therefore felt less of an obligation to Sotoshu, the Japanese umbrella organization for Soto Zen. From Sotoshu's point of view, he was a kind of maverick, as were many of the Japanese teachers who came to America. Once in a while, some representatives of the Sotoshu would come over to see what was going on, since San Francisco Zen Center was getting a reputation. Some couldn't understand what we were doing, and they bawled out Suzuki Roshi. We were rather shocked and could not understand why they couldn't understand. It brought home to us the great divide between our practice and the current condition of Soto Zen in Japan. Suzuki Roshi wanted to give us the essence of Zen practice, with zazen at the center, which had been so neglected in Japan.

Zen Master Dogen introduced the lineage of the Soto Zen school to Japan in the thirteenth century. Dogen's practice was based primarily on zazen. It was widely propagated generations later by Keizan Jokin. Keizan's disciples spread the teaching mostly to the common people in the countryside, while the Rinzai teaching became popular among the aristocracy. Rinzai Zen is sometimes characterized as like a general moving his troops, and Soto Zen like a farmer tending his crops. Both schools had to deal with the samurai. For about five hundred years Dogen's *Shobogenzo* writings, which express his deep and unique understanding of Dharma, were largely forgotten. Soto Zen continued to develop, but some of the essentials of Dogen's vision were dormant. In the seventeenth century two reformers, Manzan and Menzan, generated a renewed interest in Dogen for the Soto school. But it was not until the approach of the twentieth century that Japanese historians and scholars began to take more of an interest in Dogen, who is now considered one of the major religious figures in Japanese history. He is also considered a major figure in the philosophical world.

The practice of zazen has waxed and waned over the centuries since Dogen's time. At the beginning of the Meiji period in the late nineteenth century, there was a reform movement by the Japanese government designed to reduce the power of the Buddhist monastic community. Thousands of monks were turned out of the monasteries and were pressured to return to lay life and marry. Those who remained tonsured mostly became temple priests. The whole populace had to register with a Buddhist temple, and the practice took a whole new turn. The priests became ministers to family congregations, and zazen became a secondary activity for most of them.

The monastic system was later reinstated, but it never quite resumed its former prominence. Besides the head Soto training temples, Eiheiji and Sojiji, there were a few smaller training temples, mainly Rinzai, where foreigners could go to train in Japan, and where many of the prominent teachers are. It is only in the last thirty-five years or so that these training temples have accepted and made allowances for foreigners.

In modern times, along with maintaining temple services and related activities, most priests have done funeral and memorial services as a means of support. Although many temples have a zendo, it is often used for storage. After college, a temple priest's oldest son is often sent to one of the head temples for training for a few years. Then he returns to the family temple and eventually takes over when the father retires. Although the son practices zazen while at the head temple, mostly they don't continue when they return home. Zazen is considered by most people as something old-fashioned, which goes along with the perception of the temples as being dark and musty relics of a bygone age, associated with funerals.

But there have always been a few dedicated priests who have carried on and maintained the practice of Dogen's way in Japan. Suzuki Roshi was one of those priests. He was not well known in Japan, and he was not the abbot of a prominent temple—though his temple, Rinso-in, is over 550 years old and is the grandfather temple of many related temples in Shizuoka Prefecture.

Suzuki Roshi had a sincere and genuine respect for monastic practice, spent a year and a half practicing at Eiheiji and Sojiji, but most of his experience had been with lay people in a lay sangha. I think he felt that in Japan he could not express his inmost longing to extend his practice beyond the role of temple ministry. He wanted to introduce people to zazen and to Dogen's teaching, and he found that fertile ground in America. World War II had created so much bad feeling and misunderstanding in the United States about the Japanese people that he wanted to give us something that was the very best that Japan had to offer, something that went beyond Japan and America. He gave us a very simple way, introducing formal Zen practice while leaving out a lot of what he felt was unnecessary for us.

Suzuki Roshi wanted his students to find their own way under his guidance. So he gave some of us a big field, but he didn't ignore us. Even though we were young and relatively inexperienced, he gave us a lot of responsibility. Bill Kwong, one of his earliest disciples, had a sitting group in Mill Valley and Marion Derby had one in Los Altos, which was later led by Les Kaye and Kobun Chino Sensei. This was his way of assessing our abilities and our understanding. He wanted us to take the responsibility, with him taking the role of mentor. To say that Suzuki Roshi was the founder of San Francisco Zen Center may not be completely accurate. The Zen Center was also co-founded by his students with his encouragement.

He also wanted us to be independent of the Japanese cultural model, which is so much a part of Soto Zen. He introduced to us the practice that he knew, but he also knew that over time there would be a transformation of the practice as it engaged with American culture. At the same time, he didn't push for change, knowing that it would come at its own pace if we sincerely maintained our way. Every now and then someone would ask why we didn't just dump the Soto Zen forms and create a completely American Zen practice. Suzuki Roshi would kindly reply that we didn't realize how egotistical we were—wanting to dismiss as irrelevant seven hundred years of practitioners' totally devoted effort and development, without which this practice would never have come to us.

At the same time, he saw us as innocents, free from the cultural baggage of Japanese Soto Zen. We all felt that he knew us better than we knew ourselves.

Page Street

In 1969 San Francisco Zen Center moved from Sokoji Temple to 300 Page Street. Suzuki Roshi's Zen sangha was outgrowing Sokoji and felt the need to have their own space. The board of the Japanese American congregation made that a necessity when they gave Suzuki an ultimatum: us or them. The large three-story building on Page Street had room for a zendo, a Buddha Hall, a dining room, and a courtyard, as well as rooms for many students, including an apartment for Suzuki Roshi and his wife Mitsu. Up to this time the Zen Center had been a nonresidential practice. The members lived at home, although there were some houses across the street from the temple that were rented by students. The Page Street building, which was designed by the well-known architect Julia Morgan, had been built as a residence for young Jewish working women. Silas Hoadley and Ananda Dalenberg were asked to find a building for the Zen Center, and this was the place that they found. (Richard Baker, also integral in Zen Center's early development, was in Japan at the time.)

Tassajara, which had been purchased in 1966, was Zen Center's first residential practice place, but it was a monastery in a remote setting. The Page Street building was more like a cross between a monastery and an urban temple, with a resident program and a nonresident program. This move changed forever the kind of intimacy that had characterized Sokoji, like when a small popular grocery becomes a supermarket.

Page Street had the usual pains of transition, growth, and transformation. It took on a quasimonastic residential model together with the old lay-student nonresidential model of Sokoji. Suzuki Roshi had been a temple priest most of his life and had a deep appreciation for lay practice. On the other hand, he saw the rare opportunity for residential, monastic, and priest practice that was being presented to him. He made an effort to combine opportunities for both at Page Street.

The practice there thrived as more and more new students arrived and the older students matured. The students would go back and forth from Page Street to Tassajara for various periods of time for training. But as Suzuki Roshi's illness progressed in 1970, he was more confined to Page Street. The burden for managing the practice at Tassajara, and eventually also at Page Street, fell to the few Japanese priests who were there, and to the older students.

Suzuki Roshi's Death

On October 11, 1971, in San Francisco, Suzuki Roshi called a small number of his disciples into his living quarters. He was sitting up in bed. He told us that he had been diagnosed with cancer and that it was a relief for him to know that. He knew that it was not curable and made a little joke, saying, "Now I can eat whatever I want."

On November 21, in a very moving ceremony Suzuki Roshi turned over the leadership of Zen Center to his chosen American dharma heir, Richard Baker. Then the disciples gathered around Suzuki Roshi in his study and meeting room. There was a wonderful feeling, a love samadhi, and we were all crying, knowing in our hearts that this was the final communion.

On the morning of December 4, 1971, as we began the traditional seven-day Rohatsu *sesshin*, Suzuki Roshi passed away. We sat through the first period of zazen and the bell didn't ring for *kinhin*. I knew instinctively that Suzuki Roshi had passed away. Then Peter Schneider came and asked a few older students, including myself, to come upstairs. I had a gut feeling about why, which was confirmed when I entered the room and saw Suzuki Roshi's body lying on his back, neatly on the floor with a quilt on top, and on his chest, his *rakusu* (small robe) in its envelope.

All day long people came and filed through the room to pay their final respects. In the late afternoon we carried his body down the stairs to the vehicle that took him to the funeral home. I remember carrying his feet and noticing how bright yellow they were—a symptom of his liver cancer.

There was nothing to do but finish *sesshin*. Any mourning we had to do was absorbed into zazen. There was a general unspoken feeling that Suzuki Roshi had planned it that way. How typical of him, and how kind.

On April 17, 1972, we scattered some of Suzuki Roshi's ashes from a promontory just off the Tassajara road, where the Zen teacher Nyogen Senzaki's ashes had been scattered just a few years before. After that we made an ashes memorial on the top of the hill at the end of Grasshopper Flat. We had an interment ceremony in which the disciples each placed some of the rest of his ashes under a large stone.

The Tassajara environment is mostly stones. Wherever you dig you always encounter stones, and stonework has always been an integral part of being at Tassajara. A year or so earlier, Reb Anderson and Dan Welch had chosen a large stone in the creek, one of several that Suzuki Roshi had pointed out, and hauled it to the base of the hill.

Then Bob Walters and I, with help from others from time to time, had winched it up that hill inch by inch—around trees, chaparral, and rocks, with the help of an old one-cylinder motor, a chain, crowbars, shovels, and a come-along. It took us at least a week. Suzuki Roshi was there to make sure the stone was set just right in the exact spot he wanted. Later, we realized that he had been directing the positioning of his own gravestone.

Suzuki Roshi's Key Subjects

Everything changes—According to his understanding, this is the most fundamental, indisputable principle of Buddha Dharma. All the rest could be considered a commentary on this truth.

Beginner's mind—This became a kind of trademark term for him, which was used in the title of the first book of his talks, *Zen Mind, Beginner's Mind*. I see it as another way of expressing the meaning of *shikantaza*.

Shikantaza—This is a term that Dogen used, which basically means "just" sitting/doing. It applies to daily life as well as to zazen. It also means to let go and arise anew on each moment, or to die and be born in each moment.

No gaining mind—Our practice is to resume our original, true nature. Fundamentally there is nothing to gain or lose. That which is gained is also lost and therefore not fundamental. Our practice is to let go and trust our Buddha-nature.

Nothing fancy—Suzuki Roshi didn't want us to get lost in or confused by complicated theories, or dazzling and seductive explanations, or excessive or ostentatious practices, or distracting mystical beliefs.

Do one thing thoroughly—Suzuki Roshi, like Dogen, stressed: To do one thing, and totally penetrate that one thing; to practice one dharma and penetrate one dharma. Instead of accumulating many things to put into our basket, we strike in the same place over and over to reveal our treasure store. Suzuki Roshi liked to say that we are protected from within. When we have this kind of confidence, we can let go of our crutches and external support; without trying, our practice will give confidence to others.

Nothing special—Suzuki didn't want us to think of zazen as some special practice of some special people. Our practice on the cushion should harmonize with the practice of our daily life. Zazen is not "your" practice. It is the basic activity of the universe in which everything is participating. It is Buddha's practice. Therefore it is not something which we do just for ourselves. Since no two things can exist in the same spot at the same time, we each appear to be sitting in a solitary way.

Your difficulty is your treasure—Zazen has its difficulties as well as its pleasures, in the same way that our daily life has its difficulties and its pleasures. Sometimes our response to problems is to avoid or resist them. But if we approach our problem as a vehicle, or an opportunity, we can welcome and use the problem in a beneficial way that can deepen our practice, rather than allowing ourselves to be overwhelmed and victimized by it. Sometimes Suzuki Roshi would say that you should appreciate the problem you now have. If you get rid of it, another one will take its place, and you may wish you had the previous one.

Little Bear

When you enter the main road to Tassajara, about a mile up the road is a horse ranch run by the Nason family. The Nasons were from the Esselen tribe, and we were right in the heart of Esselen territory. It was necessary to cross a road that ran through the property run by Fred Nason. He inherited it from his family. His grown children lived there and worked the ranch. His eldest son, Tommy, who inherited the ranch from Fred, was locally known as Little Bear, even though his shoulders were about five feet across. In addition to running the horse ranch, the Nasons raised cattle and would take hunting parties into the wilderness to hunt wild boar. The land was ideal for hunting boar, and Little Bear was hired as a guide. Every time we would pass on the road, Fred would invite us in and offer us a beer. David Chadwick especially loved that. We stopped sometimes, sometimes not, and he was very friendly to us. We were on good terms with him, and if we ever needed any heavy machinery work like hauling boulders, we would call on the Nasons.

We became acquainted around 1967 and we maintained a stable yet distant relationship. Our relationship continued for decades. During the 1980s and '90s, Little Bear and Tassajara became more associated. He did a lot of work for Tassajara, like working on the road and bulldozing. So we grew closer together. It turned out that Little Bear was taught to be a shaman by his grandmother.

On his property Little Bear and his friends built a hogan. You dig down into the earth and make a large space, as big as a living room, and cover it with a stick frame and tarps. In the middle of the hogan is a small fire. Little Bear would gather everybody around; it was great to be in the dirt, like a little kid. Little Bear would tell stories, and he was always calling on his grandfather. It was very moving. "O Grandfather," he would chant, invoking his ancestors.

When it was my turn, I would do my Zen thing. I would do the Zen thing and Little Bear would do the Esselen thing. We worked very well together. Little Bear played a flute that had a capped end. It had a very soft sound. He handed it to me. I played it and he liked the way we interacted together. We had this familiarity.

Little Bear was always naturally himself. He had many associates, who formed the Four Winds Council of Big Sur, which was made up of the Esalen Institute, Tassajara Zen Mountain Center, the Esselen Tribe, and New Camaldoli Hermitage, each covering one side of the mountain. The mountain is more than just the mountain; it represents the world at large. They considered the Four Winds as the guardians of the Ventana Wilderness. They all rode horses in deference to the Native way of life. There was a Caucasian man, representing the European Americans; an African American lawyer, representing African Americans; a young representative from Okinawa of Japanese extraction, representing Asia; and Little Bear represented Native Americans. All together representing the four winds, the four directions. The Four Winds would all meet once a year at the horse ranch.

Little Bear and I shared our practices. At that time, I was teaching people to do zazen, so we were sitting zazen for various periods throughout the day, about fifteen or twenty people all together, including guests at Little Bear's ranch. During the daytime and in the evening, Little Bear gave talks and had people do various tasks and experience the life around the hogan. In the morning, when everybody woke up, we would have breakfast and zazen and get prepared for the ride into Pine Valley. We'd pack up the mules and horses. Everybody would have a horse, and a caravan would proceed over the grassy hills to Pine Valley. When we got there, we let the horses and mules loose and they'd all run into the valley at full speed and start chewing the grass. The cooks would make dinner and we would have a little powwow, and Little Bear and I would take turns giving short talks.

The next day, after breakfast and a little zazen, our little community would spend the morning gathering long, thin green branches and use them to build the framework for the sweat lodge. When the framework was done, we collected rocks and long branches and covered the framework with overlapping tarps so that it would be airproof. The stones collected were about a foot in diameter. Outside the lodge was the bonfire. The fire was kept going all day long, and the large stones were heated. Firing the stones all day made them so hot they were transparent, red and transparent. We had a basket on the end of a stick to carry the stones in. Everyone took a place inside the lodge, and whoever was capable went out and put a stone in the basket. As the stone was being brought into the center of the circle, all together everyone would say, "Welcome, Stone Person." The stone was very carefully placed down in the center of the circle. Ten or fifteen stones would come in. Little Bear had a water jar. The stones would come in one at a time and Little Bear would dip into that cold water and pour it on the hot rocks and *pfseew!* It got so hot with the steam rising, everybody dove for the floor. I had thought I would sit there in zazen the whole time, but I too dove for the floor. I remember lying on the floor, and I vaguely remember walking out. Not everybody could handle it. I remember waking up on the grass and Little Bear saying, "Oh, you had a mystical experience."

Berkeley Zendo on Dwight Way

In 1966 I moved across the Bay to Berkeley. Suzuki Roshi would come over to Berkeley on Monday mornings. He had a small number of regular students in Berkeley who would sit with each other in someone's home on Monday mornings, and Suzuki Roshi joined us. One person hosted zazen at his mother's antique store. We would do zazen, bowing and chanting, followed by Reverend Suzuki's talk, and end with an informal breakfast. It was a wonderful, intimate way to be with him, since there were usually no more than eight or ten students. It didn't feel so formal. That's where we got our Monday morning tradition. Suzuki Roshi would give a talk and then we'd have breakfast.

Being dedicated to the practice, I drove to Sokoji on the other mornings for zazen. On the way I would pick up some of Suzuki's other East Bay students. At that time, there was no zazen at Sokoji on days with a four or a nine in the date, which marked the rest inter vals or "laundry days" for monastic or temple life in the Japanese system. Sometimes we would forget and arrive to find the door locked. Suzuki Roshi might look out the window and wave to us.

Suzuki Roshi was touched by the sincerity of his students and felt a need to establish a zendo in Berkeley. One Saturday during a talk at Sokoji, he was expressing his desire to have a zendo in Berkeley and asked me if I would find a place and maintain it. He knew that I would be willing to do that, and it felt good that he trusted me to do it.

In 1967 the rental housing market was reasonable. I biked all over Berkeley looking for a place, and I found a wonderful old two-and-a-half-story Victorian. It had a basement apartment (which continued to be occupied by someone else until 1973), while the main floor was spacious, filled with light, and had ten-foot ceilings. Upstairs was a large attic. The rent for the whole place was $130 a month.

It had a big backyard, and in front was a tall palm tree, which from time to time was packed full of twittering birds. There was also a very tall monkey pod tree, the tallest tree on the block, which produced extremely sharp spikes and enormous seed pods that would explode like a bomb when they hit the ground.

During the first few months we did zazen in the front room. After morning zazen the members would go to work and I would spend my time taking care of the place.

Although at first we sat downstairs, with the fireplace going on cold winter mornings, from the beginning we wanted to turn the attic into the zendo. It was a large square room with a double A-frame roof that came down past the floor and left a narrow opening for air and light all the way around. It had one window and got very hot in the summer. The floor itself was made of wide, splintery, dried-out, low-grade, irregular fir boards. We loved this space and put a lot of work into it to make it a viable zendo.

To do that, we needed to complete the attic floor. But I wasn't about to buy new materials. One day I spotted a big piece of plywood on the freeway, which I quickly snatched up. I liked to go to the beach near the racetrack at Golden Gate Fields to comb for materials. I mostly scrounged whatever we needed. (In 1973 Andrew and Edit, a wonderful young couple from Alabama, with their baby, Ria, moved into the basement apartment. One of Andrew's favorite pastimes was dumpster diving. He would bring back incredible caches of cheese and other articles that were thrown away to make room on the supermarket shelves. Not everyone was like Andrew and me, but most of the members appreciated not being solicited for money all the time.)

But that was several years later. To come back to 1967: Once I had gotten all the necessary lumber and we had used to it fix up the attic floor, I got some members together and we had a sanding party. Some students from San Francisco Zen Center also came over. We did all the work by hand, which included sculpting and smoothing each board and bringing out the beauty of the irregularities.

The stairs up to the attic were very steep. The whole setup was way out of code for a meeting place. We had no insurance and fortunately no one ever hurt themselves walking up and down the stairs.

I had a little black dog named India that I inherited, who would sometimes lie down next to the black *zafu* (sitting cushions). One dark morning someone came in and sat on India, thinking she was a *zafu*. On another morning in stormy weather, just before zazen, a huge frond from our palm tree tore loose and came crashing through the main floor window where someone would have been sitting a half hour later.

When I saw the huge backyard at Dwight Way, I knew what I wanted to do. I wanted to be an organic gardening Zen student. I wanted to spend my days cultivating that garden, sitting zazen every morning and evening, taking care of the zendo and the members, and, if I ever became a mature student, teaching.

The feeling I had was that I wanted a grassroots zendo, a local zendo. Grassroots meaning that members would develop the zendo and support it. We turned our large backyard into a vegetable garden. One time back when I was living in San Francisco I had access to a small strip of land, and had the urge to make a vegetable garden. I had never done that before. I borrowed a shovel and turned over the soil. It was a hot day and I took off my shoes and walked on the soft warm earth and all at once had an overwhelming experience of being connected to the universe. The organic gardening movement was just taking off and I was sold on it. I made compost. I became a compost fanatic, which is not unusual among those who discover the living organisms and energy that is a compost pile. I grew a great variety of vegetables and occasionally sold them to a local organic food store, Wholly Foods, and I went out and collected cuttings all over town to make compost. Eric Storlie, a San Francisco Zen Center student at the time, would bring the garbage from SFZC to Berkeley, and I'd put it in my compost pile. When he came over he brought his violin, and he and I would play violin and recorder duets together. Sometimes students would come to talk with me, and I would receive them in the garden. I really enjoyed that kind of life. To me that was the essence of Zen practice: to sit zazen and cultivate the soil. That was great. At one point during the mid-1970s drought, I constructed a gray-water system that supplied water to the garden from the kitchen sink.

I was fulfilling my dream of a grassroots zendo (that would have been a good name for it). At first I asked for $5 a month in dues. I kept the dues in a little tobacco can, and when we or I needed something, I would dip into the can. I still keep that can as a memento of our original treasury. I suppose it's because of my upbringing, but I have always been extremely frugal with money. From the time I was twenty until I was ordained at forty, I always bought my clothes at thrift shops. I wanted to get the most use out of any object before discarding it. At Sokoji I wore the same sweater every day for a couple of years. One day, Suzuki Roshi took hold of the collar and with a soft smile said, "This is your robe." He often said that in order to become a priest, you should first be a good layperson. I think he was trying to tell people not to jump to the conclusion that they could easily become ordained and shirk their responsibility to their families and their other obligations.

At Dwight Way there was zazen every morning except Saturday and Sunday. On Saturday morning we would go to Sokoji. We also went there for *sesshins* and longer sitting days. After we had been operating the zendo in Berkeley for a while, I asked Suzuki if I could introduce an afternoon zazen schedule. He said, "Yes. You may do whatever you want." So we added a 5:30 p.m. zazen period. We experimented with informal breakfast in the dining room, and formal monastic style.

I considered myself the resident caretaker of the Dwight Way zendo, keeping the place in order, making sure that we had everything we needed, always being present for zazen, collecting books for a library, and taking care of the garden and the grounds. I wanted to build a good Buddhist library so I asked the members for used book donations, which I took to trade at Moe's Books on Telegraph Avenue, a large bookstore that gives you credit for used books. I'd get all this trade credit, and then I'd go to the Buddhist section of the store and buy Buddhist books. Then I'd read some of them. That's how I learned about Buddhism, by getting the books and reading them and building a library. Over the years I built up a considerable library. This gave me a good picture of the many aspects of Buddhist literature, and also the opportunity to educate myself.

In 1967, after SF Zen Center acquired Tassajara, Suzuki Roshi became more absorbed in its development, and the number of students in San Francisco increased. He gradually became less available to come to Berkeley on a regular basis. Instead, Katagiri Sensei would sometimes come over on Mondays. Then, as he became busier, Kobun Chino Sensei or Yoshimura Sensei would occasionally come. While Suzuki was alive, we had the benefit of practicing with these Japanese priests who had been drawn to SF Zen Center and Suzuki Roshi. Their presence gave us a more rounded experience of Soto Zen. Each of their personalities was different. Their presentations varied, but their fundamental understanding and their teachings all struck the same chord.

Suzuki Roshi sent Richard Baker, who was the president of SF Zen Center, to discuss with me what kind of support SFZC should offer us as an affiliated center. Richard came over and we talked, and the question came up, well, should San Francisco give us any support? And he said, "I don't think so. I think that if the members themselves don't support the place, then it shouldn't be supported." And I said, "Well, I agree with that." I agreed with his idea that the members should support the place; otherwise, what was it? But I didn't agree with him that SFZC shouldn't give us *some* support. I've always felt I was right about that. It would have been nice for him to say, "Well, we'll give you some support." Even if it's just camaraderie, right? But that never happened. It was really hard to challenge Richard because he was so successful.

At some point people felt that what was really happening was in San Francisco. A number of people who were practicing with me moved to San Francisco. This was fine with me. I have never tried to recruit or hold on to any students, but to let people go where they feel they should. I have always responded fully to whoever shows sincere interest and engagement. But I have never had to sit alone. The vortex of practice has always attracted practitioners without the need to advertise. I was always encouraging people. You know, "If that's what you want to do, please do." My bottom line of practice was: I sit zazen every day. If someone wants to come and sit zazen, I welcome them. If they want to leave, I say goodbye. And no matter how long they have been practicing with me, or whatever our relationship is, that's always been my bottom line. I've stuck with that and I feel okay about it. Eventually most of them came back, maybe after a short or long period of time. But that's not something I counted on. When we saw each other, it was almost like there had been no interval. Suzuki's son Hoitsu once said that a priest should be like a round glass or cup with no corners to get hung up on, presenting the same face all the way around. The Sixth Ancestor in China said that one who carries the Dharma is like the sun in the sky, radiating light in all directions without discrimination. A Dharma teacher can be someone who is content to be solitary, but when someone appears who wants the Dharma, the teacher responds and comes forth. And when there is no one to respond to, the teacher returns, content to be solitary. I've always had faith in my practice, which has sustained me. Whatever happens is supposed to happen. So I've always felt okay. If nobody came, it was okay. If people left, it was okay. I was just doing my practice with whoever was there.

Actually, when people leave I never think about them until I see them again. I just focus on what's in front of me. I've never tried to gain students, and I did not call myself a teacher. People would come, and they'd say, "Are you the teacher?" And I'd say, "Well, if you feel that I'm teaching you something, or you're learning something from me, then you can think of me in that way, but I'm not going to tell you that I'm the teacher here." I maintained that for a long time and felt good about that, because it always helped me to not get ahead of myself. I felt, if I'm going to be a teacher, someone is going to have to tell me that. I've always been very careful to be verified by others. In this busy world where there are so many possibilities and distracting enticements, my intention has been to maintain this one single path of zazen transmitted to us by Suzuki Roshi and to keep it as simple as possible.

We were at Dwight Way for twelve years.

Priest Ordination in Berkeley

Two years after I opened the Berkeley zendo, Suzuki Roshi ordained me as a priest on May 19, 1969—the day after his birthday. (May 19 was, coincidentally, the date of my first marriage and the date of my Mountain Seat Ceremony when I became the abbot of Berkeley Zen Center in 1984.) Suzuki Roshi had to consider whether to do the ordination ceremony at Tassajara or at Berkeley, and he finally chose Berkeley. We had a wonderful ceremony in our attic zendo, with Katagiri and Kobun Chino assisting. I remember Kobun showing me how to wear the robes, the fine points and attention to detail. I also remember getting all tangled up and running to him to get me out of the mess of cloth. The members in Berkeley were happy, I think, to have their own priest and to realize that it was possible for that to happen. And it gave a little boost to the practice.

Suzuki had ordained two people shortly after he arrived in San Francisco, but they left before Zen Center was incorporated. Ananda Claude Dalenberg was ordained in Japan at Rinso-in. He said that Suzuki Roshi took him into a room at the temple, said some things in Japanese, and put some robes on him, and he didn't have any idea what had happened. Then there were Phil Wilson, Graham Petchey, Ananda Claude Dalenberg, Richard Baker, Ron and Joyce Browning, Jean Ross, and myself. By the time I was ordained, Jean Ross was in Carmel, Phil was gone. Graham was in Japan and didn't come back to Zen Center. Richard was in Japan and Claude was involved with a study program in the city. So that left me as the only American priest at Zen Center at that time. I didn't know what to do, so I just copied what Suzuki Roshi did. I just followed in his footsteps. I bowed the way he bowed. I sat the way he sat.

I even unconsciously copied the way he spoke. Many of us did that. One time my dharma brother Bill Kwong and I were giving a talk together at Sonoma State College and someone said, "There is something about the way both of you speak that has a funny quality about it, what is that?" I realized it was our Suzuki Roshi accent.

There is a way of teaching and learning without words, where a student observes his or her teacher closely and follows in their footsteps. Suzuki Roshi did not explain things. He just expected me to catch on. This way is subtle, intimate, and intuitive. When talking about how he wanted to practice with us at Tassajara, he said, in effect, that he just wanted to hang out with us, moving stones, sitting zazen, eating together, and enjoying our life together. His teaching was simply to set an example and transmit the Dharma through this kind of merging. This kind of teacher-student relationship works best in a small sangha where the students have daily contact with their teacher. It is a kind of apprenticeship. The student must then find his or her own way. Suzuki Roshi felt that this old poem expressed it just right:

The Blue Mountain is the parent of the White Cloud,
The White Cloud is the child of the Blue Mountain,
All day long they depend on each other
Without being dependent on each other.
The Blue Mountain is always the Blue Mountain,
The White Cloud is always the White Cloud.

Shuso at Tassajara, 1970

I returned to Tassajara in early 1970. Suzuki Roshi had asked me to be *shuso* for the three-month practice period. The *shuso* is a mature student who shares the abbot or practice leader's seat for that time. Until later years, the shuso was always an ordained priest and, as much as possible, they assumed this position at Tassajara in order of seniority. At that time Suzuki was feeling the effects of his illness and was unable to come to Tassajara, so the practice leader was Tatsugami Roshi.

It was a well-attended practice period, a mixture of older and newer students. Most of the students that Suzuki would eventually ordain were there. Peter Schneider, who before Tassajara had been an English teacher, was the director. Dan Welch was an artist who had practiced in Japan for a year and a half at Ryutakuji, a Rinzai monastery, and knew a good deal of Japanese. He became the interpreter when Katagiri was not available. Bob Halpern was the *ino* (director of zendo activities). Dan and his wife Louise were Tatsugami's *jisha* and *anja* (attendants).

Tassajara was a radical experiment in Buddhist monastic life. I think of it as Frontier Buddhism or Pioneer Buddhism. Here we were, an assembly of men and women of various backgrounds who had been practicing with a Japanese Zen priest in an old Jewish synagogue that had been turned into a Soto Zen temple with a Japanese congregation, and we were now setting up the first successful Zen

Buddhist monastery in the West in an old remote resort fourteen miles into the Ventana Wilderness.

Return to Berkeley

When I came back from Tassajara after I had served as *shuso*, I resumed my position at the Berkeley zendo as before, going to zazen and taking care of the garden. Richard Baker had his Mountain Seat (abbot installation) ceremony on November 21, 1971. Now that Suzuki Roshi was no longer my living teacher and I wasn't accepting Richard as my teacher, I was more or less on my own. I had never proclaimed myself as a teacher—I felt that I was simply the caretaker of the Berkeley zendo—but I was teaching zazen and the zendo forms, responding to people and developing the practice. When the question came up, I would usually say that I was not the "Teacher," but I could address their questions. I did not advertise myself as the teacher. I would say that if you felt that you were learning something from me, then fine. My role was to provide a place for people to practice zazen.

At that time we still went to Page Street for five- and seven-day *sesshins* because I didn't feel that I was authorized to lead them until I had Dharma Transmission. Suzuki Roshi was very strict about what we were allowed to do. Unless you had Transmission you couldn't do weddings, funerals, or ordinations or be considered a legitimate teacher.

Given Richard's attitude toward the other disciples of Suzuki Roshi, Bill Kwong and I didn't expect much in the way of Dharma Transmission. We both felt frustrated. I won't speak for Bill on this subject, but as for myself, I resolved that I would simply give myself wholeheartedly to the practice. If I did that, then the practice itself would be my witness and my verification. Therefore, I wouldn't have to court anyone's favor and I would be free to continue to develop my own practice and the practice at BZC in the way that I felt was correct and in conformity with Suzuki Roshi's teaching. I had faith that if I was true to the practice without trying to get something, that whatever was due to me would come in its own time and in its own way. For the next thirteen years I practiced that way within those limitations. No Transmission and no colored robe.

Liz

A couple of years after my ordination, I met Liz Horowitz. She and some other students were living in a house near the Berkeley zendo and they came to zazen regularly. I was impressed with Liz. She had recently graduated from UC Berkeley, and I was touched by her dedication to the practice, her integrity, her intelligence. She was skilled at sewing and cooking and even basket making. She was good at whatever she turned her hand to. Soon she was sewing robes for the priests who were ordaining at SF Zen Center; everyone wanted one of Liz's robes. Her efficiency was a good complement to my intuitive style. She eventually moved into the Berkeley zendo with me.

Liz grew sprouts from seeds in a little hothouse that I built for her at Dwight Way. She would sell the sprouts to the Berkeley Co-op markets. Alfalfa sprouts were all the rage then. She kept up her sprout business until we went to live at Tassajara.

In 1972 Richard Baker, as abbot of SF Zen Center, asked me to be the director of Tassajara for a year and a half. I accepted. Liz and I went together and lived at Tassajara. We were not married at the time, but we did get married later at Green Gulch in 1978. At Tassajara I was the director and Liz worked in the kitchen and the garden. The Tassajara kitchen has its own schedule, which meant that we didn't see much of each other during the day. The director's work is never over, so I was always dealing with one thing or another. It was good training for both of us.

While we were gone, Ed and Meg Brown took our place at the Berkeley zendo, where Ed wrote the *Tassajara Cookbook*. When we returned from Tassajara after a year and a half, Liz didn't restart the sprouts business.

In 1988 I became co-abbot of San Francisco Zen Center at the same time as I was abbot of Berkeley Zen Center. For nine years my circuit was Tassajara, San Francisco, Green Gulch, Berkeley, and home. I don't know how I did that, but it was very hard on Liz and on our son, Daniel. If I told Liz that I would like to do something, she said okay. Daniel didn't like it so much. One time he wrote me a note saying, "Daddy, don't go away again."

Liz never favored her own well-being over what I had to do. I should say, though, that Liz has always kept me on track. She still does. She never let me get ahead of myself, or aggrandize myself, or call myself something special. Our relationship is like this: I see the glass half-full, she sees the glass half-empty. So I always encourage her, and she's always bringing me down to earth. I really want to apologize for all the inconveniences I created for her and Daniel.

Teaching at Berkeley Zendo

After Suzuki Roshi there was no other teacher that I was drawn to. There is a saying that you can't study with a dead teacher. But I always felt that I was following Suzuki's teaching, and I continued to use his example and his words as my guide and they have always proved to be reliable. Even though I didn't go through the Transmission ceremony with him, there was no doubt in my mind that I was his heir. Although my teacher is no longer living, I have always made an effort to keep his teaching and practice alive.

Little by little, the sangha grew. I can remember times when there were only four or five people at morning zazen. I remember one time when only one person came. It was the Fourth of July in the early 1970s, and it was just the two of us. This other person was so disappointed that he left in disgust. But over time a core group developed, and the sangha grew. That development is ongoing and always changing. As the practice and the members have matured, the core group has grown and become more stable and reliable.

One important element of a practice place is a dedicated person, usually what we call a teacher. "Teacher" may not be the most accurate term. In Japan the term for abbot is *jushoku*, the one who is "presently abiding." In monastic terminology, "The head of rice and gruel." But we use the term "teacher" and fit it to our needs. We say Buddha, Dharma, Sangha, the Three Jewels, or the three legs that support the practice. Dharma is the teaching, Sangha is the members, and Buddha is the *jushoku*, the one who knows the purpose, the function, and the direction of the practice and who makes every effort to maintain it for the benefit of the sangha. In that way the teacher is the focal point. But that does not mean that a sangha cannot at the same time have a democratic process (provided we understand what that really means). From time to time, we encounter sitting groups around the country that have steady members and a consistent practice, and are looking for a teacher to bring it all together.

SF Zen Center's Expansion; Richard Baker and Suzuki Roshi's Other Disciples

From the beginning, Richard Baker and I had some difficulty with each other. Competition may have played a part in it. One time

Suzuki Roshi said, "If my students quarrel with each other, I will leave." Suzuki Roshi asked me to be the *shuso* for the 1970 winter practice period at Tassajara, so I did that. He said to me, "Although I have asked you to be the *shuso* before Bill Kwong, I am giving him Dharma Transmission first." My understanding, possibly naïve, was that when you become ordained you let go of your former life and simply begin a new life, letting go of worldly ambitions, which puts you on an equal footing with your peers. My understanding was that an ordained person is devoted to bringing forth wisdom and compassion, letting go of self-promotion.

I had a gut feeling of mistrust about Richard, which was reinforced as events unfolded over time. Suzuki Roshi recognized this and made an effort, I felt, to be fair to both of us, realizing that our paths were not the same. I knew that Suzuki Roshi also had his doubts about Richard, and that his entrustment to him was based on a great leap of faith that the Dharma would prevail over personal ambition. Just prior to Richard's Transmission ceremony, Suzuki Roshi said to me, "When I go to Japan, I will give Transmission to Richard. What do you think about that?" I said, "Do you think he is ready?" He said, "Sometimes we give it when someone is ready, and sometimes we give it and hope."

Soon after Suzuki Roshi's funeral, Richard called the ordained disciples together. He said that although we had been ordained and had black robes, we were all novices, and that he, having received a brown robe, attesting to his Transmission and being installed as abbot, was the head priest of Zen Center. The further implication was that Zen Center had been endowed to him. I don't think any of us had expected him to go this far, even though a number of us were aware of his desire for power. My idea was that whoever succeeded Suzuki Roshi would include and recognize the other disciples, and make an effort to create a harmonious leadership, taking advantage of what each one of us had experienced with our teacher. I felt that each one of us represented an aspect of Suzuki, and that together we could create something unique and wonderful. That would be the fulfillment of Suzuki Roshi's legacy.

Each one of Suzuki Roshi's disciples had to decide whether or not to stay. In one way or another Richard tried to eliminate competition by his peers. He forced out several prominent leaders and tended to ignore and belittle Bill Kwong. Those who stayed became Richard's students. Anyone who was not loyal to him was not welcome to stay. Before he passed away, Suzuki Roshi had asked Reb Anderson to be Richard's assistant and to give him his full support. Reb helped to promote Richard's vision and became his right-hand and trusted disciple. Richard then promoted Reb as the ideal model of a Zen student. The disciples found themselves in a bind, because on the one hand they had their doubts about Richard, but on the other hand Suzuki Roshi had appointed him to be the abbot and they wanted to give him the benefit of any doubt. Because Richard was so successful in expanding Zen Center, it was difficult to object.

In order to win us over, Richard outlined his vision and how, with our help, he would actualize it. In addition to the City Center and Tassajara, there would also be a new center in Marin County, including an organic farm and a conference and retreat center, and we would work with Alan Chadwick, who was a rising and prominent horticulturalist from England. Green Gulch Farm, as it is called, is a long grassy slope leading from Highway 1 to the ocean, which originally included a winding creek flowing leisurely through the property to the ocean. George Wheelwright, the co-founder of Polaroid and a *National Georgraphic* photographer, owned the land and saw the property as an ideal place for raising a special breed of cattle, so he straightened out the creek to make it more accessible to them. It became just one line of water rushing to the ocean. He imported and raised prize bulls from Australia, importing just the right kind of feed. As he was getting older, Mr. Wheelwright felt a need to put the land in the hands of somebody who would appreciate it and take good care of it. Through the Nature Conservancy, which acted as a go-between, our proposal to purchase it and turn it into a Zen center and organic farm seemed reasonable and satisfactory to Mr. Wheelwright. The deal was consummated. Richard presented the foundations of his plans through the example of acquiring Green Gulch.

At another meeting he proceeded to unwrap and show us some new, expensive, fancy robes that he had ordered for himself from Japan. We all looked on, and as I remember, this was followed up by serving us an enormous piece of strawberry shortcake. All the rest of us were wearing our old worn robes and had no means with which to replace them. I couldn't remain silent. I said something like "How can you walk up and down flaunting your riches in front of Suzuki Roshi's disciples? Why didn't you order robes for your peers?" From that time on I became Richard's outspoken critic.

I found myself in a different position than the other disciples. Because I had the Berkeley zendo I had some degree of independence. I was a disciple of Suzuki Roshi, the zendo was an affiliate of San Francisco Zen Center, and I had always been a Zen Center student. But I had an independence that most of the others didn't. I think Richard felt that I would simply retreat to Berkeley and he wouldn't have to worry about me. But I had a strong feeling that San Francisco Zen Center did not belong to Richard or to anyone else, and that I was not going to allow myself to be forced out. I have always had a strong loyalty to San Francisco Zen Center as the place where I entered practice with my teacher and grew up with my peers. I also felt that SFZC was like the flagship of West Coast Zen and that the practice there and the trust that Suzuki Roshi had created should not be lost.

Abbot Richard Baker

Richard Baker arrived at Sokoji two years after Suzuki. He was intelligent, sophisticated, Harvard-educated, full of energy, and young. He had sailed in the Merchant Marine one summer, and then was enrolled as a graduate student at UC Berkeley when George Fields at Fields Book Store told him of Suzuki Sensei at Sokoji. He organized a major conference on LSD in 1966 and learned the skills of networking and information flow. He further developed that skill at Zen Center. Richard made a point of connecting with famous and well-positioned people. Two of his frequent phrases were "So-and-So is the top person in his field" or "world class."

Richard was a really good fundraiser and recruited some very sincere wealthy people to contribute to Zen Center. (I never knew how to do anything like that.) He was charismatic, convincing, and ambitious. He divided his time between Zen Center and the cultivation of important people of power, wealth, and influence outside the sangha who were inspired by his vision of Zen Center. He persuaded us to acquire the Green Gulch property in Marin County and initiated the Tassajara Bakery, Greens Restaurant, the Corner Grocery, and a print shop (the latter didn't work out). He was working on developing a spectacular bookstore, which never did happen. The SFZC began buying up properties in the Page Street neighborhood. In his own apartment on Page Street next door to the City Center, he had artists painting rococo-style floral designs on the ceilings. In the twelve years that he was abbot it seemed like he had the Midas touch. Every year Zen Center attracted more students and more outside support. But it was a bubble that was on a shaky foundation, and when it collapsed it was disastrous.

Richard was the only student in the West who received Dharma Transmission from Suzuki Roshi. Suzuki Roshi had also started the process with Bill Kwong, but he didn't live to complete it. Suzuki Roshi had asked Richard to invite Noiri Roshi from Japan in order to help Zen Center and Richard learn the Transmission ceremony for the sake of Suzuki Roshi's other disciples. This never happened. Richard set himself up as the sole authority in the community.

As time went on, Richard became more and more powerful. The original plan for the businesses was that the students who worked there would have room and board and a small stipend as a means of support for their practice. But as it turned out, the students were working long hours and had little time for zazen. Ideally the plan, if it had worked, would have supported the students to practice, and the work could be seen as an element of practice. But as it worked out, some of us felt more and more that Richard was taking advantage of them in order to build and maintain a growing empire. They were being used and getting less, while the abbot was realizing his creative ambitions and accumulating property for the Zen Center and fame. Toward the end of his abbacy, some of those who were close to him could see that Zen Center was getting more stretched and that he was getting out of control. Although he had an extended affair with a female student, it was a weekend affair with the wife of one of his close friends that touched off the backlash that finally ended with Richard's resignation and departure.

The other side of the story is that Richard was an extremely talented and creative personality. During the twelve years that he was abbot he acquired Green Gulch, developed Tassajara and the businesses, and made it possible for many people to practice in a dynamic situation. It is important not to forget that. But the question re-mains—at what cost?

Impact on the Sangha

In my opinion, Suzuki Roshi's mistake was in giving too much power to one person, allowing Richard to proceed on the basis of being the sole inheritor of his Dharma. If Suzuki Roshi had set up a council of elders with some authority, they could have provided a safeguard of checks and balances to Richard's excesses. Instead, Richard used his empowerment to create a great gap between himself and everyone else, so that he would be untouchable.

Although people began to wonder about all of this, it was hard to counter or question it openly because he was so enormously success-ful. Zen Center was becoming a visible entity in San Francisco, espe-cially in elite circles. Richard was hobnobbing with the cream of San Francisco society, including an astronaut and the governor of Cali-fornia. He was bringing avant-garde people and ideas together. At the same time, within Zen Center, he began ordaining more priests. The old Zen Center had been mostly lay people plus a few priests. Now becoming a priest seemed like the thing to do. The priest prac-tice took center stage and the lay practice was marginalized. The priests became the favored group, with greater access to Baker Roshi, and were considered the true sangha. It was understood that the stu-dents were loyal and devoted to him. They discussed their practice with him as the teacher and with no one else, which meant that he had a string to each one and they didn't discuss their practice with each other. They had a vertical connection with the abbot but lacked a horizontal connection with each other. Sometimes a student would have to wait a long time for an interview because Baker Roshi was so busy. He was also leading *sesshins*, seeing people in *dokusan* (one-on-one teacher-student discussions), giving lectures, overseeing the businesses, fundraising, traveling widely, and cultivating important connections. Most of the students were by then working in the Zen Center businesses. Altogether, this gave him an enormous amount of power. He was a living dynamo.

Although on the surface everything seemed to be going well, problems were beginning to emerge. What was clear to me was that there was an enormous amount of denial within Zen Center. In the first place, it became obvious to me that Baker Roshi's main purpose became name, fame, and the pursuit of power—three basic stumbling blocks to practice. Zen Center was becoming Baker Roshi's showplace, fostering a mystique of Zen, with all those monks in black robes doing zazen, three major practice centers bustling with activity, and a bevy of cutting-edge businesses run by the students. Without faith, which fosters humility as a balancing factor and keeps our ego in line, intelligence easily turns to self-delusion, cunning, or craftiness and loses all sense of proportion.

I felt that Baker Roshi was beginning to believe his own story. With his unlimited power he could use his students to gain his ends. Since he didn't recognize any other authority, who was there to bring him to task? I observed that no one was allowed to question his extravagance or his intentions without paying for it by being marginalized, criticized, or forced out. No one ever complained except me.

Since I refused to be forced out, I had to bear the brunt of his criticism. I sensed what his attitude was toward me at any time by the way his senior students related to me, which was often disdainfully. Berkeley Zen Center was considered a place that was tacitly off limits for his students. The hardest part was being snubbed and ridiculed.

Early on, Berkeley Zen Center was no longer listed as an affiliate.

People I had known and practiced with rarely came to visit. When Liz and I left Tassajara in 1973, we invited a number of the Tassajara staff that we had become close with to come over for dinner. They all enthusiastically accepted. A few days later each one called and said that for one reason or another they couldn't make it.

Baker Roshi appointed all the board members, and at one point proclaimed them to be permanent members, of which I was one. At board meetings I had a hard time distinguishing between what was Zen Center business and what was Baker Roshi business. The two were totally intertwined. Most of the requests he made were rubber-stamped by the board.

I do have to say that he also did some nice things for us. One time when he went on one of his numerous shopping trips to Japan, he asked if there was anything I wanted for the Berkeley center. I asked him to bring a Buddha figure for the altar. He came back with a very nice piece, which graces our altar today.

My thought, my hope, was that when Suzuki Roshi died all of his disciples would work together to create a wonderful Zen Center. I thought that surely Richard would be more unifying. But apparently that was not Richard's idea. His idea seemed to be that he was going to create whatever it was that was Zen Center. So he kind of scattered the family, rather than unifying it. This was very disappointing to me and I always felt very critical of whatever he did. I felt more isolated in Berkeley. But Richard had great plans, and Suzuki Roshi just gave it to him and said, "Do something." I didn't feel so good about that. But he was so powerful, he knew so many people, and he also had organizational skills which were marvelous.

Later, after things fell apart and most people turned on him, I tried to help mediate the conflict. By that time, I had given up my criticism and felt I could help him. I thought I had a good idea of where Richard was at.

Co-abbots and Rebuilding San Francisco Zen Center

Much has been written about Richard Baker's fall from grace, but little attention has been given to how San Francisco Zen Center survived afterward. To many, Zen Center seemed either finished or diminished after the resignation of Richard Baker Roshi. For some people, Zen Center was Richard and Richard was Zen Center. But for many of the older members who had practiced with Suzuki Roshi, Zen Center had no fixed identity. Before Richard put his stamp on it as abbot, Suzuki Roshi's influence of integrity, honesty, simplicity, and wisdom guided Zen Center. It was recognized by those outside as a rare and trustworthy endeavor. Zen Center under Richard became overextended and top-heavy, and it finally collapsed due to ambition, self-belief, and lack of attention to the karmic consequences of manipulation. As a new Zen institution, Zen Center didn't seem to be prepared to hold together its monastic and lay foundation. It seemed like it was too soon to combine the two. He was trying to put too many things together.

After Richard left, Zen Center was thrown into a kind of chaos. The students had lost their leader. The unity was lost. Those who stayed were looking for leadership, but most of the students had pledged allegiance to Richard as their teacher, and he had had a big influence on their lives. The board had been more or less a rubber stamp for his ideas, not all of which were bad, but it all got mixed up with his personal ambitions and his place in society. When he left, his senior students found themselves unempowered unless they went with him. Some of his students did go with him, but a good many of them just left Zen Center, leaving the sangha with a scattered feeling.

The Page Street building became like a quasi-transient Zen hotel, without standards. Very few people went to zazen. Those who did sat in the hallway. No one would go into the zendo. Disillusionment ruled the atmosphere. Green Gulch fared no better. Green Gulch was Richard's pet project and it was still a work in progress. No one knew exactly what it was. It was constantly finding its direction from the beginning.

Tassajara, on the other hand, fared better than the others. It had been the most disciplined practice place, and its strict schedule continued to hold the practice together. But the disillusionment and depression were still palpable. Students questioned why they had to do anything. Faith in the practice and the leadership is what holds everything together. Without that it falls apart like a broken string of beads.

Zen Center limped along like a ship without a rudder for a pretty long time. The board met every day, trying to sort it out and come to some decisions. It is no exaggeration to say that there was a cloud of mourning for about five years. At some point the board decided to ask Katagiri Roshi, who had been Suzuki Roshi's assistant and who was now abbot at the Minnesota Zen Center, to come back and be the abbot of SFZC for one year. That helped to stabilize the practice to a certain extent. Katagiri Roshi took as much responsibility as he could.

At the end of Katagiri's term, Reb Anderson was asked to step up as abbot for a term of four years with a possible three-year extension. At this point the board had taken over the leadership of Zen Center and charged themselves with that responsibility. Zen Center was becoming so large there was a need for more than one abbot, so the board invited me to be co-abbot with Reb. I had been running Berkeley Zen Center pretty successfully for a good number of years; I had Dharma Transmission by that point; I was on the SF Zen Center board; I was intimately familiar with the situation; and I lived just over the bridge.

I told the board that since Reb was already the abiding abbot at

SFZC, I did not wish to accept the position unless he too invited me—since he was the person I would be working with most closely. He did so.

I also had to consider that I already had a full practice schedule in Berkeley. I talked with the Berkeley Zen Center board, and they gave their blessing. I would have to divide my time between the City Center, Green Gulch, Tassajara, Berkeley, and my family. It was 1988, I was fifty-nine, and I had a wife and a seven-year-old son.

So Reb and I, two disciples of Suzuki Roshi who have significant differences in approach and temperament, had to figure out how to be co-abbots, how to create a harmonious sangha, and how to give the members an incentive to practice. First, we had to learn how to get along with each other. We decided that we would both be overall abbots with no special territory. This mostly worked, but since Reb lived at Green Gulch, Green Gulch more or less fell to him, and then City Center fell to me. We agreed that neither of us would make a decision without the approval of the other, and if one of us did, we would call him on it. That worked very well and kept us checked and balanced.

When Richard had originally taken responsibility, he and the board had registered Zen Center as a "corporation sole," which gave the chief priest (at that time Suzuki Roshi) the main responsibility for the leadership of the corporation—something like that of the Catholic Church with the Pope as the pontiff. The primary concern was that Suzuki Roshi would be able to have control over any decisions concerning the ownership of Tassajara. The chief priest had no term limit. Richard and the board each had one vote and nothing could happen without the chief priest's permission. When Richard left Zen Center, that incorporation was still in place. The board of directors went to Sacramento and changed the articles of incorporation in a more democratic direction. The board of directors became the director of Zen Center.

Suddenly everything had to be decided by committee. This

change of governance slowed the decision-making process to a crawl, but it was a process of transformation and empowerment that seemed worthwhile, and it gave the sangha a sense of inclusion.

A few years later, when things were beginning to settle down, Richard Baker paid a visit to Reb and me. He invited us to meet him at the Jack Tar Hotel in San Francisco, and asked if we wanted something to drink. He said, "I'd like to make a deal with you. If you let me come to Zen Center once a year to establish my position as abbot for a day, you can have Zen Center back." We both said, "Sorry. No deal." The next day Richard let us know that he had a lawyer and they had already gone to Sacramento and changed the articles of incorporation back to what he had originally set up, with the abbot as corporation sole. So Zen Center got its own lawyer and spent a lot of money to get this reversed once again.

Although I turned out to be mostly the City Center abbot, I did lectures, classes, *dokusan*, *sesshins*, and practice periods at Green Gulch. And Reb did some classes and *dokusan* at City Center. I had assumed that I would be teaching at Green Gulch as well as City Center, because at that time no one else had been authorized as a teacher. It's not that there weren't student teachers, but they had not been authorized by Richard. So Reb and Ananda Dalenberg developed a study center, and the student teachers actually became the teachers over time.

Because our study was largely self-education, we didn't import teachers. There was a time when we considered bringing some in, but Zen Center has its own customs and it's hard to import somebody else and change the culture. There's a statue of Suzuki Roshi that doesn't look like him at all in the *kaisando* (Founder's Hall). Someone asked me, "Is it a rule that we have to bow when we pass the statue in the hallway?" No, it's not a rule. It's a custom. We tend to follow things in a customary way, not so much by following rules.

And that seemed to stick. Zen Center has its own culture. Suzuki Roshi didn't think teachers from Japan would understand what we were doing. Zen teacher Robert Aitken Roshi came and made suggestions about bringing in outside teachers, but it was hard to explain to him that we didn't need to change our culture with a new abbot from a different lineage. I was convinced that we should continue to build on Suzuki Roshi's teaching. So we did not hire some other leadership, but we did create a chair for visiting scholars. The scholars would stay for a week or two and give lectures, and that was very satisfying for most people.

As co-abbots, Reb and I agreed that we would alternate the responsibility of leading the fall and spring practice periods at Tassajara. When I wasn't leading *sesshins* or practice periods at City Center, I would mostly sit morning zazen at Berkeley Zen Center and go to SF Zen Center two or three days a week, working with the students, going to meetings, and staying overnight.

At Green Gulch I would do shorter practice periods, which included the lay community. We would have an intensive three days. The rest of the week the students would follow the usual temple schedule. My innovation was to include lay students or outside students, with an emphasis on their taking positions and being supported by the Green Gulch staff. The students really liked it. It was very successful while it lasted. Usually at Zen Center, the sangha is considered to consist of the residents. So my effort was to innovate to have the residents interact with those who practiced from the outside. It worked well when it was working. I'd go there two or three days a week and would have one-day sittings and classes, including everybody working in the kitchen and in the garden.

Although I was often away from Berkeley during my nine years as SFZC co-abbot, I did always manage to be there to attend to Berkeley Zen Center's annual six-week practice periods. I really honor and respect the Berkeley sangha for taking care of the practice while I was gone, especially when I was gone for the three-month practice periods every year at Tassajara. As abbot, besides taking care of all that, there are board meetings, practice committee meetings, this meeting and that meeting. Everyone wants the abbot to attend all the meetings. Liz is good at taking care of herself and always supported my practice. How did I do this? I never worried or got upset about SF Zen Center and I always allowed myself to be interrupted without complaining.

As I said, when I was first establishing myself as co-abbot at SF Zen Center, it had the feeling of a boarding house. I asked everyone who was not willing to follow the schedule to leave Page Street. I encouraged the students to do zazen in the zendo and to have service in the zendo instead of the Buddha Hall in order to emphasize zendo practice. I also reinstated *oryoki* eating practice in the zendo on Saturday mornings. Sometimes I would work in the kitchen. Little by little, the practice schedule returned along with the students' faith in the practice. This could not have happened without the effort of three practice leaders: Michael Wenger, Paul Haller, and Pat Phelan. Pat is now abbot of Chapel Hill Zen Center, Paul became an abbot of SF Zen Center, and Michael has developed a small community called Dragons Leap.

Because of the good roots established in the past, the SFZC students and teachers, working together over time, brought back the practice. This is of course a simple overview and doesn't touch on all that went down at that time. That is another story. Reb stepped down as abbot in 1996, and I stepped down in 1997 after nine years. We have been followed as abbots by Blanche Hartman and Norman Fischer, then up to 2021: Eijun Linda Cutts, Paul Haller, Myogen Steve Stücky, Kiku Christina Lehnherr, Rinso Ed Sattizahn, Furyu Nancy Schroeder, and Tenzen David Zimmerman.

Jakusho Bill Kwong and Me

When I came to Zen Center in 1964, Bill and Laura Kwong had already been there for four years. Bill was one of Suzuki Roshi's earliest students. Bill cooked the Saturday breakfast, and as far as I could tell he was as close to Suzuki as anyone. He always sat in full lotus and never moved. He was a great example for us struggling new students. He and I became very close. He lived in Mill Valley and led a sitting group there. After a few years I was leading the group in Berkeley, so we had that in common. A few years later Bill was offered a nice piece of land with some buildings and a barn in Sonoma County, and he and Laura and their four boys moved up there. He named the temple Genjo-ji.

Suzuki Roshi started working on the Dharma Transmission process with Bill, teaching him calligraphy, but then Suzuki Roshi became too ill to continue and died. He once said that when a teacher dies before completing Transmission with a student, it often happens that another disciple of his who has received Transmission will complete it for that person. He was of course alluding to his own situation. Since Richard Baker was a transmitted heir, he could have done that for Bill. But he didn't, and Bill felt abandoned. Without Transmission, a priest who has a community is not officially authorized to perform ordinations and would have limited authority.

When Richard left Zen Center, there was no one to complete Bill's ceremony, or to transmit any other disciples of Suzuki Roshi. Richard would not complete Bill's ceremony, and completely alienated him.

Maezumi Roshi, the founding abbot of the Zen Center of Los Angeles, was indirectly a teacher of mine. I knew him over a long period of time. I was impressed by the quality of his students. You can tell a lot about good teachers from the quality of their students.

He trusted his students, even when they went in a direction different from his way. He trusted this would all come out all right. I give him a lot of credit for that. That's hard to do.

Maezumi Roshi had been observing Richard's behavior toward Bill and me. He invited the two of us to L.A. from time to time and commiserated with us. He told us that we should have received Transmission a long time ago. One time when we were in L.A. he decided to call Suzuki Roshi's son Hoitsu in Japan and ask him to complete the Transmission.

As a matter of fact, Suzuki Roshi, anticipating that something like this might happen, had asked Hoitsu to take care of Bill. Hoitsu immediately agreed. So Bill went to Rinso-in and with the help of Noiri Roshi completed his Transmission in 1978.

Hoitsu Suzuki Roshi

At first we didn't know who Hoitsu was. We had only seen him a few times when he visited Zen Center, and at his father's funeral. We thought this was Suzuki Roshi's son who had inherited his temple, just an ordinary temple priest. Little by little we could see that Hoitsu wasn't just an ordinary temple priest, but a very deep and profound person who sometimes acted oddly.

When we first started getting together with Hoitsu he would jump around and pretend he was a monkey. Then he'd sit on the ground and pretend he was a frog. He'd go through all these animal acts and we'd just crack up because he was so good at it. We thought, "This guy should be on the stage." But underneath all that we knew there was something he was trying to communicate.

He was giving us something. He didn't really know who we were, just like many Japanese priests don't really know who we are.

Also, he had some resentments against his father, who had left to go to America when Hoitsu was still young. He felt abandoned—just left with the responsibility of the temple. He had to find his own way, which he did. He became a very independent person, in some ways like Suzuki Roshi but with a different temperament.

Over time he showed himself completely to us. We came to be impressed by how intelligent he was and is, and how much he actually knows. How formal and informal he can be. As well as being a great comedian, he is a serious and profound teacher. That was a great surprise to us and a wonderful gift.

In the 1970s I had started working on Dharma Transmission with Richard Baker. I said, "This is the way it is supposed to be, this is the way it should happen." After the crisis at Zen Center, I was still working with him. Later, when the whole Zen Center staff turned against him, I felt that I was somewhere in between, as I had already been through my anger with him and come out the other side. I was willing to help Richard, but he was pretty elusive. One day he told me that maybe we should stop the process because, as he said, "You're not supporting me enough." I immediately said okay. We decided not to continue.

Now, ten years later, I was working with Hoitsu Roshi, but still I had some lingering doubts. You can't do Dharma Transmission with somebody just because you say you're going to do it. There has to be some real connection. You can't just go through the motions. I went to Japan in late 1984, and in one month we had to find that connection. During that month we got to know each other intimately.

Just before Dharma Transmission I still felt we didn't really have a solid relationship. Jakusho (Bill Kwong) and a young priest, Ekai Korematsu, were with me, and one night we really had it out: how Hoitsu felt about us, what he felt about his father, what he felt about the whole thing. Then I explained to him how I felt. We came to an understanding. At that point I knew what we were doing was genuine, so we went ahead and completed Transmission in late 1984.

I do feel that Hoitsu Roshi is my dharma teacher and that I am his dharma heir. But he will say, "Even though I did this with you, it is my father's Dharma Transmission." I think that he felt that way about all of us—Jakusho Kwong, myself, and Keido Les Kaye—the three students of his father with whom he did Dharma Transmission.

Berkeley Zen Center on Russell Street*

After we had been living and practicing at the Dwight Way zendo for several years, we wanted to buy the building, but the owner was reluctant to sell. Old Victorians like this weren't worth much then. We offered the owner $45,000, but he balked.

In 1979 one of our sangha members, knowing what we were looking for, informed us that she knew of a man who had two adjacent properties with four houses, and he would like to sell them to us. The asking price was $220,000. I thought, "Oh, that's a lot of money." Hah! We didn't have any money to speak of. We decided to fundraise. We knew nothing about fundraising.

I don't know if you remember EST. It was a self-improvement program for entrepreneurs. Werner Erhard, who was the founder, invited a number of psychiatrists and religious leaders to a free EST session—including Zen Center priests. Although I was not that enthusiastic, I was curious. The fee for an EST training session was

---

* During the early years the building on Dwight Way was informally referred to as "the Berkeley zendo." The official name "Berkeley Zen Center" was adopted in the process of moving to the larger Russell Street location in 1979.

typically two hundred dollars. I thought, "Boy, two hundred dollars to go to a session, that's asking a big price from people, a big commitment." Two hundred dollars was a lot of money back then. I thought, hey, we could ask all our members to each contribute two hundred dollars to our fund, as a way of getting seed money going. I kind of sold the idea of buying this new place, which seemed to me ideal for us. People didn't have to contribute, but that was our suggestion. It was hard for a number of people to contribute that much money, but many did. And we did many other interesting things. The San Francisco Zen Center bakery, for example, let us use their facilities to make brownies and cookies and sell them at fairs and events.

So here we were, buying a property for $220,000, and we didn't have any money to speak of. But the owner allowed us to buy the place from him. Many of our members, depending on their ability, gave us loans both small and large. Some of the loans were quite large and unsecured because the lenders trusted us and wanted to make this work. So we made our down payment and secured the deed. There was a lot of enthusiasm, and everything just seemed to work. The finance company didn't find out about our self-financing until about ten years later, and then they refinanced us at a much higher rate. That was their solution. And then later, a number of members refinanced at their own rate to bring the sale to a conclusion.

So we bought this place on Russell Street, and that was a big, new development. We could now have a good number of residents. We had four houses: one floor of one house became the zendo and the zendo kitchen, and two of the other three houses were residences. Residents from Dwight Way moved to Russell Street in the fall of 1979. We used what is now the community room as the zendo.

After purchasing the property and moving in, our next step was to create a Zen center. So in 1981 we designated one house to be the zendo, and we had to fundraise for that, because we had to tear it all apart to make it into a zendo. That was a big project. But everybody helped. Somehow when you need building done, carpenters appear out of the woodwork. When we first started Tassajara we needed carpenters and they appeared, as students. Anyway, the same thing happened in Berkeley: we needed carpenters, they appeared. The carpenters were working on the zendo—we had to pay them—and that got a little messy after a while, because the work went on and on. We said, well, it's going to cost this much, and it'll be done in this amount of time, but that was only kidding ourselves. Whenever you have a building project you always fool yourself. You always say, oh, it's going to cost only this much, when you know it's actually going to cost a lot more, and you say it'll be done at a particular time, when you know it's going to be done much further in the future. But you have to kid yourself, otherwise you'll never do it. Anyway, it really brought everybody together. Everybody contributed.

Developing the Practice at Berkeley Zen Center

We always wanted a residency program. When we moved into Russell Street, we began to develop that. In Berkeley you are not allowed to remove a living space from a property, because living space is so limited. So in order to build something like a zendo, we had to add an equivalent living space in one of the other buildings. To do this, we had to change one of the other two-story buildings to a three-story building. So in 1982 the house movers came over and lifted this building up, and we built a whole story underneath it. People were out there working around, digging ditches for the new foundation, and then we raised up that house, this big two-story house.

I remember the family that was living up there in the house had to climb a ladder every time they came home. And if you put a marble on the floor, it would roll down to one side.

Not long after we moved to Russell Street, Liz decided to go to nursing school. Around the same time, she got pregnant and gave birth to our son Daniel. When Liz was at nursing school, I carried Daniel around in a backpack during the day, and I'd feed him Liz's expressed breastmilk. He was a very good little boy. When I had meetings with people, he sat down in the middle of the meeting and played quietly with his containers, putting one inside another interminably. He was completely absorbed in his own endeavors, not bothering anybody. It was wonderful.

After Liz finished nursing school and had been working as a nurse for a couple of years, she decided she wanted to buy a house in a different neighborhood. She was not comfortable raising our son in the neighborhood we were in. I said, "I have to live at the zendo; I have to live here at the zendo, this is my life." Then some time later she said, "You know I really want to buy a house." And I said, "I know that's very nice, you know, I appreciate what you're saying." And then some time later she said, "You know, I really want us to have our own house." And I finally said "Okay." I didn't even think about it. I just said, "You want that? Okay." I didn't dwell on what that would entail for me. I just said, "Okay." Her father gave us the money for the house down payment.

It was very hard for me to move, because it removed me from contact with the sangha in the way that I was used to. But other people took up that contact that I had had. Now when I go to the zendo, I have to get dressed, go to BZC and get dressed again, putting on my robes and so on. It became my way of life. And then I started riding my bike to the zendo. I'd get on my bike at five in the morning and ride to the zendo, which is what I did for years. I got most of my exercise that way. So there are advantages and disadvantages. That was my way—go to the zendo and do zazen and *dokusan* every morning, and take care of business and see everybody. Every Saturday we have a long morning program with a talk, and then once a month we have a one-day sitting, or a five-day or seven-day *sesshin*.

It's a very vital place, with a lot of good strong activity going on all the time. And little by little the practice has built a strong core of dedicated people. The members take very good care of it. Whenever I go to Tassajara, I don't worry about Berkeley. I just think: However it's going is the way it's going. But I know it's okay. I feel that's a real accomplishment—the fact that this practice goes on without me.

Lectures

Section 1:
Practice

Just Sitting

Shikantaza (Just Sitting)

We call our practice *shikantaza*, which means something like "just to sit." To "just do" means acting without self, or ego, or some extra purpose. This is the opposite of a materialistic way of life. Much of our usual effort is materialistic, to "have" or "accumulate," or to "improve."

Shikantaza is the other side, which is just "to be." But when we practice to be, sometimes our materialistic side (desire) raises questions like "Where is this going? What do I get from this? Where's the reward?" Those are natural questions to ask. But if we want something in a materialistic sense, we should not seek it in zazen. There may be many things to accomplish, but zazen is "just to be." It's enough just to be. If you can settle on just being, you can experience your completeness. But if self-centered desire takes over, we are easily pulled off our seat.

Often, we get bored in zazen because we're not getting or accomplishing anything in the usual materialistic sense. We feel we have to have some justification for being alive. When we first come to zazen, we don't know why we like it. It feels right because it's enough just to be. If we can settle on just being in that way in all of our activity, then whatever we do is zazen. *Shikantaza*, just sitting, is just doing something without any "gaining idea," as Suzuki Roshi used to say.

Shikantaza is a total offering, holding nothing back. Merge completely. Be complete. Sit zazen with your whole body and mind, with full function and complete attention. It's hard! It's very hard to be here, completely awake and merged with reality, moment after moment. But if you're completely merged in zazen, you won't be pulled by desires. Your body and mind will be refreshed, ready, and open for the next moment.

We need to rediscover how to practice over and over again so that our effort stays fresh and we don't fall back into the realm of craving. We have to live our life in the world of desire and at the same time be free from it, choosing to continue our active samadhi. When we're engaged in selfless activity, our samadhi is very strong, and we come to enjoy pure activity more than we enjoy selfish activity. We practice zazen to learn which is which.

In a *sesshin* or a long sitting, we say we are "unifying the mind" or "embracing the mind." Strictly speaking, a *sesshin* is five days or seven days. One day is not usually called *sesshin*. We usually call it a one-day sitting. But whether one-day sitting, five-day *sesshin*, or seven-day *sesshin*, the principle is the same: to unify body, breath, and mind. We realize the basic unity of our body and mind with the whole universe. That's what we mean by embracing the mind or unifying the mind.

Mind is already one with things, but we just need to realize it, to re-mind and re-establish our balance and harmony continuously.

It is necessary to find our balance in each moment. What I mean by balance is to be aware of all of the forces that are active in our body and mind at any given moment. For instance, when we sit zazen, gravity is one great force acting on our body. Another great force is what I call spirit, which keeps our body upright. These are the two counteracting forces or polarities of our life: the pull toward the earth and the pull away from the earth. The earth pulls everything toward it, and so we say we're grounded on the earth. But the counterforce of vital spirit is pulling or pushing us away from the earth, pushing us up. We're always concerned with the balance of forces between gravity and growth or spirit—birth and death.

When we sit zazen, the whole time, from beginning to end of our long sitting, we're dealing single-mindedly with the problem of spirit and gravity. All of the problems that arise in between spirit and gravity are the factors of our practice. To sit upright and not lean to the left or to the right, not lean forward and not lean back, just to be comfortable—it's that simple. How do you just sit all day without leaning forward or backward, without leaning left or right, without moving—and remain comfortable? We struggle with this problem. *Sesshin* is to struggle with this problem until, finally, we stop struggling and allow our spirit to find complete unity with gravity.

What do we need to know in order to be able to deal in this way with the problems of gravity and spirit? Recently, I've been talking about how we keep time with our chanting, how we follow the rhythm and at the same time create the rhythm or push the rhythm, how we follow and lead at the same time. This following and leading at the same time is a koan for us. When you can follow and lead simultaneously, without a gap, then there's no following and there's no leading. To lead is to follow and to follow is to lead.

Without losing the unity, we can sometimes emphasize leading and we can sometimes emphasize following. But there must always be balance in unity. This example of chanting can be taken into every situation. When you're leading the chant with the *mokugyo* (wooden fish), one necessary thing is to listen. The other is to lead, to activate yourself. When receiving and responding is one unit, without a gap, we say there's no subject and no object—chanting chants, sitting sits. The unity illuminates both subject and object. Exhaling, we give in to gravity. Inhaling, we reach for the sky. In one complete breath, the unity of birth and death.

Zazen has two sides. One is the passive side, and the other is the active side. The passive side corresponds to awareness or being attentive—just letting things come and go. The active side is purposeful effort of body and mind, fully engaged in upright posture—total exertion and focus. The balance of these two is what we are continuously working with. The passive side allows for all difficulties. It is opening completely to everything, without trying to block anything and without trying to inhibit the difficulties and problems. It is not holding anything. The active side is the spirit of determination. It's the form side with which we maintain our posture. With the active side, we maintain our attitude of constancy, keeping a check on our activity, and returning to our original intention over and over.

The passive side goes along with gravity, while the active side provides the pull away from gravity, giving us the form which allows the spirit to be fully expressed. It's very important, in sitting practice, to maintain the form of posture—to maintain our focus without losing concentration. When we put forth our total effort to maintain the form, and at the same time open ourself up completely in a passive and accepting way, then we have the perfect balance between doing and being. It's the harmony between these two which accounts for our being either comfortable or uncomfortable. Even though we may have pain or discomfort, it doesn't succumb to suffering.

Many of us cannot maintain an ideal sitting position for one reason or another. But each of us can work within the limitations imposed by our physical formations, which is what we are all doing anyway. So when we have this kind of experience, we can enjoy our life, which includes various difficulties. We can still smile and help people. It is not necessary to be the victim of our difficulties. When we are not victims, we have freedom.

Within this most confined posture, we can exist with total freedom. This is the most stable posture in which to sit for long periods of time. We're not trying to do something extreme, like putting our legs behind our ears. To sit for a long period of time, this is the easiest way.

The unity between the active and the passive, between gravity and spirit—the basic unity between things is always there. At the bottom, all things share the essence. The way to express this harmony is through zazen. When we sit today, we should make that effort to close the gap. Within the total activity is total stillness. Within that stillness is total dynamic activity. Not "I am sitting zazen," but "just this sitting." Putting attention on posture is the most important. "How is this mudra?" "Is it being held right?" "Is the back correct (given our limitations)?" "Ears in line with the shoulders?" "Nose in line with the navel?" "Is the chest open?" "Are the shoulders relaxed?" "Is the breath deep?" If you battle gravity, gravity will always win. So don't fight gravity, but become partners with it, giving to gravity what belongs to gravity.

Let your shoulders fall. Your shoulders don't hold you up. What kind of effort is needed to hold you up? Where is the fine line, which is just balance? When we find that balance, that harmony, then total effort seems effortless.

Breath

In Buddhist meditation, paying attention to breathing is one of the most important factors. Breathing is usually taken for granted because it is so constant. The blood runs through our veins. We don't see it but we are aware of it as heat, so we take it for granted. Breath is something that is going on continuously. It connects inside and outside, so to speak.

Each one of us has this experience of breath. Coming in, going out, inhaling, exhaling. This is the fundamental movement of our life. In zazen we pay attention to posture, and we pay attention to breath. Posture is first, because posture is the fundamental structure of this body. After we establish posture, we pay attention to breath. So zazen is harmonizing body and mind with breath; all three elements. We pretty much know this. If you have been sitting zazen for a while, you have this experience. But one important factor that is easy to ignore is the role of breath, or how we pay attention to breathing in our daily life. In zazen we let go of the busyness of our daily activity, all the complications, and it's pretty easy to simply pay attention to the rising and falling of our breath. In our daily life it's much more difficult. When paying attention to the breath and sitting up straight, the breath becomes more subtle, and we then experience a feeling of liberation, lightness, settledness, freedom, and selflessness.

This kind of attention to the breath can be applied to all of our activities. When you walk, to be attentive to the breath with each step. When you are hiking it's pretty easy. Sometimes when you are hiking up a steep mountain it is one breath, one step. But in our daily life of varied activities it's much more difficult to be aware of breath in your work, to be aware of breath while sitting down at your computer; how you actually breathe with the activity and the rhythm of the breath and the activity, driving a car, turning on the ignition, the rhythm of shifting gears (some of us still have them), putting on the brake, stepping on the gas.

To actually pay attention to breath and the movement in this way is how we carry our meditation practice into our daily life. It is an activity that is common to both zazen and daily life. Suzuki Roshi said in a talk, "We should be kind with ourself and very kind with our breathing. We should have a warm-hearted feeling toward our breath." We can relate to our breath as a constant companion, not simply taking it for granted. To have this awareness focuses our attention and helps us to be concentrated on what we are doing. It's the kind of energy that's not chattery, but calm and collected. It creates a joyful mood. When we can keep coming back to the breath, our disposition actually becomes sweet and smooth and makes it easy to smile. It helps us to respond to circumstances rather than just reacting.

It is important to keep the breath down low in your hara (abdomen). Breath in Chinese is called *ki* or *chi*, and in Sanskrit, *prana*. *Ki* is the place of power or strength, when our breath is down here in what feels like our center—in our lower abdomen, at the bottom of our lungs just below our navel. This is called the Sea of *Ki*, or the key of C. Suzuki Roshi said it's also called rice paddies, which in the Asian way of thinking means "place of plenty"—the place of nourishment and the source of our energy and well-being. You notice when you hyperventilate, it can create a feeling of euphoria. And when we put on an oxygen mask and take a hit of oxygen, we feel high. It's not necessary to do that; natural breathing is enough. But often we find ourself breathing in our chest. When we become angry or irritated or frightened or anxious, then our breath tends to become very shallow and we lose our center or ground. But when we pay attention to breathing and allow ourself to breathe deeply, then the body relaxes and lets go of holding on to itself and our state of mind becomes free. Our state of mind and the breath are very much connected; this is why it is important to harmonize body, mind, and breath, and resume our natural state of mind, which is free of conditioning.

In our daily lives we meet many conditions. All we have to do is read the newspaper to drive our breathing up into our chest. When you read the newspaper, let your breath go down to your hara and harmonize with body and mind. Even though the world looks like it's going to hell, you can still have a calm mind; you still have your composure so you don't get lost.

Breathing is a kind of involuntary activity. It has a voluntary aspect, but it is also involuntary because breath is just coming and going, regardless of our desire. We can control the breath. We can hold our breath for a little while, or we can control its rhythm, but in zazen and in our daily life, if we just allow the breath to do its own thing, our mind follows the breath.

In zazen we start out by letting the mind follow the breath. This is difficult: once you focus on the breath it's hard not to feel that you are controlling it. First, we say "count the breath." That's good for getting a handle on following it; and then just let the mind follow the breath, let the breath be. Actually, we are breathed by the universe. This is just the universal activity which is inflating and deflating the lungs. We usually think "I am breathing," but actually breathing is just happening to you. This is a wonderful mystery. To inhale is to come to life as we know it, and to exhale is to let go of life as we know it. Suzuki Roshi talked about the breath at the exhale as letting go; long breath, letting go. We put more attention on the exhale than the inhale. When you inhale the body becomes excited, and when you exhale the body becomes calm.

These are the two aspects of our life: excitement and calmness. Someone said, "A movement and a rest, over and over again." And each breath is a moment of birth and death. This is how we can understand how our life continues, it's both continuous and discontinuous. Last week I was in Arcata with our dear dharma sister Maylie Scott, who is dying. For six days she was kind of gone. Lying in bed on her back, not moving for all that time, with her eyes closed. Just breathing. And we would go in and sit with her. The only movement was her breath, which was quite audible. Sometimes calm, sometimes labored. She was breathing, but it was just the universal activity making this movement; it was so obvious. And we would do zazen with her and just watch to see if it would continue, and to see if it would stop. It had just kept going on like this, day after day, breath after breath. Life living itself out. I feel sure that her great long experience of zazen was simply continuing, lying still, giving herself over to the universe, one with her breath. And at the right moment, just stopping and experiencing this wonderful feeling of release. I wondered how we would all feel at this moment. And yet it was like whew, the last breath.

This is how I think about that time, and about breathing, and about appreciating our breath, not just taking it for granted—harmonizing our breath in order to allow ourself to have that release. In the Sutra on the Mindfulness of Breathing there are sixteen methods of observing the breath or practicing with the breath. And the last one is practicing with the breath in order to understand impermanence, in order to realize impermanence, and to practice letting go of body and mind, so that the whole life is lived consciously, and our entire death is lived consciously in the same manner. We tend to grab onto life and resist our death, which is normal and natural. But to live a complete life, to be able to pass out of this world in a conscious purposeful way, is possible.

We can see death as losing our life, as losing something, or we can see it as gaining something, or we can see it as neither losing nor gaining, but simply expanding into the universe, our true body. So paying attention to breath from the hara, throughout every activity, is our practice. Sometimes I ask a student, "Right now, tell me, where is your breath?" Most students will say, "Well, I don't know." But you should know all the time where your breath is, where you are breathing from. There shouldn't be any hesitation. We don't know everything, we have fears and uncertainty and a lot of the time in our life we are puzzled by what confronts us, and our breath becomes shallow. When we accept "I don't know," and put our mind down here in our hara, in our belly, then from here something will come forth. This is to have faith in our true nature. As a Zen student, you must have faith in your true nature, and it's right there in the letting go. You can let go and have a free fall into Buddha's hand, which will always rescue you. So when we practice with our breath settled in the hara, we have the right foundation for all our activities, and even though we get lost, there is always a place to come back to.

Finding Our Balance

When I give zazen instruction I encourage people to release or let go of the tenseness in various parts of their body. Easier said than done. There is tension that holds the structure of the body-mind together, allowing for a free flow of unhindered energy. And then there is tenseness that causes knots that hinder that flow. The tenseness is extra. An important aspect of our practice both on and off the cushion is to be aware of how we hold our well-balanced unconditioned posture, as well as waking up to the corners and crannies of our body where we hold our unresolved angers, resentments, fears, frustrations, anxieties about loss and gain, and much, much more that determines our conditioned postures.

In a world where there is so much to be angry, resentful, fearful, frustrated, jealous, and self-critical about, it's a wonder that we have any freedom from ourselves at all. It is well known that our back from top to bottom is a storage compartment for anger and resentment. After all, if we can't resolve it, it has to go somewhere. The other parts of our body also hold this mental and emotional baggage. When I adjust posture in the zendo, it becomes clear that we bring our conditioned postures to the cushion.

Zazen is to resume our original unconditioned posture, which harbors nothing while embracing whatever appears without attachment. Although angry, not harboring anger; although resentful, not harboring resentment; although self-critical, not harboring self-criticism. Meeting the trials and tribulations as well as savoring the sweetness and love of our everyday activity, we follow the natural order of Mind. Suzuki Roshi once said that everything is falling out of balance and finding its balance, moment by moment. This takes continuous awareness. Responding allows us the opportunity to stay centered, while reaction usually pulls us off center. Staying centered and balanced and in touch with the profound stillness at the center of our activity is our practice.

Sitting Still in the Midst of the Waves

It is important to have a good understanding of why we practice, and to keep reminding ourselves. Buddhists have always been concerned with seeing through the illusory quality of our life and living in a way that is grounded in the bedrock of reality. From Buddha's strict example come the various practices of Buddhism, but if we try to imitate Buddha's lifestyle—a person who lived in ancient India more than 2,500 years ago—we may get quite discouraged. We have to see our activity in the light of the present day, but we can't ignore the principles of Buddha's understanding. We are easily pulled around and conditioned by our changeable, unstable feelings, emotions, opinions, partiality, and desires. In order to live our life in the light of nonattachment and non-partiality of practice/enlightenment, and to settle down in the bedrock of that reality, we sit zazen.

I like to think of what Master Dogen says in his fascicle of *Shobogenzo* called "Sagaramudra Samadhi, the Ocean Mudra Samadhi." He implies that while we are swimming in the waves on the surface, our feet are at the same time walking on the bottom. In the moment-by-moment, ever-changing events of our life, our practice is to be grounded in great immobile stillness.

Sometimes we come to a difficult place in our practice where we can't see where to go. A dark place. At that point we may have to feel our way, taking one step at a time and not giving up until we come out the other side. When we can continue in that way, we gain confidence in ourselves and can appreciate the meaning of continuous practice, what Dogen calls *gyoji*, and overcome doubt. During *sesshin*, even though we may have difficulties and doubt, we continue to sit still in the midst of the waves, riding one wave at a time. We exist in that space, offering ourself totally. Without the last gap of separation, we face the reality of our situation and can enjoy navigating the difficulty.

For beginners, especially, there is the temptation to run away, but with time we are able to settle into *shikantaza* (just sitting).

Zazen brings forth in us a steady light that isn't subject to the ups and downs associated with grasping and aversion, craving or excitement. The light illuminates our direction so that we know which step to take next. When we question our practice, we should look at the details of our life more closely. Where am I and what am I doing? What was my original inspiration, my intention? And remember to let go of our gaining mind and resume our fundamental beginner's mind.

When someone asked Suzuki Roshi, "What is nirvana?" he replied, "Seeing one thing through to the end."

Acceptance

During our last *sesshin* the word "acceptance" came up. I didn't think so much about that before I began practicing zazen. During my early years as a novice, there were times when zazen was excruciatingly painful. Suzuki Roshi was always encouraging us to sit still and not move. Our zazen periods were forty minutes, just like now. At that time, in the early 1960s, his students were mostly novices. He had only been here for five years when I came. Sitting zazen for one period once or twice a week was a significant experience for me. Then I came to my first Saturday morning, which was a longer program. After the first period and *kinhin*, everyone sat down again. I thought, "They are going to do this *again*?" I said to the fellow next to me that this was really painful. He said that yes, it always is.

But somehow I kept coming back. I knew that even so, there was something else going on that I was not able to explain. So coursing through a forty-minute period of zazen, when the pain would arise I would hope that the bell would ring and save me from my suffering. My whole life at that moment was waiting to be rescued. Saved by the bell! I simply could not be where I was. But in fact, I had no alternative because my intention was to stay through the forty minutes. Sometimes, just when we thought the bell would ring, Suzuki Roshi would say in his soft voice, "We will sit ten more minutes." We're bursting at the seams, how are we going to do this for ten more minutes? But we did. This was our basic training.

Suzuki Roshi taught us the meaning of acceptance: We must open ourselves to each sensation and become one with it. If you try to escape you will suffer. But it is not so easy to be one with the pain, because of the embedded associations of our discriminating mind. Most of us have to go through the painful process before we can truly open up and be free from our conditioned responses. Instead of shutting down and resisting, we open up and accept whatever appears, and instead of narrowing our borders we allow them to expand and include whatever appears. It is counterintuitive. Instead of gritting our teeth and clenching our fist, we relax our jaw and open our hand. Suzuki Roshi would encourage us by saying that those who have the most difficulty and see it through will have the most benefit.

As soon as an "uncomfortable" feeling arises and we don't "like" it and don't "want" it, we form an attachment and begin to suffer. Wanting to hold on to a "good" feeling, it is painful when it leaves. So in this sense, acceptance means letting go, or freedom from attachment, which is the bedrock of practice. There is no special state of mind to attach to and no special feeling to desire and no special self to hang on to. This can be called bliss.

Posture and Breath

Today is the fourth day of *sesshin*. To begin, I want to remind us about breathing. I know you won't forget to breathe. Whether you forget or not, you will breathe. I want to remind us to allow our breath to be deep, and to let go of tenseness when we find our breath rising up in our chest. When we inhale, our lower abdomen expands. When we exhale, it contracts. This is where we should focus our attention. If you have pain in your legs and don't know what else to do, put some strength into your exhalation, focus your attention on one breath at a time. In Soto Zen we mostly follow our breath. Rinzai students put a lot of strength in the lower abdomen on the exhalation. When you don't know what else to do, rather than uncrossing your legs, you might try putting some strength in your lower abdomen when you exhale.

Question: If you don't know what to do and you don't want to uncross your legs, do you just grit your teeth and bear it?

Sojun: Instead of gritting your teeth, try letting go. You can't fight it. It's not a battle. It's a letting go. Whatever appears, let it be without attaching to it. There's a saying: "The cool breeze blows through the empty hall." The only approach that works is to open up and let whatever appears pass through. This is where I have to find the balance between ease and effort.

Question: But is it better to uncross your legs than to fight it?

Sojun: No. It's better to keep your legs crossed and not fight it. Better to have great patience. Otherwise, you'll never find your way. You have to find the ease without turning away from your difficulties. Sit still, don't move, and concentrate on one breath at a time. Dogen calls this the comfortable way. You have to go through your difficulties until you give up and let go. So let your mind follow your breath. The first thing is posture. Establish your posture. Put effort into posture, and then let the mind follow the breath with the rising and falling of your lower abdomen. You can tell that you're getting tense when your breath becomes rough and shallow. Be aware of that. Realize when your shoulders are getting tense. Fear or anxiety makes us tense up. At some point we have to drop our resistance and say, "It's okay." Then we rise to a different level. Our resistance is the problem. We usually have to go through many painful, difficult periods of zazen until we allow ourselves to let go. That's why seven days is a good opportunity, because it wears us down.

Question: I keep hoping that the pain will go away as the week goes on.

Sojun: That's the problem. That's why it doesn't go away. Anything you hope for is a problem.

Question: And I'm afraid that, as the week goes on, it's going to get worse.

Sojun: We should have a sign over the zendo door: "Abandon all hope, ye who enter here." Hope is resistance, hope is fighting. It's saying, "I wish it would go away. I hope it goes away." But the more we hope it goes away, the more it's right there! The more we hope it goes away, the worse it gets. Instead, we should say to our fear or our pain, "Okay, you can be here with me. You can stay here. I'm sitting zazen. You're welcome to stay here too. Howdy." But if we say, "Please go away," this is becoming attached to your pain. And pain answers back: "Says who?" Give up hope of anything you want. The Second Noble Truth says that wanting is the cause of our suffering. When we say, "I wish it would go away," that's the cause of our suffering. Having what we don't want is the cause of suffering. Zazen is to drop body and mind. Let go of ego. Let go of self. It's not just words. We have big strong egos which keep us from realization. The important thing is to be compassionate with yourself and not blame your surroundings, not blame the practice. Sometimes we have people come to *sesshin* and blame us for making them do these things. They say, "It's all your fault." But the most compassionate thing we can do is look for the problem within ourselves and, at the same time, not blame ourselves for it. When we really take on our own suffering and our own difficulty, we have compassion for everyone. We look around and see that everybody is having a hard time, and we feel compassion for their difficulty. The suffering that we are going through is the basis of our enlightenment. I know that is not what we picture as enlightenment. We think that enlightenment will be the end of our suffering, but enlightenment abides right in the midst of it. Our suffering will bring it out. We have to get to the bottom of our suffering. We have to go down all the way to the bottom of it. Then enlightenment will spring forth.

Question: I feel like I am flunking Buddhism over and over.

Sojun: Me too! We're all in the same boat. I'm a failure. We're all failures. The main thing is not how successful you are at being perfect. I'm not talking about how to be perfect. I'm talking about how to "be" completely. Each one of us does the best we can. That's the main point. If we do our best, that is already an expression of enlightenment. Enlightenment is not at the end of the road. It's within our effort. When you have the hardest time and it seems like you are failing, that's actually pure practice. To have this difficult time and stay with it and do your utmost, that's pure practice. Suzuki Roshi used to say that the people who have the hardest time often turn out to be the most enlightened Zen masters. So you never know.

Question: When I listen to you, I think, "Someday I will have this giant letting go and everything will be great."

Sojun: Just let go, and everything will be what it will be.

Question: But aren't I just going to fall back into hoping?

Sojun: Maybe and maybe not. You are already predicting the future. You are already predicting that you'll fall back into your old ways. Just stop the whole thing! Be where you are. Just be where you are with what you have. That's all. There will always be something missing. That's okay. It's not how much you have. It's not a matter of quantity. It's a matter of thoroughness. It means to unify your body and mind so that whatever you do includes everything. When you do one thing without ego, without self-centeredness, that's thoroughness.

Question: And the results don't make any difference?

Sojun: It's not that the results don't make any difference. It's just that we're not attached to the results. Of course results make a difference. But if it doesn't turn out according to your dream, don't be attached to that. Each one of us has our own perfection which includes all of our so-called mistakes.

Question: What about when our mistakes hurt other people?

Sojun: When you hurt somebody, you have compassion, you feel repentant. "I'm sorry." That's a form of repentance, an aspect of enlightenment. What to do when we hurt others, what to do when we hurt ourselves, and what this means in a deep sense, not just a superficial sense—these are good questions. Just acknowledge. Turn around and continue on in a careful way.

Practice-Enlightenment

Chasing Enlightenment

Suzuki Roshi used to say that all of us are part of one being. When we are completely merged with reality, we're all part of the one complete being called Buddha. This is enlightenment. We experience that through zazen. But sitting cross-legged is just one form of zazen. Zazen has many forms. We continually come back to the *zafu* because sitting in zazen is a most fundamental way of understanding or experiencing our nature. But there are many ways of practicing zazen—if we know what we are doing. It's really up to each one of us to find out how to practice in this way.

Chasing enlightenment is like running across the desert. We want to get to the other side of the desert so badly that we are tempted to run. But we don't get very far running in the desert. After a few feet we find that it's too hard to run, so we try walking. When it's very hot, we walk very slowly, one step at a time. If we're carrying too much, we just leave it lying on the sand. Piece by piece, we unload our excess baggage, and we just take one step at a time. Finally, we find a comfortable way to get through the desert, walking steadily day after day. And it takes a long, long time.

From time to time, we may come to an oasis. We drink the water and it's just wonderful. The oasis is a kind of awakening. At some point we may have a wonderful refreshment called understanding.

But we can't stay at the oasis. We have to leave it behind and continue on in the desert. The desert is just as hot as it always was, but now we have some confidence because we got to the oasis. We find that the desert doesn't end, and we have to continue forever in the desert. But we know how to walk in the desert, so we find out how to do it continuously. The only way we can continue is to bring forth a strong, true spirit. If we can't bring forth that strong spirit, we can't continue. Since there's nothing else to do, we do it. And in the process we find out that everything we need to know is right under our footsteps.

Practice-Enlightenment

Our Zen practice is very simple. And yet the focus is easy to miss. As a matter of fact, it's so simple that sometimes we don't see what's right under our feet, or in front of our nose. To be able to take hold of and seize this moment and not get lost in the world, not give way to confusion and doubt, is pretty difficult, and yet this simple practice is not so difficult if we always question, "Where am I and what am I doing?"

This "What is it?" is a koan for each one of us. I have always felt that this "What is it?" was Suzuki Roshi's unstated koan for us. I could sometimes hear him saying this in a casual way, but loaded with meaning. If someone pointed something out to him, he might say, "What is it?" After all, what is this bow? How do we become aware of the absolute quality of our life in each moment's activity? It's maybe not so difficult to be aware of what we're doing, but to be aware of the absolute quality of our life in each activity is easy to miss. How to express Buddha-nature in the simplest acts of our life. How to express our whole being, which is not just our personality.

Whenever someone asked Master Gutei a question, he raised one finger. When he raised one finger, he was saying, "This is it!" This is it! Everything in the whole universe belongs to this one finger, and this finger belongs to the whole universe, the *Dharmadhatu*. The whole universe is supporting this finger.

When we say that we are doing something such as walking or eating, what does that really mean? What is that? In one sense, there's "Hey, leave me alone and let me enjoy my meal," but in another sense, the universe is eating potatoes with a knife and fork. *It* is a little word, but it has a big meaning. *It* has no special name or object, but we can point to anything and say "This is it." If I point to you, I can say you are it—depending on the situation. Yet each it, John or Mary, the table or the chair, has its respective name. And at the same time, each one of them is it. So if we say "What is it," it has no special name, no special form, no special characteristic, but every name, every form, every color is *It*. What is it? What is it? What is it? As Ganto says, the answer is always "This is it."

If we can keep our attention on *This is it*, then we have our practice. It's not that we know something, but we express right understanding. I may know what something is, yet not know that this is it. Even though I don't understand it, I know it. The barbarian knows it, even though he doesn't understand it.

Question: You say that after enlightenment begins hard practice. So if this is it, what's going on before?

Sojun: We think that delusion precedes enlightenment. We tend to think in terms of before and after. Delusion is first, and we work hard to get something called enlightened. It does look like that, but enlightenment is our nature, our true nature that is always with us. When we say we "get enlightened," it's not that we actually get something. It means to bring forth light, to let go, so that light can shine forth. Enlightenment is an expression of our true nature, but that doesn't mean that we necessarily realize it.

So what's before realization? There is obscurity, confusion, dualistic thinking, yours and mine, right and wrong, good and bad. After enlightenment, there's confusion, right and wrong, good and bad, but it's not the same. We sometimes think that enlightenment means the reconciliation of all dualities. You and I may be angry with each other before enlightenment, and when we become enlightened we reconcile anger with serenity. After enlightenment we may still get angry, but that anger is not the same. You are not attached to that feeling.

Enlightenment is the beginning of our practice. Enlightenment is what motivates us toward practice. The fact that you want to practice means that the enlightenment that is always with you needs to somehow be expressed. It is usual to think that we enter practice in order to get enlightened, but enlightenment is actually driving our practice. We have a tendency to see it the other way around. "If I work real hard, I can get enlightened!" That's good, but it's enlightenment that's motivating you to work real hard to seek enlightenment. What we are all looking for is what we already have in abundance, but we don't know that until we wake up to it. And then we might say, "Now that I've awakened to it, I don't have to do this troublesome practice any more." But if it's actually enlightenment that you have awakened to, you won't want to stop, because enlightenment is within our effort, within our practice. Practice brings forth enlightenment, and enlightenment creates practice. Practice is the basis; enlightenment is its expression and extends everywhere. It's not confined to a certain place or activity. This is it. Now please pass the salt.

Buddha-Nature

Baika's question: One of the most important questions of my life in
the past couple years has been: If my nose is vertical and my eyes
are horizontal, then why Buddhism?

Sojun: That's a good question; that's exactly the question that Dogen
carried with him to China. He said that if we all have Buddha-
nature, if everything is Buddha-nature, why do we have to do
something like practice? Why sit zazen, or do anything special,
if Buddha-nature is our natural endowment? What Dogen woke
up to was that although Buddha-nature is our essential nature,
if we don't do something to bring it forth, it doesn't manifest
as realization. Even though electricity is everywhere, if we don't
induce it, we can't make use of it. It's all around us. But we have
to channel it somehow so we can use it. Once we realize our
nature, everything will open to us. Since Buddha-nature is the
fundamental nature of all things, we realize that all things are
essentially aspects of our true self.

For us humans, Buddha-nature manifests as human nature.
Even though we're born with the ability to be truly human, it
doesn't necessarily follow that we will turn out to be completely
realized human beings. We may manifest the characteristics of
an animal while having the outward appearance of a human. It's
also true that some animals are more compassionate and loving
than many humans. That's why many people prefer the company
of animals. We may become a fighting demon, a hungry ghost,
or a hell dweller. Which world do we live in? We may think that
we live in the human world, but do we really know what a human
being is?

What does it mean to be born, live our lives, and die as human beings? When we look around we may wonder. Although

we think of ourselves as complete human beings, we are also evolving into being or becoming human. The theory of evolution is, I think, correct. We started out as something and we're evolving into that something very slowly. At the same time we are complete human beings. Each one is at a unique stage of development. We're human beings evolving into human beings; myself becoming myself. But very few of us have reached that completeness.

Although we all are Buddha-nature, each one of us has human nature as well. But we don't necessarily realize that we are Buddha. Very few of us have become the Buddha that we are—a fully evolved human being. We are both Buddhas and ordinary human beings.

When we raise the thought of enlightenment or way-seeking mind and enter into and turn the practice, the Buddha comes forth; human nature and Buddha-nature merge, and an evolving bodhisattva is born, one who arrives with every step and never stops arriving. This is why we are drawn to practice, in faith that we are Buddha.

Dogen understood that realization stimulates practice and practice sustains realization. Eyes are horizontal and nose is vertical. A moment of practice is a moment of awakening.

Unborn Buddha Mind (Big Mind)

A Zen student came to Master Bankei and complained: "Master, I have an ungovernable temper. How can I cure it?"

"You have something very strange," replied Bankei. "Let me see what you have."

"Just now I can't show it to you," replied the student.

"When can you show it to me?" asked Bankei.

"It arises unexpectedly," replied the student.

"Then," concluded Bankei, "it must not be your own true nature. If it were, you could show it to me at any time. When you were born you did not have it, and your parents did not give it to you. Think this over."

Bankei makes it look like anger is an acquired taste. It can be delicious or bitter. The student says "I have" something that is "ungovernable" (a feeling that has a life of its own), a "temper" looking for a "cure." Bankei was a very effective seventeenth-century Zen teacher in Japan. "*The only thing that you really have is your Unborn Buddha Mind*" was at the root of Bankei's teaching.

This Unborn Buddha Mind which we all share is also called Buddha-nature, or essence of Mind, or Big Mind, by Suzuki Roshi. Daikan Eno says, "In all circumstances don't stray from your essence of Mind." Suzuki Roshi says, "When small mind becomes calm, Big Mind starts its true activity."

To take refuge in Buddha is to return to Big Mind. It is a cooperation between small mind and Big Mind. Just like in zazen, the mind wanders off and we wake up, let go, and bring it back. Enlightenment is to recognize the dream as a dream. Anger arises in everyone. That's why it is such a juicy subject. When it arises we have a choice (a kind of koan): If I react, I am caught by my reaction. If I don't react, I may be disloyal to my feelings. To step back and respond with a calm mind between reaction and loyalty is to work to save all beings.

When small mind operates without the cooperation of Big Mind, we call it ego or delusion—the root of suffering. Bankei admonishes us not to be a slave to our emotion-thought by trading off the freedom of our Unborn Buddha Mind for the addictions of greed, ill will, and delusion.

Aspects of Practice

The Rhythm of Practice (How to Keep Our Daily Practice Fresh and Vital)

Sometimes I think of a simile to practice as the difference between the sprinter and the long-distance runner. When I was in high school I ran the hundred-yard dash with a burst of speed as fast as I could, while some ran the mile and others even did the marathon. I couldn't understand how they had the patience, much less the stamina, to run that far. In the Buddha Dharma there is the example of the three animals: the rabbit, the horse, and the elephant. The rabbit is like the sprinter, hopping all over the place as fast as it can. The horse is running around too, but is more settled. The elephant is very careful, taking slow and deliberate steps without being scattered or hasty, and if it is careful, it will live a long, wise, and useful life. The elephant represents Buddha Dharma.

When I practiced at Sokoji Temple in San Francisco in the 1960s, the Japanese American congregation would trot out the white elephant cart on Buddha's birthday, load it with flowers and children, and we would have a parade through Japantown. Later I came to learn that the foundation of our practice and our very life is dependent on the same principles as those of the long-distance runner and the elephant.

Establishing a rhythm for our sitting practice is essential. If the runner goes too fast, he gets tired too soon. If she doesn't have enough momentum, her energy leaks out and is not renewed. When the runner maintains upright posture and the breath is deeply centered and in harmony with the movement of the limbs, it is no longer a race. This is true winning. Body and mind drop away and it is just here and now. Just this. A moment of exhaustion and a moment of renewal, and the runner is able to go on and on. One becomes a vehicle, allowing the inexhaustible universal energy to freely fuel the activity. In the same way, for daily practice it is necessary to balance the rhythm of our sitting with the other activities and responsibilities that form our lives. Unless we can simplify our lives, knowing what is important and letting go of what is not, we will wear ourselves out dragging around useless physical, emotional, and mental baggage.

What does it mean to have a practice? Simply speaking, zazen is the touchstone, the center. It is not just another activity like running or studying. It is not just another add-on to our agenda of activities. Complete practice is total integration. Unlike many similar ways that depend on periodic concentrated events, we have been given the problems of the long-distance runner. Daily practice, plus the periodic concentrated events called *sesshins*, require a certain amount of dedication, intention, and time. If "time is money," how will we spend it? Will we fritter it away or spend it wisely?

Lest we forget, the fruit of practice is compassion for all beings. When we give selflessly, there is no self to get tired and this no-self is continuously renewed.

Establishing a Practice

When Suzuki Roshi asked me to establish a zendo in Berkeley in 1967, I found a wonderful old Victorian. I determined that I was going to sit there every morning and every evening. And if somebody else came, that was wonderful. If nobody came, that was okay, too. But someone always came, and little by little we had a community of practitioners, a sangha. It took many years before the sangha actually matured, and we still have some of our original members practicing regularly. Together we have been through many changes and phases, and I think that kind of mutual support creates something wonderful.

Perhaps the most important thing that makes a sangha work is at least one dedicated person—one person or more who, no matter what, is totally dedicated to this practice. Through that dedication and continuous effort, that person or persons maintain the inspiration for practice and a stable base.

The other thing that makes things work is the members taking responsibility for the sangha. Each member should have something to do to take care of the place itself. Someone's assignment may be to take care of a certain space, or to take care of one of the altars, to sift the incense ashes, or to take care of a section of the garden. All these small things add up and that responsibility ties us all into mutual stewardship. Then everyone feels appreciative for everyone else and feels "I'm supporting your practice, you're supporting my practice." Otherwise, a few people may be doing everything while everyone else just comes and goes, which is not so good.

As a mostly lay community, we sit together and we study together, but we lead our daily lives independently. When the members take responsibility, they become part of the sangha. Our center in Berkeley is more than just four houses—it's a zendo, a community space, and a residence, with most of our members living in the surrounding area. When we come together to do this practice, there is a kind of cooperative, mutual support that is most valuable. It's important for everyone to figure out "What is my practice?" "How can

I do this practice?" "How can I arrange my life so that my practice harmonizes with my other responsibilities?"

We have Zen philosophy and we have Zen doctrine and we have Zen this and that, but the important thing is how to practice. How do we actually put our behind on the cushion? Or if we can't sit cross-legged, then how do we sit in the chair or some way that works for us? The community is shaped by geography. You can get anywhere in the Berkeley flatlands by car or bike within fifteen or twenty minutes. At the Berkeley and San Francisco Zen Centers, we are used to daily practice. We get up early in the morning and zazen begins between 5:00 and 6:00, and there is evening zazen before dinner. I've seen other practice places where everybody liked to sit at night. There's something about a place and the people that create a rhythm of practice.

The two sides every practitioner is dealing with is the balance of how to establish a zendo practice and how to practice in our daily life. I suggest that you take a certain period of time—it could be a week, it could be two weeks, it could be a month, or six months—and in that time period you look at your calendar and decide "I'm going to sit this time every week." It may be one day a week, it may be five mornings, it may be two afternoons, or whatever. You decide that this is what I'm going to do, and this is the way I'm going to do it. This practice schedule fits in with my life. You have the bottom line (no pun intended).

What it all hinges on is what your commitment is to yourself. The most important aspect of practice is your commitment, because you can't practice without some kind of commitment. When you sit zazen you're committing yourself to sitting still for the period of zazen. To commit yourself to that is a very important factor. Then zazen becomes an integral part of your life. If zazen is not an integral part of your life it is not true zazen, because zazen is nothing more than the way you live your life.

Suzuki Roshi would say that Zen practice is living your life moment by moment—living your life completely, thoroughly, moment by moment. You have to be careful how you make your commitments. Many people have a tendency to overextend themselves. You may say, "Well, I will commit myself to sitting zazen five times a week." But if this is not realistic, you will become discouraged. Making your commitment carefully helps you make realistic choices.

After the week, or the month, or whatever period you chose, then you review how you did. "Did that work? Yeah." So you extend it another week or month. Or you change it: "No, that didn't work so well." Or your life changes but you have the same commitment, and find your previous commitment is no longer working for you, so you get discouraged. But all you have to do is change your commitment to work with the way your life is now. This is why I suggest making the commitment for a limited period of time. That way you have a beginning and an end to a particular commitment, and it's very realistic. You keep experimenting until you find your proper rhythm, and it's up to each one of us to find out how to do it.

If you're in a monastery, you commit yourself to whatever the monastic schedule is, and you just follow that. But here, everyone has to make their own practice schedule, and it's your responsibility to create it with your teacher. It's good to go to your teacher and discuss your zazen schedule and what can be expected of you, because sometimes the teacher thinks that you're doing one thing while you're actually doing something else. If the teacher doesn't know that, they may expect something from you that shouldn't be expected. So it's very good to keep in contact with your teacher and discuss your practice. When you share what you're doing, it makes your commitment more realistic.

Practice needs that kind of intentional commitment because otherwise it is based on the way we feel. "Today I feel really good, wouldn't it be nice to sit zazen?" Or "Jeez, I just feel awful, life is terrible. What can I do? Maybe I should sit zazen?" These feelings are important, but if you only depend on your feelings, it's not a real practice because our feelings are not reliable. We depend on our commitment, or what we have determined. Then if we feel good or if we feel bad, or no matter how we feel, we honor our commitment, and that takes it out of the realm of preference.

Real zazen is when we practice without any preference. We are not trying to get something good. We're not trying to get something bad. We're not trying to get anything. We're just giving ourselves to ourselves in order to establish ourselves on ourselves. And that's a wonderful kind of gift.

Question: Is the commitment just to seek the Zen, or does it include that my room will be tidy also?

Sojun: In zazen, it means that you don't move from your position. In your daily life, it means that you don't move from your intentions.

Question: Can you say something about what you mean by "sitting still"?

Sojun: What I mean by that is, once you make your commitment, you don't move from it. That's what I mean by sitting still.

Question: For the most part it seems like that would work well, but then when my daughter comes in and says, "But I have this and this to do," then I find myself saying, "But I have zazen this morning."

Sojun: Your daughter comes first. This is an immediate thing. But if she says that every time you want to do zazen, then you have to make some agreements. I have to deal with that too, because I have an eleven-year-old son and as he gets older, I have to do more things with him. When he was born, I thought, "I'm not going to let my taking care of him interfere with my obligations." But I also thought, "I will include him in what I'm doing."

I carried him around on my back for a long time. Whatever I was doing, he was there on my back. He was a very good baby.

I can't believe it now. He's changed a lot. But he was very easy up until he was five, just a model kid. When my wife went to nursing school, she would leave him off in the zendo in the morning during service. Sometimes he'd sit zazen, and sometimes he'd do service and once, while everybody was standing waiting for service, he and his little girlfriend, both naked, whizzed by showing everybody their drawings.

It's a kind of give and take. When your life is involved with various things, they all have to intermingle somehow. So there has to be space for children, and space for family. You know, you'll go off to sit zazen, and someone else resents it. That's a problem that a lot of people have to deal with. It's like you're taking yourself out of someone's life when you're doing that. That's not what's actually happening, but they feel abandoned sometimes.

You're gone all day to a *sesshin*, and your husband or your wife is doing something else. It's good if your spouse or your family is very understanding. But you have to be careful how you regulate your practice so it integrates with your other responsibilities. Lay practice means that you have to take the responsibility for integrating it with your family, your work, and other activities, and it's going to be something that is going to create a little problem, and everybody has to be able to accept the problem.

Question: It sounds like it's just more practice—you can either escape your family responsibilities by saying, "Oh, but at such and such a time I sit zazen," or you can use family or whatever as a means of saying, "Oh, well, I can't sit zazen because I have to do such and such." It seems like it really has to be continuously weighed and reassessed.

Sojun: That's right—it does have to be continually weighed and reassessed. People within a family have to give each other space to do something without feeling that somebody is running away. It's really good if you can take the quality of your practice and extend it to your family, extend it to your workplace, to your world, that's what makes practice not self-centered. It's not something that you do just for yourself, even though you do it by yourself. If you're doing it just for yourself, it's not practice.

Actually, we come to practice trying to do something for ourselves, but after we mature we realize that the practice is not just for ourselves. The first stage is that we do this practice for ourselves. The second stage is that we do the practice for everyone else. The third stage is that we just do the practice for the practice, which includes us and everyone else. Practicing just for myself is a little bit egotistical—it's a lot egotistical. Practicing just for others is also kind of egotistical. But to do the practice just for the practice is "no self," and then others get taken care of without our taking care, and we get taken care of, so these three aspects are always working together. Of course, something is for me and something is for you, but it is out of the realm of you and me. If we all take care of the practice, then everything gets taken care of. The practice takes care of everyone.

We come to practice for various reasons, but we don't always know what it is that we come for. I don't think I knew exactly what it was that I was coming for. But when we make a sincere effort to practice, sooner or later we realize what it is. We realize that there is nothing to "get." And this "nothing to get" has to be "found" by each one of us.

Aspiration and Inspiration

What is it that we aspire to in our life? What is it that leads us and gives us direction, and how do we decide? Or do we decide?

Aspiration gives us purpose—and inspiration gives us momentum. Two of the fundamentals of Soto Zen are that Buddhas and ordinary beings are not two, and that we practice with no idea of gaining something.

When we begin sitting zazen we may not aspire to become Buddha, but it is not unusual to want something from practice. Suzuki Roshi's teaching never strayed from these fundamentals. Sometimes we confuse "no gaining mind" with no aspiration or no goal. Gaining here is associated with selfishness or self-centeredness. So "no gaining" means not adding something that obscures what is fundamental. Don't put another head on top of your own, don't stick some idea of enlightenment on top of your original endowment.

When our aspiration is pure, that is, not self-centered, it naturally becomes Buddha's practice. That is why it is important to practice for the sake of practice, without expectations. So our goal is not the usual goal of getting something, but rather of letting go. It is not wrong to aspire to enlightenment. What brings us to practice is our own light that needs to be revealed and developed through practice in order to express itself fully. It is like a piece of incense that is burning all the way down. It is the same light at the beginning and the end, and goes through many transformations as it burns. The light and the incense are one column, inseparable. Our original thought of enlightenment is the light that stays with us through our entire life of practice and illuminates our everyday activity. Nothing special.

Our bodhisattva practice is to help all beings in their quest for fundamental maturity and realization. Enlightened practice is to stop seeking enlightenment, and to practice for the sake of practice, which matures one's self and others as well. Dogen calls this *jijuyu zanmai,* self-fulfilling or self-joyous samadhi, which is complete when we let go and extend our light to others.

Some time ago I ran across a little kids' book from Singapore called *The Adventures of Leo: Rahula Leads the Way*. It's about a boy named Leo. One day his mother said, "Why don't you go to the temple and offer flowers to the Buddha?" So he went to the temple, and behind the Buddha statue was a boy who looked a lot like him and seemed to be his own age, ten or twelve, but he was a little monk named Rahula. He had a shaved head and a robe. They became friends and traveled around together. And whenever they encountered a tricky situation, Rahula always gave Leo a message or teaching about it. They got into a fight with some kids and Rahula helped him to understand it. Whatever situation Leo found himself in, Rahula was always there to teach him how to deal with it. Leo and Rahula are like the two sides of one person: ordinary and Buddha.

When we are mature enough to let Buddha lead, we can help people. When these two sides become one, we can forget our self and teach others. So aspiration is just to find the path and stay on it no matter how difficult it is, or how discouraged we may get.

Enlightenment includes inspiration and determination that keeps us going. When we fall down, we get back up. That is the rhythm of practice. Negotiating our way through difficulty and adversity gives us the strength and confidence to live our life one moment at a time in faith that we are Buddha. This is our aspiration: no gaining mind, but strong practice to express the way and to embody the way. When you have this, nothing can stop you, even though you have many obstacles and seeming barriers. When you become one with Dharma, it is transmitted to you by the universe and you have your own true way.

Gyoji and Dokan

Gyoji and *dokan* are two terms in Soto Zen that we should be familiar with. *Gyoji* is a term that Dogen used that means continuous practice, and *dokan* means Way Ring—the cyclical daily form of practice. Without using this Japanese nomenclature, *gyoji/dokan* was the fundamental practice that Suzuki Roshi introduced to us. In a talk, Suzuki Roshi said, "If you lose the spirit of repetition, your practice will become quite difficult." He also said that if you chant the Heart Sutra once you may feel okay about it, but if you chant it over and over every day you might lose your original attitude toward it. You might maintain your beginner's mind for a few years, but after a while you are liable to lose the limitless meaning of original mind.

This presents an interesting koan for us. In an unrepeatable universe, how can any act be repeated? The only way is to be fully present in each moment in each activity as *just this*, *just now*, without comparing. I remember observing my teacher's behavior: nothing special, living each moment with total presence, not getting ahead, not lagging behind. Suzuki Roshi sat zazen every morning and every evening, bowed nine times and chanted the Heart Sutra three times (that was our original service). In between he simply responded to circumstances with the same attitude. His life was all of a piece. He did not have a lot of dependencies. His demeanor was relaxed, soft, flexible, and upright. He was always shining, and his presence was nourishing.

Dokan, the ring or circle of the Way, is the nonrepeatable rhythm of daily practice. It is to follow the cosmic order. Every day the sun appears in the sky, and at night the moon, while the planets circle in their orbits. At night the world sleeps, and at dawn we awake. This is the basic cycle, the formal alternation we call night and day. It is the turning of the world in harmony with the cosmos. All creatures follow individual and collective patterns and the various formalities and structures that support our unique situations.

The life of a Zen student revolves around zazen, while zazen opens us up to the cosmic order. *Do* (Tao) means the path or the way, and *kan* means ring or circle, the cycle of practice: doing something over and over again. When sitting we hold our hands in the "cosmic mudra." The form of the hands creates the empty circle that creates the form of the hands. All is empty and empty is all. Although there are many things that are important in our lives, receiving our nourishment from the source has to be primary. When we survey the cosmos, we see an infinite variety of circular forms. We experience the cycles of the seasons and the cycles within the cycles within the cycles and we realize that each one of us is the place where heaven and earth meet. We can also see that circles of energy emanate from us and mix and overlap with those of others. What kind of vibe do we want to send into the world? The way we think and act has an effect. To sit upright in the center of the empty circle as a vehicle for light is the Zen student's life. The cycle of continuous practice, of sitting zazen and allowing that selfless freedom to be expressed in daily life is the turning of the wheel and the basis for harmony.

Responding to Conditions

In Case 16 of the *Mumonkan*, Master Unmon says, "Why at the sound of the bell do the monks put on their robes and go to the meditation hall?" To expand on this: Why, when there are so many other things to do in this world, at the sound of the bell does everybody put on their robe and go to the zendo? In other words, why do this? On what basis do you choose what you're doing when there is an infinite variety of interesting activities? What brings us to this activity?

The fact that we are here is a pretty good indication that we understand something. In our Zen practice we talk about realization or intuition, some kind of direct understanding, but why we actually practice is because of our realization, even though we may not have a clear picture or we may not be able to verbalize or even understand it. Still there is something very deep that corresponds to and wants to meet itself in practice. I think a *sesshin* or a one-day sitting like this is a very important part of our practice. In this kind of intense embracing, *sesshin* means something like "embracing mind." We meet our self in a way that we cannot do in any other way. Even though all of our activity, of course, is meeting, we don't have the same realization. It is hard to have the same kind of realization as we have when we sit. And even though *sesshin* or sitting long has its difficulties, our desire for it is very strong.

Today, this morning, almost everyone was late. If we have sincere effort then our realization will be pretty deep, but if our effort is half-hearted, our realization will be very shallow. We may have some realization, but strictly speaking our realization will probably be very shallow. And usually our realization is proportionate with our amount of effort and sincerity in practice. That's why we don't stress your understanding, but what we stress is your actual practice. We don't ignore understanding. But understanding without real effort, without real practice, is just like a picture book. So we say that how we learn our Zen, how we immerse our self in practice, how we get true understanding, is through our pores—not so much through our ears, but through our pores. Unless we present our self whole, body and mind, nothing happens.

If we want to learn nondiscrimination in its true sense, the easy way is through this practice. The comfortable way is through this practice. Dogen talks about zazen as just this comfortable way. Not learning meditation, but just a comfortable way to enter the door of nondiscrimination. If you think that zazen is uncomfortable, you should look at the rest of your life.

Without the thought of good or bad, what happens to us is what happens to us. Our life is our life. How we accept our life. How we accept this life in its true sense beyond our discriminating mind, just as it is. If we know how to do that, no matter what happens to us, we always feel comfortable.

Dogen's comfortable way is a kind of koan. When we first hear about Dogen's "comfortable way," it always makes us laugh. Oh, ha, ha, ha. That Dogen's always joking. But comfortable way is a big koan. How can you be comfortable in this life? Pretty hard. How can you be comfortable with all the difficulties? If you can be comfortable in any situation, then you're your own master. If you know how to have composure, if you don't lose your composure in any situation, we'll all bow down to you.

We sometimes talk about lay practice, lay person's Zen practice, Buddhist practice, and practicing Buddhism. Sometimes people make a distinction between lay practice and priest's practice. I don't like so much to talk about lay practice. I'm getting really tired of that kind of term. It means people who live at home and practice. People who live in the world and practice our lay practice, so-called lay practice, is not the same as practice that people usually associate with Buddhism. It's just practice. Any of us can practice wholeheartedly and with sincerity if we really want to.

The demands of life are very strong and in order to practice we have to make special effort to do this instead of something else, so I really admire all of you for practicing. And I think that the effort that you show or that's put forth in your practice is and will be a good example to people. When they see the benefit of practice manifesting in your life, your life will be a good example. But Zen practice takes a long time.

Usually in the beginning we have some immediate result and our life changes somewhat. And because of the contrast between our old way and our new way, you can see some immediate results, but as we go along in practice, the contrast between our old way and our new way gets obscured and we just find our self in practice without any obvious change or obvious benefit. And we wonder, *Is there something to this or not?* We kind of wonder about it. *Maybe I should go on to something else.* Usually in our speedy life we're looking for various kinds of highs, and we see Zen practice as another kind of high. And then when it looks like the usual, we start looking for something else. *Well, what's the next thing that will get me high?* But Zen practice is more like a glacier than a landslide. It moves like a glacier and your whole life of practice moves like a glacier. But if you move with it, your life will have the power of a glacier. Maybe three-quarters of an inch a year. If you want to measure your movement, maybe an inch and a half or three-quarters of an inch in a year. But since our practice is endless, we shouldn't worry about it.

But whether we have lay practice or monk's practice or just practice, the quality of our practice cannot be different. We have the opportunity to practice quality in all of our activity. The quality of our practice should be in all of our activity. When you sit, you just sit completely with total freedom. When you wash the dishes, you just wash the dishes with total freedom. When you're driving your car, you're just driving your car with total freedom. Total immersion.

I notice little things about how we take care of our practice in the zendo within this sphere. And I see how careless we are. Zen practice means mindful, careful practice. When someone sees somebody practicing mindful, careful practice, that's an example. The only way we can teach and learn is by example. And the only way that we can actually practice is mindfully and carefully. Strictly speaking, when we walk, say during a *sesshin* when we are walking around, we should have our hands in *shashu*. Not in our pockets. If you walk around with your hands in your pockets, then you are thinking about something. You're thinking about something else. During this time, you should only be thinking about just exactly what your body's doing. What is my body doing now? It's walking around. So the hands have got a place. This is the form of the hands. Not like this, in your pockets. As soon as you put your hands in your pockets, you're someplace else.

This is how we keep our attention up, how we keep our attention focused. And zazen is just this form. So all day we keep our attention on just this form. And when we walk, we keep our attention focused on just walking. There's no time during *sesshin* that's out of time, that's out of the practice. So walking, sitting, even speaking. We only talk when there's some necessity, but that talking, that speaking should also be mindful speaking. And when we sit down to rest, that resting should be mindful resting. And when you go to the bathroom, that activity should be mindful activity.

We make the effort to do one thing at a time. Just this thing, and in the next moment, this thing. Sometimes we have to do two things at a time. But if we are doing two things at once, then we should be mindful of two things at once. And when our mind starts wandering any time during the day, we should bring our attention back to what we are doing. Just like when we're sitting. So moving around is the same as sitting down. And we bring our attention back just in the same way we do when we're sitting. If we practice this way consciously over and over, we'll be able to penetrate zazen, but we have to have a strong desire to penetrate zazen. That should be uppermost. A strong desire to penetrate all the way through.

And how we extend this kind of activity into our daily life, either consciously or not consciously, how we manifest or bring some benefit to some people, is important. When we really become totally free, we can give our self to people. Before we are totally free, we are always holding back, holding our self back. But real freedom means to be able to give yourself unreservedly. That's the freedom, the real freedom that we have through practice. If someone asks for something, we give it. At least what we can, we give.

When you really penetrate through and through, you'll realize that there is nothing else. And then you'll realize what a great relief it is to be rid of the burden of our self. Buddha, Shakyamuni Buddha, if you read the old scriptures, he's always talking about laying down the burden. So-and-so laid down the burden, has done what has to be done and has laid down the burden, the burden of their self. We have this weight on our shoulders, which is our self that we're carrying around. We carry this big sack of our self around and it's quite heavy. When we can let that go, we will feel light and unburdened and free to do anything.

The benefit of this practice should be to help us to get rid of the burden of our self. That's the goal of practice.

Stand Up in the Middle of Your Life

There is this question: What is our practice? What are we doing? Is it vital enough? Are we sinking into complacency? Do we have enough pressure to feel that we're doing something vital?

It's important to have pressure. Some people feel the pressure more than others. One person may feel that pressure is a burden and another may feel that it's okay, or that it's not enough. Each one of us is in a different place in our practice, in our dispositions, in our character, in our strength, and in our ability, in particular in our ability to accept things as they are and to have equanimity and concentration. We're all different. Even though we have the same practice, there is something about the practice, the fine-tuning of our practice, that has to be tailored to each person.

What is it that we can all practice that is vital for each one of us? What is the koan that covers everyone? There are a couple of koans that I sometimes give people, and there are a couple of practices that

I sometimes give people. If someone has a very angry disposition and suffers a lot from self-alienation, I may give that person a *metta* practice, either reciting the Metta Sutta or practicing the four aspects of *metta*. The first aspect of *metta* is to bestow love or acceptance or light on yourself, the second is to focus love on someone you know. The third is to focus on someone you don't know, and the last is to focus on someone you consider an enemy, and then extending that love to the whole world, to the whole universe. In any case, all of this begins with knowing yourself and accepting yourself. I introduced the *Metta Sutta* into our service at Green Gulch because I felt it was something we really needed to think about as a balance to our wisdom practice.

Dogen Zenji gave us the *Genjokoan*, the koan of our daily life—how we meet every aspect of our life as the koan; the fundamental point where sameness and difference meet. We have collections of one hundred koans, fifty koans, and so forth, and those koans are examples from the daily lives of the Ancestors. In the same way, our true koan appears within the intimacy of what is actually happening in our life. So when we study the old examples, they are not just stories about someone else. Because these stories are so fundamental, we can relate to them as our own.

"What is *metta*?" is a koan. It's a wonderful koan. "What is gratitude?" is a koan. I often give people the koan of gratitude. No matter what happens to you, just bow and say "Thank you," whether you feel it's a good thing or a bad thing. If someone insults you, just bow with gratitude and say "Thank you." If someone compliments you, just bow with gratitude and say "Thank you."

Sometimes it's hard to accept a compliment. Someone may say, "Oh, you're nice," or "You did this well." It can be very hard for us to accept that. What are we supposed to say? Anything we say makes us feel either egotistical or evasive. Every time I take my dog for a walk, someone will say, "What a beautiful dog you have!" The dog doesn't care, and it's no compliment to me, but I feel obliged to come up with something. So sometimes I say thank you and sometimes I just agree. How do you accept a compliment without being egotistical? As someone said, "How do we cut through?" Right there is our practice. It's not thinking it over, it's "How do we cut through?" If we're dealing with this kind of koan all the time, we don't have any problem about whether there is pressure or not enough pressure, or whether we're at the edge or not at the edge. If you can accept this koan that is always right in front of you, you will be right at the edge all the time. The only problem is the problem of ego. We don't have to know so much. We don't have to be so smart. We just have to be able to stand up in the middle of our life and accept whatever it is.

Like Water

Someone asked me:
What is the practice of a Zen student?
I said:
Like water.

Water always seeks the lowest place
It goes with gravity
It takes the shape of whatever boundaries it meets
Sometimes it looks like a cup or an ocean
The sweat on your hands
The snot in your nose
Clouds
Raindrops
Lifeblood
Constantly flowing
In and out of
Your body.

We meet it with plumbing.
Strong pipes with tight joints.
Water is truth
Plumbing must be honest
Water can't be fooled

Water makes everything truthful
That is its pure activity
Sometimes it appears as slime
Or poison
Or tears
It goes through infinite transformations
When it dries out it appears somewhere else
It is never lost
Or gone
It is purified by coursing through rocks and boulders.

Water is drawn to the rarified realms by the sun
Gravity pulls it to earth
It has the qualities of spirit and matter
Water becomes vapor
Becomes cloud
Retreats from earth
Loses its shape
Lets go
Returns to the dusty realms
To nourish all beings
As drops
Mud
Hailstones
Snow
Dew.

The monk is called *unsui*
"clouds and water"
The *unsui* sits upright,
Doesn't lean right or left backward or forward

Gravity pulling down with all its force
Spirit rising with all its strength
Mind open, vast as space
The life force blooming like a flower
Equilibrium of all the forces and powers
The unconditional realm in the midst of
All conditions.

The lowest place is the highest place
The shape of the cloud and water person
Is determined by the direction of the wind
Water has no special shape or form
It responds to prayers
Its love pervades everywhere and is not limited by
Self-interest.

Eno says That One is like the sun
Shining light in all directions
Illuminating the way
Facing challenges
Not turning away from difficulties
With purity
Like a lotus in muddy water.

Engaging
Formal Practice

The Formal and the Informal

It is commonly thought that Zen practice is very formal and rigid, and that thinking and emotions are cut off. Formal, yes. Rigid? Not really. For every activity there are rules, directives, and procedures. The formality of our practice allows access to our ineffable, fundamental, formless nature. What looks like narrow confinement becomes, with maturity, vast freedom. What is formal becomes informal.

Submitting to the zendo forms enables an attentive student to move and sit gracefully with ease and naturalness. Over the course of our lives we develop habits and tensions in our body and mind caused by fears, resistance, defensiveness, and biased views. Zendo practice can help us, through awareness, to overcome these hindrances.

Moving in the zendo with awareness of the subtle sound of our steps, the upright movement of our posture, and the relation to our surroundings reflects a natural, unaffected choreography. It is not a matter of getting it right or being perfect. Working in the tight space of the kitchen, attending to the various tasks, we move around each other with sharp knives and hot pots in a harmonious improvised dance, concentrated and attentive, getting out the meal on time with a calm, settled mind and relaxed body.

The life of a Zen student is mostly improvisation. Improvisation works best within a solid structure or container. It is so in music and the arts. A well-trained Zen student feels comfortable within the forms and approaches the activity with gratitude, awareness, and confidence.

There is a saying, "to sit zazen with warm feet and a cool head." People often say, "I am a very emotional person." It sounds very special. I have never met anyone who is not a very emotional person. The ones who don't show their emotions are often the most emotional. To control or not to control? To have a cool head while sitting zazen is to think the thought of zazen. The nature of thinking is to think (or to dream). It doesn't make any difference what it is thinking as long as it can do its thing. The point is: who is the boss of the thinking? Feelings are both physical and emotional. Emotional feelings are mostly mental.

When we can maintain a well-balanced posture of uprightness and flexibility, our feelings tend to harmonize with our present situation. Why should we be thinking about something else or holding on to feelings that have nothing to do with the present situation? It is possible to let go for a while and allow our body-mind the freedom from the fetters of emotion/thought.

Formal and informal. They are just two sides of the same thing. My teacher said, "Even though there is no self, still there are rules."

The Form of Our Life

Recently a student said, "You know, if we didn't have all that formality in the zendo, there wouldn't be anything to this at all. It's like the Emperor's New Clothes."

From one point of view that looks like a very accurate statement. Although we talk about the form of Zen, there is no special form. Since Zen is nothing more than the practice of our life, it follows that whatever forms our life takes can be the forms of practice. Even though that is so, it doesn't mean that we are always aware of them as such. Our predecessors developed certain recognizable forms like zazen, bowing, and chanting, and holding our hands this way and our bowls this way. And when we enter into these forms, we can recognize practice. We can see it because it has a shape. We call it formal practice, and we can use it day after day and find our way in it. We can touch it, embrace it. But because formal practice presents such a contrast to ordinary worldly life, it's sometimes hard to know how to bring forth the mind of practice within the forms of everyday life. How can we do zazen all day without crossing our legs?

In a lay community we are always concerned with how to initiate practice using the forms that are at hand. How can we use the common forms we encounter in our ordinary lives at work, within our family, and amid the myriad complications of present-day life? Our complete life of practice is to merge the spirit of formal practice with the forms of the dynamically changing world.

I once suggested to a student that she sit zazen in a chair because she was having trouble sitting on the floor, but she didn't want to do it because if she did she would feel like she was cheating. A common complaint is that it's hard to find time for zazen in our busy lives, but if we know how to sit zazen in a chair, we can do it anywhere, especially since we spend so much time in chairs.

Our postures are indicative of our attitudes and states of mind. Standing in line at a Safeway checkstand, grumbling about how slowly the line is moving, I give up, shift my weight evenly to both feet, adjust my posture. Following my breath, I return to myself. Sitting in the car waiting for the signal to change, I sit up straight, let go of my grip on the wheel, put my hands in my lap, and, taking a few deep breaths, return to zero.

Simple awareness of posture and centering within each activity is a fundamental mindfulness practice. If actualized in the most common, everyday situations, it can be the basis of a calm foundation of mind. The way we move within time is a kind of dance. We are always keeping time within one rhythm or another. Music, of course, is exemplary. One reason we love music so much is that it's so complete and it always comes out right. The notes harmonize with one another in time to make a beautiful, complete, ideal statement; not like our daily life where the rhythms are more subtle or hard to find or are constantly being interrupted or changed in ways that aren't so easy to handle. In music, as in our dance of life, if we get ahead of time or behind, we have a problem.

One remarkable example of Suzuki Roshi's life was that he never seemed to be in a hurry. No matter how much pressure he was under, I don't remember ever seeing him in a hurry. I don't mean to imply that he was a perfect person. He was always the first to acknowledge his faults, which is one reason why we trusted him, but he had a way of not wasting time. He seemed to be settled in time almost casually, never ahead or behind. In his quiet way, fully filling each moment, he appeared to be tapped into some fundamental rhythm which was independent of circumstances yet totally one with them.

The tempo of monastic practice, with its constantly changing rhythms, is somewhat relentless. Throughout the day you have to let go of the present activity and take on the next one. It's not hard if you allow yourself to adjust to the changes, but if you don't, then you become your own obstacle. Monastic practice helps us maintain a life of nonattachment in the present, but there are not as many variables in that practice as there are in our city life. For instance, how do you keep a calm mind when there are demands from too many sources at once? How do we keep our composure in the face of the world's atrocities without being overwhelmed? There can be many ways to deal with these questions, but we should allow ourselves the opportunity to bring forth a response based on a mind of equanimity. Our zendo practice can give us a way of being in touch with our fundamental self, but the practice must find its completion in our everyday activity of "drawing water and carrying wood." Dogen Zenji says that *Genjokoan* is zazen as it is extended into our life. The opposite is also not only true but necessary. It is our daily life as extended back into zazen. When I make a real continuous effort outside of the zendo, my practice in the zendo becomes stronger and more vital.

Sacrifice and Ceremony

The other day I looked up the etymology of the word "sacrifice." I was surprised to discover that it meant sacred ceremony. We usually associate this term with giving up something valuable or denying ourselves. This is somewhat related to renunciation, which is related to denunciation—*nunce* or *nounce* means to announce or declare an intention. As we know, giving up something we like or are attached to is common to all religious practices. This includes celibacy, fasting, and self-denial of all sorts. In the past there were animal as well as human sacrifices to gain the favor or assuage the fury of the gods.

Buddhism has its own renunciation practices and takes a middle path leaning toward austerity. Buddhism has no deity. Buddha is not a god. According to the literature, Buddha neither denied nor affirmed a deity. In our practice we do not make a separation between spiritual and mundane. Walls, tiles, streams, and pebbles are all continually preaching the Dharma. Each being is an expression of the entire universe. So what does sacrifice mean in our practice?

For me, in the original sense of sacred ceremony, our zazen and zendo practice resonates with that term. Zazen is a sacred ceremony of *shikantaza*—stepping free of our conditioned postures and resuming our true nature: just this! Zazen itself is our human offering, without expecting anything, just pure generosity. There is also the offering of incense and flowers. Putting our palms together and bowing expresses our letting go, and merging sacred and profane as one. The ceremony of cooking, serving, eating, and cleaning up reveals the enlightened nature of pure activity devoid of selfishness. Sweeping the grounds, driving a car, interacting with creatures of all kinds. It is *gyoji*, continuous practice. Maintaining this attitude wears down our ego.

To sit zazen is to receive Buddha's teaching. The price we pay, as everything has a price, is our ego suit, our false coverings. Zazen is the great teacher. It teaches us how suffering arises, the cause, and the cure, without saying a word. We have to give up our usual comfort level in order to access true comfort.

Master Joshu asked the question, "Does one who dies the great death come back to life again?" Master Touzi replied, "Don't go by night, one should go by day." When our ego is cut down to size and is no longer the boss obstructing our original light, our true life begins and we can enter the world in the light of day with helping hands. Then true ritual is nothing but the most ordinary unselfconscious daily activity, in accord with and guided by Big Mind, our own Buddha mind.

Practicing Within the Limitations of Our Life

When I first came to Sokoji Temple in San Francisco, I was surprised by the formality of the practice. I had never encountered anything like it before. As a matter of fact, I always tried to avoid any kind of formality. So I can understand why many newcomers are put off by it. But intuitively I knew that I had to do this, and when I experienced my teacher Suzuki Roshi's composure, his magnanimous mind and totally informal presence, I began to appreciate the limitations that the structure provided. I came to understand that we are always practicing under various restrictions and limitations.

There are rules for everything. The laws of gravity are determining every move we make. I once saw a photo of a light plane stuck nose first into a tree. The caption said, "The laws of gravity are strict and unerring, and must be precisely obeyed." Gravity is pulling us down and our life force is welling us upward. The interaction and balance of these two forces control our physical body, as well as the way we think and feel. We are all living under the influence of this fundamental restriction as well. When we examine our life we can see that we have other restrictions and boundaries—inner restrictions, outer restrictions, mental, social, emotional, imaginary restrictions, restrictions of circumstance, time, truth and falsehood, conditioning, fear, and self-deception, to mention a few.

So the question is how to find our freedom within the restrictive parameters of our life. Caught by partiality, ignorance, circumstances, emotional exaggerations, and cerebral dead ends, our freedom is compromised and our suffering increases. Top athletes need strict rules and discipline to accomplish their goals, as do scientists and artists. A painter has to be able to find complete expression within the parameters of a canvas. A musician must find complete expression using a limited number of notes. People get up in the morning and go to work on time.

Zen students also have patterns that enable their practice. These patterns, which some see as formalities, allow access to a gate of a fence around an empty field. When the gate is open to the empty field, we can leave the false barriers aside—the conditioning, the fear, the self-deception—and return to the field of our original unbound nature, beyond form and emptiness. Within the so-called formality, we can find our perfect informal freedom. As our practice matures, we are able to find that freedom in every circumstance and make it available to others as well.

Good Morning

Sometimes when I arrive in the morning, I pass sangha members emerging out of the darkness and fading into the darkness. When we pass, I bow. Some bow back, some look surprised, and some just walk past without acknowledging my presence at all. It often feels like ships passing in the night, or like disembodied ghosts drifting in their own worlds. Do I know you?

One of the primary practices we learn at the monastery is bowing whenever we meet or pass someone. There is no need to think of something to say, no need for platitudes; just simply connecting on a deep, fundamental level. It means that we have an opportunity to stop and let go of our self-absorption for a moment, which allows us to meet as equals; the barrier of subject and object is gone. This is *shikantaza*, our active form of zazen. It is letting go and merging, just doing, without any other motive. Time stands still for that moment. I think bowing is sometimes ignored in the afternoon because there are people coming and going who are not familiar with this practice. But if we practice bowing to our familiars, they will begin to understand.

Master Dogen said that as long as there is the practice of bowing, the Dharma will flourish. One time I entered Suzuki Roshi's room and he prostrated himself to me. I was so taken aback and flustered that I just stood there. He admonished me, saying that when a teacher bows to a student, the student should also bow. He also said that a teacher should not feel above prostrating himself to a student. The angle of the bow expresses our state of mind at the time. One angle expresses our stinginess, holding back, or not giving ourselves completely. Another posture is ostentatious, overly generous, trying to look sincere. When neither of these is present, we can actually meet without fear or judgment. When we put our palms together, ordinary mind and way-seeking mind become one. This is a moment when everything stops, and we can experience and share, as Master Bankei says, our original, clearly illuminating, Unborn Buddha Mind.

Why and How

Why Do You Practice?

Sometimes I am asked, "Why do you practice?" There are many possible responses. In the old days in China, the question was "Why did Bodhidharma come from the west?" This became a well-known koan that appears often in the koan collections, and there is a variety of seemingly puzzling responses. Sir Edmund Hillary's response to "Why do you want to climb the mountain?" was "Because it is there." That is a little nugget one can keep unloading for a long time. When Dogen returned from China, he was asked what he brought back to Japan. He said that all he had learned was that his eyes were horizontal and his nose was vertical.

When I sat down the first time for zazen, I knew I was home. I was like the prodigal son in the Lotus Sutra who had stumbled into the doorway of his father's house. This is not an uncommon experience for a Zen student. I had found zazen and a teacher whose practice was patience and sincerity. He said that those who have the most difficult time, and who persevere no matter what obstacles they meet in the way, in the end usually become very good teachers.

Someone asked me what my teacher was like. Well, he was very gentle and kind, and at the same time very firm and strict. During zazen, he would say, "Don't move." Once he said, "Don't chicken out." We liked it when he used our colloquialisms. We had to come face to face with our difficulties, and through our own effort find the way through. And there was no escape. This is an example of his compassion and strictness. He knew how to push and how to ease off, when to hold firmly and when to let loose. He never stopped encouraging us and never gave up on anyone. He never made a judgment as to who was the best horse and who was the worst. For him the worst horse in the long run might actually be the best horse, or was already. Sometimes the one who is having the hardest time and practicing wholeheartedly and unselfconsciously is actually stimulating the practice without knowing it.

In my early years of practice I had a very hard time. I feel that I have experienced most of the difficulties that everyone does—the pain, the frustration, sitting through emotional problems, mental stress, and so on. I was never suspicious of the practice; instead, I looked at my own shortcomings as practice opportunities. When we can offer ourselves to practice wholeheartedly, together with all our defilements, the Dharma can do its work of transformation. Why wait?

I think I practice for the sake of practice. As a longtime gardener, I love to make compost—wonderful loamy soil. As a by-product, wonderful plants come forth from the soil. As a Zen student I like to encourage others. In Soto Zen a teacher is like a farmer carefully raising his or her crops. Through steady, constant practice we cultivate the ground, nurturing the wonderful variety of flowers, and enjoy helping them to mature and bloom, each one singular and beautiful.

People sometimes ask if offering so much *dokusan* [one-on-one student-teacher discussion] is tiring or exhausting. Actually, I thrive on encouraging others, so *dokusan* is actually energizing. When I give a talk, I mostly want to encourage people. This is the practice of *jijuyu zanmai*, the joy of fulfillment and our offering to everyone. When we give in this way, unselfishly and without a motive, we are one with the ring of the Way. I often think a Zen student is like that ice plant on a cliff facing the ocean. The winds blow, the sun beats down, the ocean mists and storms, and the ice plant simply weathers it all. What a life! My old teacher once said to me with a smile when I was having a really difficult time, "If you can find something more difficult, you should do it." Such compassionate encouragement has kept me on track for a long time.

Why and How

In this *sesshin* we have been sitting continuously, eating, cooking, doing *kinhin*, serving each other, working, and little else. We have been sitting with our silent dramas, our joys, our pains, our confidence, our complaints, and our doubts. And during this time of concentrated continuous practice, two questions often come up. One is Why? And the other is How? Even for older practitioners it can be difficult to stay in our seat, dealing with painful legs, painful mind, and the continuous loop of our emotions and thoughts or attachment to habitual states of mind.

It's hard to let go of the desire for some ideal state or a great transformative experience. What can we bring home to justify this commitment of time and effort? It may feel that all we got was painful legs. Students sometimes ask me how to prepare for *sesshin*. I always say, "By not thinking about it at all." When the time arrives, just go and sit down. It's seven days of letting go, of dropping, no clinging, no discriminating, not chasing away evil thoughts, not coveting good thoughts, not holding on to wonderful states of mind, not rejecting painful states of mind. Just being fully present. That's all. Maybe the most difficult thing we can do.

In the beginning we may feel that we know why we do this. It is actually beyond our reasoning, but somehow we know. Knowing knows. But when we start to reason about it, we don't know. And when we try to match our reasoning with our knowing, it brings up this question of *Why?* In the midst of *sesshin* the question *Why?* becomes meaningless.

Suppose we take a ride on a boat. What a pleasure. Suddenly a storm comes up. Pretty soon the boat is leaning over, then the storm gets worse, the sails are starting to rip, and the waves are swamping the boat. The question arises, "Why did we do this?" But it doesn't help. The next question is "How can I deal with this? How do I keep my composure and make it to shore?" *Why?* may have validity, but the Zen student's question is always *How? "How* can I do this?" *"Why* was I born?" It doesn't matter. Here we are. How do we deal with this situation, this life right now? When we hold that question *How?* it's continuous practice. When we hold the question *Why?* we haven't entered yet.

Within the question is the quest. Suzuki Roshi would say, "We are following our inmost request." One day one of his students asked him how he could be a good Zen student. Suzuki Roshi answered, "Just keep asking that question."

Fall Weather

Fall weather at Tassajara is usually mild in the beginning, coming on the coattails of summer. There have been some rainy days and a few cold ones as we settle in for the ninety days of practice period. The *tangaryo* for the new students, when they sit continuously for five days with few breaks, is over. I think of it as the entrance exam or the transitional passage from one world to another. Now they're happily chatting away now like little birds, and enjoying the cool, sunny mornings of the mountain forest; it's a special treat for them, like newborns, free of conditioned responses.

For most of the students, the first few weeks are spent getting used to the rhythm, which includes a good deal of zazen, work, ceremonies, services, *sesshins*, and the relentless demands of the daily schedule that starts with the wake-up bell at 3:50 a.m. People are tired and often have to deal with their resistances, but as time goes on the students will find their rhythm. And it now comes together in a harmonious way.

I saw an article in the periodical *Buddhadharma* asking the question, "Is monastic practice necessary in America?" My response is that monastic practice is the fountainhead, the source from which all modified practices, such as temples and dharma groups, trace their origin.

Tassajara is a model for San Francisco Zen Center and its affiliates in a fundamental way, a model that allows for variations that accord with the circumstances of individual practice places without losing sight of the essentials. The monastery is a training place for students and teachers, both priest and lay, where we absorb the fundamentals while practicing together in a concentrated environment. When the students come to Tassajara, both priest and lay, I think of us all together as monks.

I modeled Berkeley Zen Center on the principles of Tassajara and City Center and Suzuki Roshi's teaching. What a wonderful treasure we have, indeed! We continue to follow, in our own way, the Japanese monastic model that was introduced by Suzuki Roshi and other Japanese priests. This affords a valuable continuity, bridging both worlds so that we do not lose the root in a whorl of change.

Japanese Zen is embedded in Japanese culture, and although we are in the process of distinguishing the two, we should know what we are doing and not throw out the baby with the bathwater. The more we can absorb the ancient way in our bones, the easier it will be to achieve that. As Suzuki Roshi would say, "It will be accomplished little by little. No need to be hasty. When you are hasty you will make mistakes."

I am grateful to be here now with so many BZC members and a wide range of dharma relations. All is well.

The Heart Sutra and the Mantra of Our Life

At the end of the Heart Sutra we chant the mantra, *Gate, gate, paragate, parasamgate, bodhi svaha.* The sutra refers to the "great bright mantra." According to Edward Conze, a mantra is literally a kind of spell. But "spell" means various things to us. We tend to think of a spell as an enchantment by a witch or a magician. It is something which takes us over. If we listen to a piece of music, we come under the spell or influence of the music. If we go into the woods, we come under the spell of the trees and plants. If we go to the beach, we come under the spell of sun, wind, and water.

Watching a movie, we become absorbed in the story. It doesn't have to be seductive, but we tend to think of it that way because of our associations. But a mantra is not exactly a spell in that way. Maybe you could say it's a kind of samadhi, a concentration or absorption. Something that contains the means for absorption or compels our attention.

There are no mantras in the six hundred volumes of the Prajna Paramita Sutras. So to have this mantra at the end of the Heart Sutra is rather unusual. It is the mantra that expresses Prajna Paramita, or crossing to the other shore. *Gate, gate, paragate, parasamgate:* gone, gone, gone to the other shore. *Svaha* is not exactly translatable. It's a kind of exclamation, something like "well-gone." This mantra is

called the great bright mantra, the supreme mantra, the unsurpass-
able. What does it mean and how does it apply to the sutra?

I used to think of Suzuki Roshi's life as a mantra. We tend to think
of a mantra as a phrase that we repeat over and over again in order to
evoke or to maintain a certain concentrated or pure state. Sometimes
people ask, "Can you give me a mantra?" But when I observed Suzuki
Roshi, it seemed to me that the way he lived his life was as a mantra.
His life had a very obvious form. Every day at the old Sokoji Temple at
Bush Street I would see him enter the zendo from his office and light
the incense, sit zazen, and do service. Every day he did the same thing,
which was amazing to me. I had never seen anyone do that kind of
activity before. His life was devoted to sitting zazen, bowing, lighting
incense, and the various other things that he did. When there were
so many other things to do in the world, here was this person simply
doing these things over and over again every day. And he had been
doing them over and over every day for most of his life. I never thought
of myself doing anything like that in what seemed like such a narrowly
disciplined way of life. I was impressed by it.

After a while it occurred to me that his life was a mantra. Every
day he had these tasks that he would do. He was always concentrated
and went about his activity in a light and easy manner. Somehow, it
was not just repetitive. It was a dynamic that was always producing
light. One way to produce energy is to have something going around
in a circular path. If you hook up a conductor to that energy producer,
the energy flows from it as a dynamo. That's why he had so much
spiritual power. The form that he gave to Zen Center is what made
Zen Center work so well. The schedule is also like a mantra. The
mantra is a powerful basis. There also has to be sincerity and some
incorruptible leadership. With good leadership and the strong, powerful, dynamic mantra of form, the Prajna Paramita reveals itself and
is lived through the form, and the forms we meet in our life.

Lectures

Section 2:
Insight/Wisdom

The Fundamental

Unity Within Diversity

This zazen room is a very special room. It's interesting that we have this special room where we just do zazen. And in this room our activity of zazen is taken care of very mindfully. Of all the things that we do in this special space, zazen is the one thing that we really take care of most single-mindedly. So it seems like a very special practice to us. When we sit, our body, mind, and breath become unified, become one. We call this unification *shikantaza*. In the morning we get up and come to the zendo, unifying body and mind, dropping all barriers. That becomes our starting point, our zero point. From this zero point we take a step out into the world. This process of unification and then stepping out into the world of particulars is the rhythm of our practice. Dogen Zenji calls it the practice of *Genjokoan*.

Sekito Kisen, in the *Sandokai*, describes that unity as "In utter darkness all is one, and in the light, all forms are revealed." Zazen, this starting point, is that darkness without boundaries. These two sides of our practice, of our life, fit together like a box and its lid. This is the most basic kind of religious practice. I feel very fortunate to have this most basic religious practice, which is verified by our own effort and experience. I think the reason most of us come to this practice is because of its truthful simplicity. There are people here from different cultures and backgrounds, and yet every person here can meet in this space. Every person here can meet and feel a unity in this space.

I began to practice Zen for this reason. It became obvious to me that zazen was a universal religious practice that everyone could enter into. Even though zazen is a so-called Buddhist practice, you do not have to be a Buddhist to practice this unification of mind and body with everyone. I am a Buddhist priest and I engage in this practice of zazen, but I don't have to be a Buddhist priest in order to do it. Why I can be a Buddhist priest is because I feel that I do not have to be a Buddhist priest. Because I do not have to be a Buddhist, I can be a Buddhist.

I feel strongly that zazen is a universal way. I think that the world needs some universal way; not that everyone has to do some one thing, but everyone can enter into this leveling, into this most fundamental existence.

Sometimes people ask, if they are Christian or Jewish or some other religion, do they have to give up their religion in order to practice this way? They ask, "How can you practice the Buddhist way without being Buddhist? How can you practice the Buddhist way while you still adhere to some other religion?"

When we enter the zendo, whether we are Buddhist, Christian, Jewish, or any religion, when we sit down, everything falls away; there is no Buddhist or Christian or Jewish person. There is just sitting. Everything is one. When we get up and take a step, we become Christian, or Buddhist, or Jewish, or man, or woman, or Black, or white, and then we can fight and kick or argue with each other. But when we sit, it does not make any difference. So I feel that zazen is the basic religious practice before religious practice.

When we get up from zazen, we have service: we bow and we chant the sutra. This is a kind of Buddhist service, but I don't know if it has to be. Somehow we have to allow unity in this world. If our religion creates divisiveness, that's a sign of our misuse and misunderstanding. We notice people's differences when they quarrel. Even Zen students have differences. Zen masters have differences. Someone reminded me that Zen masters often have trouble getting along with each other, but actually this is just on the surface. When they sit zazen, all differences disappear. The first step out of zazen is the most important step. Then our next step after that, being careful how we interact in the world of differences. How to keep that zazen mind in the world of differences is the other side of practice.

When I was studying with Suzuki Roshi, even though he asked me to be ordained as a priest, he never talked to me about being a Buddhist. He always encouraged people not to give up their religion to be Buddhist, but to just practice freely. I feel he had a very generous big heart. Even though he himself was not interested in some other religious practice, he felt that he was Buddhist through and through. Because he found his true heart and true mind, he could find that kind of generosity and that kind of broad openness. If we have confidence in our own way we can learn to appreciate our own roots and the roots of others. I feel it is important for everyone to appreciate their own roots and to understand the essence of those roots. So many people, it seems, leave the religious practice of their background to seek something. If you really find the truth of zazen practice, you can appreciate your own roots, your own background. I always encourage people to rediscover their own background and to make peace with that and then continue however they need to. I think that most young people leave their own religious practice because they misunderstand its true meaning. If you look back and penetrate to the truth of Christianity or the truth of Judaism you can appreciate what they really are and you can appreciate yourself and your ancestors.

Some Buddhist priests who come to America say, "You have a

religion already, why do you want to study Buddhism?" I have had many Japanese priests say this to me. They try to understand why Americans want to study Buddhism or Zen when they already have great religious traditions. Many of us know why we do, but we do not always know the truth about the religious background that we come from. Anyway, when I sit zazen, I do not have to call myself anything. This is already a wonderful place to be. And when we proceed from zazen, we can enjoy everything and maintain our freedom. If our practice is, indeed, the practice of truth, we will not have to worry about anything and our practice alone will touch people without having to proselytize, advertise, or convince. So it really depends on our own attitude and our own true conviction and our willingness to drop everything and appreciate our unity as well as our diversity.

Mind-Refresher Cakes

Daowu was a master during the ninth century in China. He had a student named Lungtan as a young boy, and recognized something extraordinary about him, perhaps his seriousness and his affinity for the Dharma. So Daowu took an interest in him and invited him and his family to live in a house that belonged to the monastery. The family was poor. Making little cakes for a living was the family business. These little cakes were called "mind-refreshers," as they may still be today. So out of gratitude for what Daowu did for the family and for his interest in Lungtan, his mother would send Lungtan with ten little cakes every day for his generous teacher. When Daowu received the cakes, he would bow and thank Lungtan and give him one back, saying, "This is for your posterity." One day Lungtan said to himself, "I wonder if there is some hidden meaning when Daowu gives me back one little cake every day and says, 'This is for your posterity.' I think I will ask him about it."

He asked Daowu about it and Daowu said, "Is there anything wrong with me giving back to you that which is originally yours?" At that point Lungtan had a very nice understanding. He understood his teacher's intention. So, he became Daowu's disciple, and when he was old enough he became a monk.

One day Lungtan thought, "I've been studying with Daowu for quite a long time, but he's never really taught me anything. It's strange. I think I'll ask him about it." So he went to Daowu and said, "I've been here in the monastery for a pretty long time, but I've never received any teaching from you." Daowu looked very surprised and said, "I've been giving you the fundamental teaching ceaselessly ever since you arrived." Lungtan asked, "On what points have you been teaching me?" Daowu said, "When you serve me tea, don't I gratefully accept it and drink it? When you serve me food, don't I take it carefully from your hands and eat it? And when you bow to me, don't I lower my head and bow in response to you? On what points have I failed to show you the essence of mind?" At that point Lungtan had a very deep realization about his own mind and his teacher's mind, and the fundamental way.

Later, when Lungtan grew up and became a teacher in his own right, he had his own monastery and became rather well known. As a matter of fact he was known as "Well-Known Lungtan."

There was a Vinaya monk named Deshan. He was a powerful and dynamic kind of person who was very learned on the Diamond Sutra, but his understanding was all academic. He was not a Zen monk, and he had a big resentment against Zen teachers because they were teaching sudden enlightenment and the fact that one could have realization in one lifetime, whereas the old way of thinking was that it took many lifetimes of bone-crushing effort to become enlightened. What were these Zen monks doing, talking about going beyond the sutras and directly seeing into one's own nature and purposely misleading people?

So one day Deshan packed up all his commentaries on the Diamond Sutra, put them on his back, and set out to challenge the Zen world. One day he stopped on the road at a little bakery. Inside was a sagely woman. He saw that she had these little mind-refresher cakes for sale. He thought that's what he wanted and asked, "How much are they?" She looked him over and asked, "What is that you're carrying on your back?" He said, "These are my commentaries and the commentaries of famous commentators on the Diamond Sutra. I'm a famous lecturer on the Diamond Sutra myself," implying that if she wanted a lecture on the Diamond Sutra he could certainly give her one. She said, "Oh, that's very interesting. I'll tell you what. I will ask you a question and if you can answer my question, I will give you some mind-refreshers. Otherwise, you can pay for them."

"Fine," he said. "Ask me."

She said, "Well, in my understanding of the Diamond Sutra"—he wasn't expecting that—"it says, 'Past mind, future mind, and present mind cannot be grasped.' With what mind will you eat these mind-refreshers?"

He was completely stumped. He had come up against a wall. She pulled the rug right out from under him. He was embarrassed and dejected. This was Lungtan's mother. She was at the base of the mountain and Lungtan was at the top. It was the family business. She said to Deshan, "Well, where are you going, anyway? Where are you going?"

He said that he was looking for a Zen master so he could challenge him. She said, "There is one, Lungtan, who lives on top of the mountain about five leagues from here. Why don't you go see him?"

He said, "All right." And Deshan put his pack on his back and went up to see Lungtan. The characters for Lungtan mean "Dragon Pond." A deep pool, a very deep, clear pool. Dragons are associated with water. Tigers live in the mountains or the forest. There is a saying, "The tiger in the forest and the dragon in the water." This is their home.

When Deshan met Lungtan, he saw a very ordinary-looking man. He didn't have any special visibly masterful characteristics; perhaps he could be a peasant. Deshan was not very impressed and said, "This is the famous Lungtan? I don't see any dragon pond."

Lungtan said, "What you see directly is Lungtan." This was a bit of a hint. Because his mind was not free, Deshan was not able to see directly.

Deshan was meeting with Lungtan with a preconceived idea of him. He always had some idea in front of him about what he was seeing, rather than just seeing. Although he went to Lungtan so that Lungtan could help him see directly, he didn't know that was why he was going. He thought he was going to show him something. He didn't realize he was going to Lungtan in order to be able to see. He stayed with Lungtan for a while. He was humbled when he began to see who Lungtan really was.

One night he was having a long talk with Lungtan. Lungtan was getting a little tired and said, "It's time for me to retire. It's very dark out there and I think you'll need some light to find your way to your room." So he took a lighted candle and handed it to Deshan. As soon as Deshan took the candle, Lungtan went "Whoo!" and blew it out. The entire world was pitch dark. Everything gone. At that point, Deshan dropped everything. Gone. New Deshan.

There is something called "pecking and tapping." When the chick is ready to come out of the shell there's a "tap, tap, tap, tap," and the mother bird goes "tap, tap, tap, tap" on the outside just at the right moment. If the mother taps too early or too late, it won't work. Lungtan probably wasn't planning to do it. He was just handing him the light. It was a spontaneous act, a total surprise for Deshan. The next day, Deshan took all of his sutra commentaries and burned them, very gleefully burned them all, and felt liberated. All preconceptions had dropped from his mind. All points of view had dropped away. Any opinion had dropped away. He was just left with this clear light, which permeated the darkness.

When everything became completely dark, he could see his life, which illuminated everywhere. Then Deshan left Lungtan's monastery, but he later came back and studied with Lungtan for thirty years, refining his practice gradually.

That is a significant part of the story, because the pitch darkness is only one side of enlightenment. To have this kind of experience is wonderful. But the other side, after this realization, is learning to live your life as a new person. So the commentators say that Deshan was a little too hasty in leaving Lungtan's monastery so soon after his realization. He should have stuck around and not been so hasty to leave. Sometimes we have a realization, and we think, "This is it!" We leave and lose ourselves in the world, and it all kind of fritters away. Unless you cultivate the realization, you can lose it. This kind of experience is very good, but on the other hand, it's not the end. It's only the beginning. Any kind of realization or opening experience is only a beginning for the rest of your life of practice. You can't stay in the newborn stage. So we let go and stay present in beginner's mind, not trying to do something extraordinary, but realizing the extraordinariness of our ordinariness.

These folks are all in the lineage of Sekito Kisen. Daowu was Sekito's student, also a student of Matsu. There are many good stories about them.

Nothing Special

Today I was looking through a book for a spark to set off this talk and ran across an old question from a student who asked, "The phrase 'Nothing special' keeps coming up for me. Could you please talk about its meaning?"

It is a good question, which is at the heart of our practice. Suzuki Roshi used this phrase a lot. Back in the sixties, when young people were looking for profound experiences in psychedelics, some were investigating meditation. D. T. Suzuki was popularizing a side of Rinzai style that emphasized koan training leading up to *kensho*, or sudden awakening. Shunryu Suzuki Roshi's training in the Soto school led him to understand that what brings us to practice is our inherently enlightened mind.

Suzuki Roshi did not encourage attainment. He said that when we are always looking "over there" for something, it is harder to appreciate where we are right now. With this understanding, grasses, pebbles, and streams are always preaching the Dharma and teaching us how to act. So there is nothing special to achieve. And yet, everything is special in its own unique form and way, and should be fully respected and appreciated as a form of Buddha-nature.

Recently we were studying the Buddhist precepts of different schools. Some have 250, others have 16, and some have none. Suzuki Roshi respected them, but his understanding was that precepts are simply our way of navigating our life. When we pay attention to our surroundings and keep our senses and mind unassuming and open, everything we encounter brings us back to our compassionate, joyful, and harmonious practice. It is not that we ignore enlightening moments. But even when they are extraordinary, they are at the same time not more extraordinary than the ordinary sight of the divine light of a periwinkle by the side of the road.

Nansen's "Ordinary Mind Is the Way"

I had this all worked out yesterday. When I give a talk, I don't write it out or anything. I just think about it and then during the day things fall into place and I have really happy thoughts and so forth. I had that, but when I woke up this morning, I thought, "What am I gonna talk about? That's not worth talking about." But actually it is, and I'll tell you what it is.

I'm going to use a koan as my basis. This koan is from the *Mumonkan* and it is Case 19: Nansen's "Ordinary Mind Is the Way." Anybody who's been practicing Zen for a while knows this koan, I hope. That's a little exaggeration. This koan is between Nansen and Joshu; Nansen is Master Joshu's teacher. These are two of the most well-known Zen masters of the Tang Dynasty in China. Joshu, who is said to have lived to be 120, was Master Nansen's student for a long time.

This koan was when Joshu was quite young. I don't know how old he was, but he was young and he was searching for the Tao, or the Way. There are many ways, but this particular way was the way of liberation.

There is the way of karma and the way of Dharma. The way of karma is our ordinary dualistic life. The way of Dharma is pursuing the way of liberation, which is sometimes called enlightenment. I like that word, but I don't like the way it's expressed. For me enlightenment means light, implying that someone who is on the path of liberation is expressing light. There are many different ways of expressing this. When we speak of Tao in the Dharma, in Buddhism, we think of liberation or enlightenment or being a vehicle for light.

So Joshu asked Nansen, "What is the way?" This is what you ask your teacher in some way or another. "What is the way?" This is a setup, you know, this particular koan. I mean, who goes around asking that question?

Nansen replied, "Ordinary mind is the way."

We usually think of the transcendent mind as something like supernatural powers. But when we come to the Dharma, when we come to Buddhism, when we come to practice, we come for various reasons. Some people come to practice because they want to alleviate their suffering. Some come to practice because they want to get their head straightened out. Some come to practice in order to improve their sex drive. People come for various reasons, but it doesn't matter what reason you have when you come, it doesn't make any difference, because people don't usually come for the right reasons. But after we practice for a while, we should understand what the right reasons are.

The Dharma has open arms. Anyone can come. We don't necessarily know why, but actually it's enlightenment that brings us to practice, so seeking enlightenment is backwards in a sense.

Master Dogen says enlightenment and practice are one. One moment of practice is one moment of enlightenment. Two moments of practice are two moments of enlightenment.

Practice is the most important thing. When Suzuki Roshi came to America from Japan, there were a number of other teachers who came around the same time, and they were always trying to get their students to have *kensho*—this big opening, a moment of realization or enlightenment. But Suzuki Roshi didn't buy that. He said, "The main thing is how you practice." He emphasized practice, instead of enlightenment.

People have felt that he wasn't interested in enlightenment. It's not that, but the important thing for him was practice. So while many of the other teachers were emphasizing enlightenment, he was emphasizing practice. If you practice, enlightenment is there, but if you start worrying about enlightenment, you tend to neglect what's in front of you.

Let's say it's a hot day and you really want an ice cream cone. Your thought goes to the ice cream cone and you find your way to the ice cream store and you get your ice cream cone, but you don't think so much about how you get to the store. You don't think about each step that takes you to the store. So in a sense, you're going after the prize. Until you get the prize, your present activity is in the background and your idea of the prize is in the foreground. Your effort to get to the store is because you want the prize.

But when we get the prize, it's over. And then you have to get the prize again, or another prize. This is our ordinary life, where we are constantly working to get what we want, or to avoid what we don't want. But there's something unsatisfying about doing this over and over again.

So Joshu asked Nansen, "What is the way?"

And Nansen said, "Ordinary mind is the way."

Joshu replied, "Shall I try to seek after it?" Shall I go for it, shall I go for this thing? Shall I go for the ice cream cone?

Nansen said, "If you try for it, you will become separated from it."

I like to use the words "stumble past." You stumble past the enlightenment that is right under our feet. Suzuki Roshi says that usually when we want something, something spiritual maybe, we go *that* way to find it, but actually if you want to find it, you have to go *this* way, which means you're not going anywhere. You just sit down, and then when you take a step, that step is the way, and then you take another step.

So, as we know, the way is in the walking, not in the goal. Although you can't say one is right and one is wrong. You have to find yourself in each step. This is what Nansen is saying to Joshu. You have to find your way in each step.

So: "If you try for it, you will stumble past," replied Nansen.

Joshu persisted: "How can I know the way unless I try for it?" That's a good question.

Nansen said, "The way is not a matter of knowing or not knowing. Knowing is a kind of delusion. And not knowing is a kind of confusion."

I don't know about those terms, but knowing is kind of elusive because you think you know something. Suzuki Roshi didn't like to explain too much. Back in the 1960s and '70s, we had about four or five Japanese teachers, and in Japanese practice you don't say much to the students. The students have to observe the teacher. It's a kind of apprenticeship: You observe the teacher and you observe how things are done. You can ask questions, but usually things are not explained so much, and there's a kind of intuitive understanding that emerges in that situation. As Americans (I'm not criticizing), we want to know everything before we do anything, but in our Japanese practice you just do it and find out what it is.

I like to describe it as the teacher pushes you into the ocean and you start swimming. You find out through your own effort. It's not that wanting to know is wrong, but needing to know before you do something is not always the way.

When I see the development of our practice without the Japanese teachers, I see it not as progress, but as change. It's a cultural change. And it's inevitable.

Suzuki Roshi was a very unusual teacher. He didn't try to impose anything on us, which a lot of teachers do—"This is the right way and this is the wrong way and these are the rules." Suzuki Roshi wasn't like that. He watched us and we watched him, and it was a gradual emerging between the teacher and the students. He didn't try to impose a lot of rules. He showed us his practice, which is what he knew, and he gave us the essence of that practice. He wanted every moment to be our practice—not our understanding, but beyond our understanding.

Knowledge can actually be a block to our practice. Knowledge is important, but it's not the main thing. There's a saying that *not knowing* is the highest. Which doesn't mean ignorance; it means being open to everything without presumptions. Sometimes Suzuki Roshi used the example of the frog sitting on a rock, just very still. He'd say, "I wish I could be like a frog." The frog just sits there perfectly attentive, not moving, really still. And then the fly goes by *buzzzzzzzz*, and when the fly gets here, the frog's tongue shoots out and gets the fly. If the frog likes it, he'll go *gulp*, and if he doesn't like it, he'll go *ptui*. And then he just remains sitting. This is like our Zen practice. The frog's mind is perfectly still and ready for anything.

Then Nansen says, "The way is not a matter of knowing or not knowing. It's beyond knowing and not knowing. When you really reach the true way, beyond doubt, you will find it as vast and boundless as outer space; how can it be talked about on the level of right and wrong?"

With these words Joshu came to a sudden realization; a happy ending.

So this is a very interesting kind of koan. What is the way? Ordinary mind is the way.

So what is ordinary? And what is mind? We get up in the morning and we brush our teeth—some of us brush our teeth—and then we do various other ordinary things. We eat our breakfast, we read the paper, we sit zazen. Even zazen becomes ordinary in that way. So what is ordinary and what is holy? Holy is here and ordinary is there.

Any Zen student knows that ordinary and holy are one. That's what we're taught. Holy and ordinary are one. We tend to split between ordinary and holy. We have a split between them unless we become enlightened. Enlightenment means there's no split between ordinary and holy. Washing the floor, taking out the garbage. These are holy acts, holy activities. This is enlightened activity.

In a monastery, we study a little bit, but mostly we sit zazen and do ordinary work. Carrying firewood. We used to do that actually. Carrying firewood and hauling water, washing the lamps, cleaning the toilet. The *shuso* is a head monk for the practice period, the head monk who shares the abbot's seat. And the work of the *shuso* is to clean all the toilets or sometimes, as at Tassajara, to take out the garbage and turn the compost. That's considered the highest activity in the monastery. The highest activity is taking out the garbage, cleaning the toilets, turning the compost. That's holy activity, ordinary activity, but what makes it that?

What creates the split between ordinary and holy? Well, you know, it's the ego. The ego is the curtain between ordinary and holy, so when we take the ego out, it all comes together. It's like there's water on two sides of the dam, and if you take out the dam it all flows together. It's not two things and it's not one thing. It's one thing and it's two things.

When we're doing our ordinary activity, we don't say, "Oh, this is holy stuff." You don't say that. As soon as you say that, it's not. You can be it, but you can't see it. So this is a very important aspect of our practice. Show me your enlightenment. If you say, "Well, I'll show you my enlightenment," as soon as you say that, there's no enlightenment because there's nothing there.

If you have enlightened activity, you're being a vehicle for light. But as soon as you try to see it, it's gone. You can only be it and you can't see it, but you can see it in others. If you see the light in everyone, that's enlightened activity. Realization is to be able to see the light in everyone. But you don't look in the mirror. As soon as you look in the mirror, your ego jumps in. As soon as you want something, it's gone. So it has to be not wanting, but simply paying attention.

There's another story. Dogen talked about this story. Master Guishan (Isan in Japanese) had two disciples, Kyogen and Kyosan. They both became wonderful Zen masters, but Isan is very important. He and Kyosan had the Ikyo school of Zen in China. Anyway, it was a hot day. Really hot. I was recently at Tassajara and it was 103 degrees. You don't want to move around very much when it's that hot. You just kind of lie down. So this is what it was like at that time, and Guishan was lying down, taking a siesta in the middle of the day. The door was open and his disciple Kyogen came by and looked in. Guishan turned toward the wall. Kyogen said, "Oh teacher, you don't have to turn around and face the wall; it's just me, your disciple."

Guishan turned back over and said, "Hi, come on in." Kyogen came in and Guishan told him, "I had a dream. What do you think my dream was? Can you tell me what my dream was?"

Kyogen didn't say anything. He went and got a bowl of cool water and a towel and he came back and said, "Here's your water and your towel." Then he put it on top of Guishan's head and wiped off his brow.

You know, in the hot weather, that's great. I used to do that with Suzuki Roshi. During the summer of 1971 we'd walk around in the extreme heat and I'd have this cold towel and I'd put it on top of his head. Very refreshing.

So there they were. Then Kyosan came along and looked in and he saw the two of them and he said, "Hi." Guishan said, "I had a dream and asked Kyogen to interpret my dream. I had another dream. Do you know what that one was?"

Kyosan went away and made some tea and he brought the tea with three cups. He brought it in and then the three of them drank the tea.

Dogen says, "This far surpasses Manjushri and all the other sages in the world." So this is the ordinary mind of Buddha interpreting the dream of the teacher.

There's no self-centeredness in any of this. So what is it that takes the place of self-centeredness? Well, it's called samadhi. Samadhi takes the place of self-centeredness because it brings everything together. Samadhi literally means concentration. I don't want to call it a *state of mind* because it's actually no special state of mind. Samadhi is no special state of mind. That's why it's hard to grasp. There are many different samadhis, but it's your mind when it's not attaching to anything. There's no aversion and there's no grasping and every moment is a brand new state of mind. There are so many states of mind that they're uncountable in one moment. Mind is always changing. So samadhi is allowing the changes and not attaching to any state of mind. So when we sit zazen, it's called samadhi. This is the samadhi of sitting still and letting everything appear, but holding on to nothing. Samadhi is a state of being free. That's called freedom, because there's no attachment to anything and yet it doesn't mean escaping from the world. The mind is totally open to everything, but hangs on to nothing. When enjoyment arises, it's just enjoyment. When difficulty arises, it's just difficulty. That's all. It's just one thing at a time, following each other. Suzuki Roshi called it living completely, one moment at a time, without any aversion or grasping.

What is the way? The way is to always be in samadhi. So there's the samadhi of sitting still, then there's the samadhi of work, the samadhi of moving around. When we sit zazen, we enter the samadhi of stillness. Actually, zazen is called great dynamic activity. We tend to think that zazen is passivity, but actually it is activity. Every part of your body-mind is totally present in zazen if you sit correctly. There's nothing left out. So the whole body and mind is in harmonious dynamic activity; sitting up straight, breathing, letting breathing breathe. You don't breathe. Breathing breathes. The universe is breathing me. If you think about it, how could it not be? The blood runs through the body. You don't have anything to do with it. We're cosmic beings. Samadhi is allowing our self to be moved without restriction by the cosmos. We're cosmic dust. And because of the causes and conditions of this earth, we appear as people and animals and plants and other things. To be in harmony with the universal activity, which is called our body. The body is just universal activity. It's not mine. It's not me and mine. But it also is mine—it's mine to cooperate with its creator. When we can do that, we disappear. And at the same time, we're totally here. It's not one thing or other. It's called cooperation. And when we cooperate, then we have enjoyment. Enjoyment is something that's always there, but we cover it over.

Enjoyment is our natural state and samadhi is our natural state. It's not something special. Suzuki Roshi's mantra was "Nothing special." And yet everything is special. Everything is special and nothing is special. As long as we think one thing or the other, we fall into duality. We have to include the opposite in order to be complete. In order to be holy, in order to be whole and complete, we have to include opposites. That's called nonduality. But at the same time, we have to appreciate duality. We have to appreciate our ignorance.

Master Mumon has a verse for this case. He says, "The spring flowers, the autumn moon, cool breezes of summer, the winter's snow. If useless things do not clutter your mind, you have the best days of your life."

So what are useless things? Things that are vain. Vain means comes to nothing in the end. Joshu turned out to be probably the most famous Zen master, and he learned this from his teacher Nansen.

So ordinary and holy. As Zen students who work in the kitchen, the kitchen is one of the most wonderful places to actually practice because you have a number of people working together in a small space carrying knives. And things get busy, so you really have to pay attention. You have to pay attention to what you're doing. You have to pay attention to what everybody else is doing. You cannot have your own way. When you totally cooperate, when you are totally cooperating, then you have your own way. Truly you own it. You have your own way.

Suzuki Roshi says you should always be the boss, which doesn't mean you should boss everybody around; it means you should be the boss of yourself, which means cooperating. Cooperating to create a harmonious situation.

That's called a Buddha field. Each one of us has a Buddha field, which is the aura with which we relate to everyone. And we have an influence. We're all influencing each other. People say, "I've been around here a long time, but I never get to teach." That doesn't matter because we're always teaching. We're always teaching each other how to relate. And we're always teaching the Dharma in our actions. When you can teach the Dharma through every action, then you can teach others publicly. But we're always teaching anyway. How do you become a teacher? Not by somebody telling you to teach, but by your actions—how you harmonize with everyone and how you let go of self-centeredness. Suzuki Roshi's teaching was to let go of self-centeredness; that was the basis of his teaching. Don't be selfish. He used the word *selfish*. I said, "Don't you mean self-centered?" He said, "No, I mean selfish." That was the way he expressed it.

I remember Phil Wilson, who loved Suzuki Roshi dearly. Suzuki Roshi used to take the stick and beat him, saying, "Ego, ego, ego!" They both laughed. It was such a pleasure for everybody to be hit by Suzuki Roshi's stick. Everybody felt blessed.

I just want to say one thing. This little story about Guishan and his disciples is about supernatural power. What is supernatural power?

"Please pass the tea."

"Oh, I know what you want: a cup of tea."

For Dogen that was supernatural power. Nothing special, but very special because there was nothing to it.

Letting Go

Teaching and Letting Go

From time to time I talk about a list of ways of letting go, and today I want to comment on it again. What does it mean to let go? As well as letting go, there must be the way of taking up. How do we take hold and let go at the same time? What is there to hold on to and what is there to let go of?

We talk about abiding in our essential nature. The Sixth Ancestor, Daikan Eno, talks about not straying from our essence of mind, and Suzuki Roshi talked about it as well, saying that we should always abide in our Big Mind in all circumstances. Observing the breath, we can see that exhaling is letting go, and inhaling is taking up. As Suzuki Roshi liked to say, "Exhaling is more important than inhaling." Though you can't prove that. They're equal. But he put the emphasis on letting go, on emptying out. And, strangely enough, coming back to life. Exhaling, we expire, and inhaling, we inspire and resume our activity. Birth and death on the blank screen we call life.

Another way of expressing it is as wisdom and compassion. When we say essence of mind, this seems more abstract or intangible, like emptiness. We say essence of mind and function; essence and function. Essence is the source or background, so to speak, and function is the activity. We use wisdom, or prajna, to express the function of our essence of mind. And the function of wisdom is compassion.

So how do we let go, which is an act of wisdom, and at the same time take hold of what's necessary with compassion? In other words, how can we actually relate and help each other and ourselves through wisdom and compassion? We learn to think of this as maintaining our composure. Maintaining composure is how we balance our feelings, our emotions, and our thoughts so that, although we may be upset, we can always let go and reset our balance, like the Daruma doll that always rolls back up after you turn it over.

The next way is "To let go does not mean to stop caring. It means I can't do it for someone else." This is a subtle aspect of our teaching. Practice is something you have to do yourself and no one can do for you. Your life has to be lived by you. Nobody can live your life for you.

Sometimes within our practice it looks like the teacher is not caring about the student because the teacher will not answer all the student's questions the way the student wants them answered, or take the student's side in every instance. Sometimes people have problems with each other or want verification for themselves; they'll come to the teacher and the teacher will not agree with what they think. But that does not mean the teacher doesn't care. It may look like rejection. We have some kind of disagreement and it looks like we don't care. But actually, the friend or teacher is very compassionate. Suzuki Roshi said that when he was paying a lot of attention to working with one person, some others might feel neglected. But to work with one student is to work with everyone.

What is compassion? Sometimes what looks like rejection is actually compassion. Sometimes we may criticize, but it is out of compassion. Sometimes we will not accept certain traits of a person, but we don't abandon the person. We are mirrors reflecting each other, and it is up to us to see our reflection clearly. It looks like we are not caring, but actually it is compassion.

Compassion is to let go and take in someone's suffering. But misguided compassion can actually be harmful. The teacher, out of compassion, will sometimes give and sometimes withhold. This is something the student must deal with. I can't give you what you want. I can only give you my support, my caring, and most of all my patience. It doesn't mean not caring; it is letting go and helping you by not helping.

The next way is "To let go is not cutting myself off, it's the realization that I can't control another person." Suzuki Roshi has a well-known statement that you should give a cow or a horse a wide field in order for them to find themselves. But that doesn't mean the teacher is not caring about the student. Although the student has a wide field, the teacher always knows where the student is, and the teacher is always ready to help the student at just the right moment. On the other hand, sometimes the student needs a very narrow corral and restricted movement.

Timing is very important in dealing with a student or a friend. We say a teacher fishes with a straight hook. The fish has to jump on. The fish has to want something. If the fish bites, the teacher responds. If the fish swims away, that is okay too. The teacher responds according to the spirit of the fish. There are many stories about a teacher's coolness. Sometimes when a student wants too much too soon, the teacher has to be a little cool. That may be felt as rejection or withholding, but it is simply teaching about finding out for yourself, or about relationship. We are all the time teaching each other how to relate. Every time we meet somebody or have an interaction, we are teaching each other how to relate. So we have to be sensitive to each other's sensibilities. I teach you how to relate to me and you teach me how to relate to you. But we don't always think that's what we are doing; we're just doing it.

Next is "To let go is not to enable, but to allow, learning from natural consequences." In other words, leaving someone to learn

206 / Seeing One Thing Through

from their own mistakes. We see someone going off, and we want to say something, but we can't really control them. We have to be able to contain our impulse to save. You know what's going to happen. Boom! It's like teaching a baby to walk; you know they are going to fall down. But you let them do that, because if they don't fall down they can't learn to get up by themselves. So it is letting something happen to a person that you would rather not have happen, but that is in that person's best interest. It's difficult. We want to express our compassion and our help, but when we do that we prevent the person from learning something and actually progressing.

One controversial example is teaching someone to sit zazen. When I was learning to sit we never put any props under our knees. We'd sit with our knees up, but eventually, as we kept sitting, our knees would go down and little by little we would be able to progress in our sitting position. That's the way we learned how to sit. Of course, this does not work for everyone, but no matter what position we take there may be discomfort. If we don't let it hurt, we can't go beyond it. So we have to learn how to receive pain in order to be free from it. And to be able to receive pain without attachment is zazen. Otherwise we can't learn how to develop true composure. Making it easy is a kind of hindrance, though it looks like a help.

Disclaimer: Go slowly and don't try to be a zazen hero. Avoid extremes.

Next is "To let go is not to change or blame another; it's to make the most of myself."

During Rohatsu *sesshin* I recited the Sixth Ancestor's long poem in which he emphasizes not blaming others, but rather paying attention to your own practice. Don't look at the faults of the world. He doesn't mean you don't see what is going on around you, but that, instead of trying to fix or blame others, you work on yourself. Because when we work on our own character, that influences the world.

Blaming others is not a good influence. But working on ourselves encourages everyone around us. Sometimes we feel that we have no effect on the world, but it is impossible not to have an effect.

This is why we say, "Who is a teacher?" We don't always know who our teachers are. Sometimes the teacher looks like the worst student. It's not who knows the most. It's the person who is sincerely dedicated to practice and is having the most difficult time. The person who has the most difficult time, but who is totally dedicated is often a wonderful teacher. People who have an easy time are not necessarily good teachers. But we're all good teachers, because we're all having a difficult time. Everybody has a difficult time. Staying with the practice, and staying with the difficulty, using the difficulty, that's what makes a teacher.

Sometimes after a student who is a lay person has been *shuso*, I'll give them a green *rakusu* as a recognition of her practice—someone who has practiced a long time and is a good example. That person may ask, "What does this mean?" What it means is that unbeknownst to them, their practice is exemplary. And that's what encourages us. That's what makes the practice work. So it's not so much what you know or how smart you are, it's more how you express the essence of practice through your life.

Next: "To let go is not to care for, but to care about." I think both are important. To care for is important, and to care about is also important. But I think you can care for people independent of your relationship to them. Maybe you are a nurse or a doctor and when you see patients you primarily care about their welfare, even if you don't know them personally. I think this is to rise above personality and to treat everyone with dignity, free of preference.

Next: "To let go is not to fix, but to be supportive." Very often we want to fix something. But how do you really help somebody? That's been a big question for all of us. How do you really help somebody?

One extreme answer is that it is hard to really help anybody. But you can support everyone. Indiscriminate compassion is to simply support everyone. We support our group, our friends, our family, or our lovers. But how wide is our support? How far-reaching is our support? *Metta* is like wide-reaching support for everyone.

Do we support our enemies or do we slay them? That's an interesting question. It is often easier to slay them, which brings us into the realm of the Middle East. Instead of working things out, we fall back on and attach to righteous indignation, emotional reaction, an eye for an eye, a tooth for a tooth, blow for blow.

As the world shrinks, the eyes of the world focus on this one spot. Some blame one side and some blame the other side. And it's so tangled and so impossible. Someone has to start repenting, apologizing, and expressing remorse. It's the only way that anything will happen. Someone has to be the first to back down. But then you become afraid of losing your honor. How do you back down or give up without losing your honor? How can that happen? Suzuki Roshi said that to be truly weak is to be truly strong.

All these people are sacrificing their lives for whatever they believe their cause is. All have to be honored who sacrificed, and then "getting even" takes over, and so it goes. The conditions get worse and worse. They've lost their footing altogether. They have strayed from their essence of mind. And they can't include each other in their Big Mind. So they care for their families and their country, but their caring is not universal. I don't believe transformation can happen until people let go of everything and start anew.

So next is "To let go is not to judge, but to allow another to be a human being." We have to recognize that everybody is not just like me, and yet everyone actually is just like me. I remember Suzuki Roshi talking about Japan and America. He said Japanese people think

American people are different and American people think Japanese people are different, but actually we are all the same. There are differences, but we are all the same.

So how do we include everyone in our Big Mind? How do we allow others to be themselves without being judgmental? We don't try to make everybody be the same, even though, when we come to the zendo, we all sit in the same way, and in monastic life we all wear the same clothes and it looks like we are making everybody be the same. But within that conformity everyone stands out as different. And you see the differences and accept the differences we all have. When I am open, it helps people be who they are and I can understand them better. Otherwise we just cut people off and we live in our little channel.

The next one is "To let go is to fear less and to love more." In recent years our society has been coerced into fearing more and loving less. We have to open that up so that we fear less and love more. If you hit a hornet's nest with a stick, you have to expect that the residents are going to come out to sting you. And as we keep enraging the hornets, putting them back in there is really hard.

Next is "To let go is not to regret the past, but to grow from there for the future." True repentance is to acknowledge, turn around, and go straight without turning back. Suzuki Roshi taught about a woman walking with a large jug of water on her head. The jar fell backward off her head and smashed on the ground and she just kept walking straight ahead and didn't look back.

I will tell you a little story. Some years ago, maybe about forty-five years ago, we were in Hawaii. We went to the beach. It was isolated. There was a restroom and it was getting late. There was nobody around, no telephones, no cars, nothing, and I went into the restroom. Somehow the lid for the toilet dropped. It dropped. I dropped it. And it fell into the toilet and broke it. Then the water just kept shooting out, and it was flooding everything, and there was no way to turn it off, and there was nobody to call. And there I was. This is a great example of admitting to being totally helpless. And so we got in the car and ran away.

The Host Within the Host

At the conclusion of Master Tung-shan's *Precious Mirror Samadhi* (*Hokyo Zanmai*), he says to "work secretly, like a fool or an idiot. To do this continuously is called the Host within the Host." "Secretly" means something like to practice selflessly as an ego-tamer without asking for credit. The Buddha said that the purpose of his Dharma is to help people understand how suffering or dissatisfaction arises, what the causes are, how to see them through, and to see through them. Suffering and pain are important components of our life, as are happiness and contentment.

What is a fool or an idiot? Someone who does the secret activity of zazen, of course! When you don't understand it, it is a secret. When you do, it is vast open freedom. One who has this freedom is often considered a nonconforming fool. We are taught to build up and depend on our so-called ego: the acquiring mind, the cause of suffering. So when we come to practice we are told to let go of it. But hold on! That's not so easy.

We don't want to kill our ego, we just need to train it. No matter how often we tell ourselves that we don't have one, we constantly refer to it as me, myself, and I. It does after all have a function. It is our inter-actor. It can lead us to kill or nurture. It is the sufferer. It can be blown up like a heavenly balloon, only to pop and send us into depression. It suffers from the effects of its own self-importance. The problem is that we set it up as an icon, place our faith in it, and follow it around like something that smells good.

But the ego should be our servant, not our leader. It has a wonderful and vital function. When we put it to use to serve the Dharma, it becomes the mind of the Way. It takes the position of the Guest, serving and doing the work of the Host. Master Tung-shan calls this the Guest hidden within the Host. When Guest and Host are not two, this is called the Host within the Host. The Third Ancestor Sosan said, "A hair breadth's difference and heaven and earth are set apart."

No matter how talented or intelligent we are, no matter how well we are educated in the Dharma, or our position in the sangha, or our many years of practice or authority inside or outside the gate, if we let our ego take center stage, it has a negative effect on the harmony of the sangha. Every time we completely let go and bow with sincerity to the altar, or to each other, or to those we have a problem with, we enter the Big Mind of the Host and the ego is purified.

Life (Birth and Death)

I am able to not hang on to anything. That's my secret. I believed my teacher when he said, "Don't get caught by anything." I really believed it. And then, not only did I believe it, I started acting it out. So that's where I'm at. Don't get caught by anything. I'm able to not dwell on something. The news is what the news is. My anger is what my anger is. That's all. And I try to do what I can to assuage my ... everybody's anxieties. I don't have much anxiety. I'm gonna die. I'm on my way. What should I do, worry about it? Everybody does this. Nobody escapes. This happens to every single person that's ever lived.

What should I worry about? What's there to worry about? I am just not that kind of person. This is what I decided when I was young. I said, "I'm just gonna live my life all the way up to the end. And when it's time to go, I go." That's part of . . . that's life. Life is death. So we experience it every moment. Here we are. Next moment, here we're not. This happens every moment.

Insight/Wisdom

Happiness Is Not in the Pursuit Of

Happiness is not in the *pursuit of*. Peace must be found within ourselves. That is why we don't say to get rid of your pain in order to be happy. Happiness doesn't depend on the circumstantial causes of pleasure and pain. Buddha Dharma goes deeper than just being happy. The pursuit of happiness is a false pursuit, because happiness is a result of something and not an object. Since everything is impermanent, if you construct happiness out of an ephemeral situation it will eventually crumble and unhappiness will be the result. True happiness is like the sun, which is always with us and shines through even when the clouds of like and dislike, grasping and aversion, and the trials and tribulations of our life seem overwhelming.

When we can settle ourself and open to our own light, that light illuminates our self and permeates outward to all beings (*jijuyu zanmai*). If we can open the source of joy within ourself, we can touch it in others. True joy arises from wholeness, but we lose it in partiality. It is easy to believe that if we were rid of all our problems, we could have a happy life.

Have you ever noticed those big kelp beds in the ocean? The ocean moves and the kelp moves with it. Whatever the waves do the kelp does, even when it is rooted to the bottom. Often we try to escape the waves, but our resistance is a cause of suffering. Samadhi is like playing in the waves without getting pulled under. If you can do that, your life can be happy even though you have many problems. This is the joyful path that cannot be extinguished by circumstances. If you follow this path of *shikantaza* (just this) and with no avariciousness, appearing new on each moment, your life can be fundamentally happy beyond all circumstances.

Sesshin is a practice of great patience and endurance. Patience is the ability to stay still in the center of each moment. It is fundamental in helping us endure the painfulness of our life. Pain and suffering are not always the same thing. Pain is a feeling and suffering is more of an attitude toward pain. If we can allow for our pain, it is easier to be free from suffering.

It is hard to open our self to pain, but when we do, transformation is possible. When we are not controlled by emotions and thoughts, we have the opportunity to rely on our original nondual Buddha mind and allow our emotions and thoughts to function in a beneficial way, free from partiality. This is how happiness arises without looking for it.

Does Life Have Meaning?

This morning, March 19, a warm and sunny day, I walked out of the house and wandered into our fenced-off vegetable garden. I walked over to visit the lemon tree that I planted in January. It had been in a pot for two years. It was doing quite well, producing nice new soft, shiny leaves and new buds. Then I spotted our new cat, Willow, lying under the shade of the yellow pepper bush. She seemed very happy that I was there with her in her territory, her garden. I just stood still, silently participating with her zazen. It then came to me that tomorrow, the twentieth, is the first day of spring.

Little by little the whole garden was coming alive and revealing itself. The new small lettuce, the green carrot tops, the new leaf buds on the blueberry bushes. I could feel the tremendous energy of the earth, all at once reaching for the sun, being expressed through this multicolored world.

A few years ago I made a little housing for Liz's garden figure of St. Francis, the patron of the animals. She had hung a ceramic sign on it that said, "We come from the Earth and return to the Earth and in between we garden." I remember one time reading somewhere something like "Cultivating the Dharma in the Garden of the Heart." This reminded me that the seeds of all our thoughts and actions are stored in our subconscious mind-ground, the *Alayavijnana*, the garden of the mind. These wholesome and unwholesome seeds sprout and manifest according to our actions and thoughts, causing happiness or suffering.

A question was presented to me the other day about the meaning of our life. What is that? What could be more meaningful than dropping our self-absorption and devoting ourself to cultivating the Garden of the Mind? We are vegetable, animal, mineral, and human. When we take off the coverings and open our eyes we can realize all of these qualities in ourself. Our body-mind is not separate from the world. When we take care of the world, we take care of ourself, and vice versa.

The blood runs through our body. The heart beats, the breath-door swings, the thought bubbles come and go, the body ages, and none of it is controlled by "me." It is the universal activity. This is what we belong to. There is a deep satisfaction that comes from co-operating with this universal activity, which is our true self. Maybe this is what self-respect is. Our practice is to find the meaning in each moment, taking nothing for granted.

A monk asked Joshu, "What is the meaning of Bodhidharma's coming from the west?" He said, "The oak tree in the garden." He also had a great awakening when he saw a peach tree in full bloom.

Dharma

The Three Doors of Liberation

This morning I am going to talk about a subject that is three subjects, which are really one subject that is divided into three parts. This is a Buddhist understanding of what is called emptiness. We talk a lot about emptiness. We read a lot about emptiness. So I hope it's not a boring subject for you.

These are called the three doors of liberation: emptiness, signlessness, and wishlessness. We are very familiar with emptiness, but maybe not so familiar with signlessness and wishlessness. I will start with emptiness, which is what the Prajna Paramita Heart Sutra is all about.

The sutra is not just about emptiness, it's about form. It's about the emptiness of form, and about the form of emptiness. So we use this term emptiness, and the problem with the term emptiness is that it means so many other things. So when we're talking about emptiness, we have to focus on what we really mean by emptiness. Because we can mean a lot of different things.

In Buddha Dharma there are twenty meanings for the term emptiness, but they're all related. In order to easily, *easily* identify what we mean in the Dharma: it means interdependence. Right? All created dharmas, or things, are empty of their own inherent existence. In other words, we're all dependent. There's nothing in this world that is not dependent on everything else. That's pretty easy. The problem is, how do we practice this? Is it just a theory? Is it just something that we chant every day? How do we actually practice emptiness? Do we want to practice emptiness? Is it worth practicing emptiness?

You can practice emptiness right here, right now. We understand it and we don't understand it. So emptiness is a big koan for us. Form is a big koan for us. What is form? What are forms? What are the things that emptiness is the emptiness of? Forms being emptiness means that all forms are interdependent with all other forms. That's why there is no special self. When we understand this and can practice it, it is the form of liberation. Because we are trapped—we're trapped in our bodies, we're trapped in our circumstances. I don't want to say trapped, but we are contained within—and those containers can either be a trap for suffering or a doorway to liberation. It just depends on our own understanding and how we actually deal with the circumstances of our life. This is all connected with what we call karma. If our actions are directed toward liberation, that's what we find. If our actions are directed toward confinement, then that's what we find. We put ourselves in jail, actually. You know, people are really caught, no matter what their circumstances are. Suzuki Roshi, I remember, always said, "Don't get caught by anything." What is our practice? Don't get caught by anything. But we get caught by desire and delusions.

Emptiness is a doorway to liberation if we practice it. This morning I was sitting zazen. You were all lucky because you were sitting in the quietness of your home. I was sitting in the *dokusan* hut and around the end of the first period someone started a construction party over the other side of the fence. And my first reaction was, "Oh my god, is this going to go on all day?" I mean it was really loud—everybody shouting and digging with shovels—and it was quite an interesting situation. I said to myself, well, I'm not going to get up. I'm just going to sit here and see what happens. My first thought was, How do I save myself? Should I get up or not? But I just sat there.

And it was a little bit annoying. If I didn't like it, it was annoying. If I didn't care whether I liked it or not, it was a lot easier. Not that I liked it, but instead of trying to escape from it, I was able to go right into it. This is how we find our freedom. There's no escape. The only escape is to be one with something. As long as we are involved in our dualistic thinking, there's no escape. The only escape is to be one with everything. So I didn't try to be a hero, it's just that I found myself not worrying about it. Even though it was pounding in my head, I just didn't worry about it. And so I thought: This is what I'm going to talk about today. How to find our freedom within an impossible situation.

How do we practice free from desire, free from desiring too much, and free from self-pity? We're full of self pity "Oh me, oh my." Which brings us into the other two aspects, which are signlessness and wishlessness.

You know we see indirectly. Most of the time we see indirectly. When I say "see," I mean that we see through signs. We invent words to stand for something. So then we *name* something. Russell Street. I'm on Russell Street. That's not untrue, but it limits my understanding. We have to limit our understanding in order to do anything. If we don't have signs, if we don't have representations, it's really hard to move around with each other. So signs are representations. They are little posters, or big posters, that we invent in order to move with each other. "It's on Russell Street. Yeah, I know where that is." So we need those things, we need signs. But the signs are representations, and our thinking is representational. I don't want to say we're trapped in our mind, even though we are, but we need that kind of confinement and differentiation, right? It's important, but it's still a veil. It's a veil because we design our life to conform to the signs and then we live in a life of signs or signatures instead of breaking through to directly understanding or directly touching.

In consciousness there are three aspects. One is directly touching.

This is called intuition. Intuition, directly touching without having to go through the machinery of thinking. It's just *There it is*. Period. And that's a doorway of liberation. We cling to the signs as our real life. And that's the problem we have with birth and death. We don't want to die to the signs. As soon as the signs are taken away, we feel jittery because we depend on them. So instead of depending on our intuition or our direct touching, like animals do, we depend on the signs that we agree on as reality. We all agree on these things. We agree or disagree, of course, but everybody has some idea about how our society should act, according to the signs.

Lao Tzu said that before there were rules and regulations, everybody adapted to life perfectly. Something like that. That's direct seeing. That's intuition. That's freedom. The next level of consciousness is where we start to think. And the thinking is there and it's discursive, but it's simple. And then the third level of consciousness is where you elaborate on the thinking. That's my understanding. All three are necessary, but if we lose or are not aware of the first level, which is intuition, we're still living in a world of signs.

So here are four signs that the Buddhists pay close attention to. The first sign is I have a self. The second sign is I am a person. The third sign is I am a living being. The fourth sign is I have a life span that goes from the day of my birth to the day of my death. That expanse—that's the fourth sign. We say when we realize the nonself, that's the doorway to liberation. We're liberated from our self. But we don't want to be liberated from our self, and we don't want to be alienated from our self, but we have to accept that fact. That's why it's so hard to die. When you realize that you're connected with everything, and that you are not a separate entity, it's not so hard to die. But we hang on and those things that we can't handle, we just suffer with. That's why this is called the life of suffering, the *saha* world, the world of suffering. And Buddha says, I only teach you how to deal with suffering. That's my message. So that's why we talk about these things. And of course, we hear this all the time, right? Till we're sick of it. We have no self, no self, no self. But it's true. And we're sick of it because we can't do anything about it.

But we can. We can do something about it. The idea of a person, meaning a separate person—that separation is necessary, otherwise we couldn't walk around, right? We couldn't eat and do all the things that we do. So it's necessary to realize that we have a self. It's necessary to realize that we are a person. It's necessary to realize that we have a life span. But these are all signatures, they're all signs. They're not true reality. They're secondary reality, they're not primary reality.

Nirvana is reached when we're no longer fooled by signs. So we keep making more and more signs and keep struggling and struggling to make life more complex. We think that we're doing a great job making life more complex. Do you remember when the pandemic first started? Everybody was rushing around like crazy without realizing that that's what we're doing. And then the pandemic hit, and boom. "Ahhh." Everybody drew a big breath. "Ahhhh." It was wonderful. The first month was great because you couldn't do anything. And it wasn't our fault, maybe. In trying to make things work better, we have to be careful that we don't keep making ourselves more complicated, our life more and more complicated. This was a great treasure, this pause in our life. The skies cleared up, the water became less poisonous. Everything was getting better. And we kind of realized that, but everybody's still worrying. The main thing is that there is something called a life span, but it's not a true life span, it's just a life-span for this particular world at this particular time, which concerns you and me because everybody goes through this. Nobody escapes.

The third doorway is called wishlessness. You see how these are all connected. Wishlessness means letting go and appreciating. Letting go and being able to appreciate everything around us just as it is. To accept myself just as I am. This is called virtue. Everyone has their own virtue, which is not the same as value. Value is comparison. So we stop comparing ourselves to other things. One of the driving factors in our life is that we are always comparing ourselves to other things, and we like to think of progress as the energy that comparison or competition generates. Wishlessness is beyond competition. It's actually called nirvana. Just dropping. Just letting now be now. Just letting this be this. We live in our dream and letting go is letting go of the dream, and that's scary. We depend on the dream. If we didn't have the dream, what would we do? We'd just have to go find another dream. Dreams are important. Absolutely. Dreams are important. To have a goal is definitely important, but find your freedom within the goal that is beyond our wishes.

Wishlessness is also characterized by not running after things. I often walk the streets at night. Believe it or not. Every night I walk the streets with my dog and I come across all kinds of stuff on the corners. I think, "I would like to take that home. Gee, that's such a nice chair." I did find a really good chair the other night and I took it home. I often bring things home and Liz, my wife, says, "Why did you bring that home?" Why did I bring that home? At the time it looked really good. I bring all these useless things home. So I'm very conscious and aware of how I should control all my wishes. And, believe it or not, after ninety-one years I realize that if you follow what you want, that's what you get. So you have to be very careful. The problem in our society is that there's so much that's being pushed on us, and everyone has a better one than the one before. So we are very confused. I remember when I sent my son Daniel to college, he roomed with four or five other students. And one of them was very wealthy. Actually the guy that owned the house. His parents were very wealthy. So you opened the garage door and there's a motorboat, a bicycle, a motorcycle, and everything you can possibly think of that would please a kid. And the kid was so miserable. He was really miserable. There's all this stuff that you use for a little while, then go to the next one for a little while, there was nothing basic about his life.

So these three doorways, these three characteristics are actually how we bring peace into the world. The world depends on these three characteristics. Understanding the empty nature of all things, all beings, the interdependent nature of all beings. Getting beyond signs so we can directly touch reality, not be fooled by signs or ideas, but getting our juice directly from the source. And toning down our wish list and being able to appreciate what we already have. That's why we practice zazen. I'm an advocate for zazen. That's why we're sitting here, with nothing. We have nothing, and when you can actually deeply understand that, you don't have any suffering. This is plain-Jane Buddhism. Don't cause yourself a lot of problems.

In zazen we let go, we offer ourself to emptiness, and to signlessness, and to wishlessness. We don't hanker after anything. We let go of all the verbiage and all the signs, and simply give our self to reality, which is emptiness of form. Enjoying our forms even if we're not well. You can do that.

I have a little poem here by Thich Nhat Hanh. He says, "Waking up this morning I smile. / Twenty-four brand new hours are before me. / I vow to live fully in each moment, / and to look at all things with the eyes of love." Four lines: very simple, very direct, and very true. That's all you need. And that's our thought just before we sit zazen first thing in the morning. And then when we sit, we let go of all that. And then when we get back up, we take it up.

The doorways of liberation are nirvana. Dropping everything, wishing just for the well-being of all beings, is enough. That's nirvana. But because we're people with busy minds, we're busy bodies and busy minds, and so we need something for our busy bodies and our busy minds to do. But our busy bodies and our busy minds can just practice nirvana. Emptiness and form, the forms of emptiness and emptiness of forms, are the most important things in our life.

So practice. Prajna Paramita is not only to be studied, but it's actually to be practiced. If you only study it, there's something missing. When we practice it, it's helpful to study it as well, because although we directly touch, it's also important to share our understanding with the Ancestors. What did they say about this? How did they approach it? How did they understand it? And all that comes down to us, to help us to practice. So, study and practice, but study the right things. So that you stay on the right track. You feel right. We all want to feel right. I can't say that I'm a great advocate, or that I'm a pretty good example. I'm okay. In any case, I don't worry about that too much. I just do what I do. And I try hard to stay on track.

One of the things that I'm a little concerned about, I don't know if it's correct or not, but I worry about our practice falling to pieces. Not falling—I don't think our practice will fall into pieces, but I'm a little concerned because the only thing that's keeping us together is our memory of practice together. There are other things that keep us together, too. We all have really sincere practice, but I'm worried that we will lay back too much, because there is nobody pushing us, nobody propping us up. And I am concerned that we will just take it easy, you know. I think to a certain extent it's good because we're recovering from the pandemic *before* the pandemic, which was our being pushed around by our desires. That was a real pandemic—it killed a lot of people. It made a lot of people sick. Now we're kind of healing, even though we're in the midst of this terrible pandemic and sickness. And everything appears with its opposite. If we understand that everything appears with its opposite, we won't worry too much. This too will pass. And its opposite will appear as the dominant. And then that too will pass, and its opposite will appear as the dominant. That's the way it is. One thing follows the other like the cart follows the horse. The cart doesn't work without the horse. And the horse carries all the baggage. So wasn't it great to not have any baggage for a month? I mean, you didn't have to go hiking, you know, or camping or anything like that. Just free. So we had our freedom for about a month and now it's coming back, you know, how can we trap ourselves more. So be careful!

Do you have a question? If anybody has some kind of burning question or something.

Ellen: I also really noticed that month after we were all kind of locked down and many, many people I know spoke to me about how wonderful it was to suddenly stop or pause. And I'm curious about what the enticement of busyness is. What is it that draws people, even though they were so clear about how great it was to not be busy, they were drawn back in to being busy, and I think they wanted to be drawn into it. I'm just so curious about that.

Sojun: Yup. Remember back in 2000 or whenever it was when we had the earthquake and the Bay Bridge lost its roadway? Unless everybody drove way around, they had to go by ferry. And I used to take the ferry. I was abbot of San Francisco Zen Center at the time. I would ride my bike down to the Berkeley ferry, then put my bike on the ferry, and it was the most wonderful trip across the bay. All these ships, and the water, and the birds—it was a whole different world of refreshment, the most refreshing thing that had happened to me in years. And I would do that three or four times a week, and then ride my bike up Market Street to the Zen Center. And as soon as the bridge became repaired, everybody, everybody went back to the bridge, which is smoky and trafficky and, you know, stop-and-go and all. We tried to have that ferry stay open, but all the ridership disappeared into hell. They exchanged heaven for hell. So to speak.

Ellen: So what's the appeal of that? I know that some people need to move faster, but during this time people really wanted to.

Sojun: Well, yes. The problem is you have to go to work. Sorry. That's the way it is. It's part of our interdependent life that everybody has to work so that everybody can eat and so forth. That's what we're working with right now. There's nothing for people to do. And they have to start doing something. So that's the other side.

Ellen: Well, that is the other side and I really honor that, but I'm talking about people who are not working, for one reason or another, and still they're drawn toward just accelerating their lives.

Sojun: That's because they're used to it. We just depend on what we're used to. It's hard to switch from depending on what we're used to, to letting go. It's not easy.

Ellen: Thank you.

Sojun: Nevertheless, that's the road. But it's the road less taken. That's all.

Karen: When you correct someone's posture in the zendo, how is this done wishlessly?

Sojun: You see a need and you respond to it.

Karen: Thank you, Sojun. Last Saturday you said that thinking is imagination.

Sojun: Mm-hmm.

Karen: Could you please talk a little more about that?

Sojun: Yes. Well, imagination is creating images, right?

Karen: Yes.

Sojun: So, we're always creating images. That's called signs. We create the image to represent the thing. Representations are called signs. They are the imaginative representation of the actual. It's really hard to separate what is directly touching and what is imagination. It's not always easy to separate those. It's a wavy line. It's not a fine line. When you go to the beach and you run into the ocean and that cold water hits you, that's directly touching. That's just one example. You're dreaming about the beach . . . I remember when I was kid, we used to drive to Venice Beach from Hollywood. I was about six or five or something. And as soon as we got down to where the beach was, my imagination would just go crazy. "When will we get to that place where there's a V?" (which is where the road hits the beach). "There's the beach! I can smell the salt water!" I could smell the salt water two miles away. That's directly touching. Being outdoors is really good for people.

Karen: Does the dualistic track that we live in—does that begin with thought?

Sojun: Yes. Thought is discrimination. Anything you say is discriminative. We can't help ourselves, unless we become conscious of what we're doing. It's so easy to fall into discriminative thinking. That's why we have koans. The koans that we study are about nondiscrimination, and about the discrimination of nondiscrimination, and the nondiscrimination of discrimination. That may sound garbled, but it's the truth, because every time we open our mouth, every time we talk, we're separating ourselves. Even if we don't speak, we're thinking discriminatively and acting discriminatively. But it's necessary. We're discriminating constantly. There's not a moment when we're not discriminating. I decide to do this rather than that, right? So discrimination is important, but because our mind is always discriminating we don't pay attention to the nondiscrimination, which is directly touching the truth. Because there's no division. There's a secondary truth and a primary truth. The secondary truth is discriminating truth. The nondiscriminating truth is when we're not thinking—or when we're thinking nondiscriminatively, which is difficult.

That's why when someone asked Joshu, "Does the dog have Buddha-nature?" he answered "No." Well, I thought the dog had

Buddha-nature. No. Another time Joshu is asked the same question: "Does the dog have Buddha-nature?" He says, "Of course." Which is true? That's why it's a koan. Do you exist as a person? Well, yeah. Joshu would say, No. And then, ask him again, he'd say, Well, of course. So which is it? Is it yes or is it no? Do you exist as a person or don't you? It's both. Where does the history, or the past moment, meet the next moment? In a universe where everything is changing without stopping, if there's no stopping, how can one thing meet another? It's all just one whirling ball that never stops. Except that it's perfectly still at the same time. That's why when we drop our wishfulness, which is discriminating, we enter the realm of nirvana. Just drop our discriminating mind, and it's all one. That's why we sit zazen. Just to stop our discriminating mind. Meaning: Don't pick things up. Don't get caught by anything. We live in the whirling ball of everything, of chaos within order. And order within chaos. You can't have one without the other. You can't. That's our song, should be our song. [*Sojun singing mellowly*] "You can't have one without the other. Sorry. The way it is." Change it if you can.

Karen: Thank you so much.

Sojun: You're welcome.

On the Heart Sutra

The full title for the Heart Sutra is the Great Wisdom Beyond Wisdom Heart Sutra. Wisdom here is not our ordinary knowledge; it is innate knowledge, or our innate, intuitive connection with the fundamental principle, which is called *prajna* in Sanskrit. In the prologue, Shariputra asks Buddha how one courses in perfect wisdom, and Buddha, in turn, asks Avalokitesvara to explain it for him.

Avalokitesvara is practicing deeply—one of the translations actually says he is "coursing"—coursing deeply in the Prajna Paramita. Practicing is a good word for coursing. He is not just thinking about it, he is actually one with it. When we sit zazen, we are practicing deeply Prajna Paramita, and when we leave the cushion, we are hopefully still practicing deeply Prajna Paramita.

So there are two aspects of this. One is that there is an Avalokitesvara Bodhisattva who is doing all this, and we are watching the scene. But actually each one of us is Avalokitesvara Bodhisattva, and each one of us is Shariputra as well. This is the kind of dialogue between two aspects of ourselves. The one who inquires and the one who responds. "Practicing deeply" means to be able to see beneath the surface.

In Sanskrit, the five *skandhas* are forms, feelings, perceptions, mental formations, and consciousness. These are called the five streams of existence. Usually when we talk about "me" and "mine" and when we talk about "myself" and "who I am," we are talking about some idea we have, some concept of "a being." When we look at ourselves, our mind creates some image through either hearing or seeing—through one of the five senses—and then we decide what that is that we see or hear, etc. We have a kind of partial view of what this person is. But do we really see something in its total reality? In Buddha Dharma we say there is no self, no permanent self-nature. This being that we encounter as ourselves, or someone else, is a "confection," something "put together," consisting of forms, feelings, perceptions, mental formations (which means thoughts of various kinds), and consciousness or awareness. Within these five categories, what we call a human being is to be found. But there is no permanent self, or no inherent self, within the five skandhas.

"Avalokitesvara Bodhisattva, when practicing deeply the Prajna Paramita, perceived that all five skandhas in their own being are empty, and was saved from all suffering." The important word or phrase here is "own being." Nothing, no entity, has its own being. Emptiness means interdependence. It means other things too, but for this purpose it means that nothing stands by itself. If we make a cake, we have flour, eggs, sugar and salt, etc. We beat them all up and we bake it, and then we say we have a cake. We eat the cake and it is a real cake eaten by a real mouth. But the cake is empty and the mouth is empty of its own being. What makes the cake is the mouth, and what makes the mouth is the cake. What makes the cake are all the ingredients. So we have a real cake, but the cake is illusory. It looks like a real cake. Today it is a real cake, but if you leave it on the table until tomorrow, or next week, it's not a real cake anymore. So it only has momentary existence as a cake. Not only the ingredients, but the oven makes the cake, the table makes the cake, the spoon makes the cake, the sky makes the cake. The cake is dependent on everything in the universe for its existence, and it is one expression of universal life. In the same way, a human being is one expression of life.

We can use the analogy of the water and the wave. The water is life itself, and the wave is an expression of the water. The wave is no other than the water, and the water is no other than the wave, but the wave doesn't have its own being: its own being is the water. A wave is dependent on wind and weather conditions for its existence, and, of course, it is dependent on a great body of water. So each wave is an expression of a body of water just like each one of us is an expression of life itself. This is called "being empty," and "being empty" also means being full. I think it is important to remember that whenever we say something in Buddhism, its opposite is also included. This is called the nonduality of duality. If you say "I am alive," "I am dead" is also included. If you say "I am dead," "I am alive" is also included. Otherwise, you fall into duality and you only see in a partial way.

To see things as they are completely is to end suffering. Not that there is not some pain; life is painful. Even though we may be saved from suffering, it doesn't mean that there is no suffering, or that we won't suffer, but we should know how to accept that suffering and know how to accept our pain, and know how to accept our joy. Whatever arises, this is our life. True life is more important than any one aspect of life. Fundamental life is more important than any one aspect of life. If we understand this, then we can appreciate our life no matter what happens. This is maturity and this is what we experience in zazen. In zazen we say, Well, what was it like? Well, it was painful, and it was joyful, and it was whatever you want to say. But each one of those aspects we accept equally. This is what zazen is. Whatever comes up, this is it. When it is painful, it is just painful. When it is joyful, it is just joyful. We just accept each moment as it is, with what it is, with deep appreciation. This view is the aspect of enlightenment. So we say zazen is enlightenment/practice. The practice is not discriminating, not picking and choosing.

"O Shariputra, form does not differ from emptiness, emptiness does not differ from form; that which is form is emptiness, that which is emptiness form." Whatever form arises is empty of its own being, even though there it is. You may have a glass of water and when the glass is full, you say, the glass is full. After you drink the water, the glass is empty. Actually, the glass is empty whether it is full or not. The glass gives form to the water. Water has no special shape. When it drops from the sky we call it a drop; and when it hits the earth, it falls in rivulets and pools and puddles; and rivers and streams flow to the ocean. When we drink it, its form takes shape within our bodies. It takes shapes within bottles and myriads of "containers." It is in everything, but it has no special shape; whatever form it encounters, it takes that shape. This is the secret of zazen. Even though we have the most confining form for zazen, our feelings come up, consciousness comes up, thoughts come up, perceptions come up. Whatever comes up takes that shape. Our body takes that shape, our consciousness takes that shape. Our zazen is quite empty, quite open, just like water.

"The same is true of feelings, perceptions, formations, consciousness." You apply the same formula: feelings do not differ from emptiness, emptiness does not differ from feelings; that which is feelings is emptiness, and that which is emptiness is feelings. The same is true of perception and mental formations and consciousness. In the sutra he first uses form as an example, but the others conform to the same formula. Consciousness does not differ from emptiness, emptiness does not differ from consciousness. Each one of the skandhas is explained in the same way, and each one of them is empty in its own being. Then the sutra goes on to talk about dharmas: "All dharmas are marked with emptiness." Not only are all skandhas marked with emptiness, but all dharmas are marked with emptiness. "Dharmas" means things or objects. Technically, dharmas means thought formations like greed, anger, and delusion or happiness—all the thoughts and feelings and emotions that are associated with the mind and feelings. But in a wider sense, "dharmas" means "all things." This is with a small "d." Dharma with a capital "D" means "Buddhist teaching," the "truth" or "law." "Marks" means their characteristics. For example, the characteristic of fire is heat, so the mark of fire is heat. The mark of water is wetness, and the mark of dharmas is emptiness. The true mark of all things is emptiness.

"All dharmas are marked with emptiness, they neither appear nor disappear, are not tainted nor pure, do not increase nor decrease." Although everything has an appearance, there is nothing that appears or disappears. That's the point. What appears and disappears is empty. With all dharmas, although they seem to appear and disappear, there is no real "thing" that appears and no real "thing" that disappears. If something could appear and disappear, it couldn't be real in that sense. So all things that appear are real, but their reality is their emptiness.

If we understand that all dharmas and all skandhas are empty of their own being, then we can call them real in the sense of nonsubstantial. Substantiality is an aspect of nonsubstantiality; substantiality only exists within nonsubstantiality. Everything only exists because of its opposite. Everything is dependent on something else. Although things seem to appear and disappear, ultimately nothing has appeared or disappeared because things don't come and go. We talk about waves in the water: "Oh, that wave was a great roller and it smashed on the beach." But actually, waves just go up and down. I think this is a scientific fact. Energy moves. When we see things on the surface, we say, "Oh this is moving and that is moving," but actually energy is moving, and even energy is empty of its own being.

Tainted and pure—people are always looking for the form of purity. We look at garbage, and then when we look at food we say, "This is pure." It does have a certain kind of purity. When we look at garbage we say, "That's impure," and compared with what is pure it is impure, but only by comparison. Ultimately, everything is garbage. Sorry to say so, but as you know, everything is garbage and everything is pure. There is nothing that is not really pure, and there is nothing that is not really garbage, because everything is decomposing and everything is coming to life and decomposing. It's composing and decomposing at the same time.

We are always measuring in terms of more or less. But more or less aren't just comparative terms. We say a mouse is small and an elephant is big, but an ant is even smaller than a mouse. So we can say a mouse is small and an elephant is big, but it is not necessarily so. It is just a comparative way of speaking about things because of our position. We are always looking at things in terms of our position, and we are trying to figure everything out from the point of view of our position. The only way we can really know is to get off of our position, which is very difficult. As soon as we start to think, then the mind starts to discriminate, and to discriminate is to separate and to "dualize." We are continually confronted with discriminating and dualizing our world. The duality is important, but we also have to be able to see from the other side. The Heart Sutra is viewing from the other side; that is why it seems so strange.

Buddha-Centered

The basic understanding of Soto Zen is that ordinary beings and Buddhas are not two. So we have to investigate what is meant by "ordinary" and "Buddha." Since we speak of ordinary and Buddha, they are two things, but the understanding is that they are one. Although this is a basic understanding, what does it really mean for our daily life?

One day as I was sitting in my office my eyes fell on my bicycle as it was leaning against the wall, and my gaze wandered to one of the wheels, and I saw it as a mandala. The axle, the hub, as the center, and the spokes radiating in all directions, and attached to the spokes, the rim with its tire (for absorbing the hard knocks).

Circles and cycles are fundamental in describing Buddhist understanding, and especially in Zen. There are the ox-herding pictures, Tozan's five ranks, Isan's one hundred circles, and in early Buddhism we have the twelve links of conditioned co-arising. The Tibetan model pictures the hub of the wheel of karmic life as greed, ill will, and delusion as characterized by the pig, the chicken, and the snake, which are known as the three poisons. There are six spokes emanating from the hub that divide the six worlds, or realms: heaven, hell, fighting demon, human, hungry ghost, and animal. The rim that binds it all together is made of the twelve *nidanas*—the karmic conditions that continuously turn the wheel and lead to suffering. So this wheel illustrates the human condition, turning on the three poisons and driven by karma and self-centeredness. The pig, the chicken, and the snake are symbols of self-delusion, which include greed and ill will and are the basis for ordinary human suffering.

In order to free our self from turning and being turned by our karmic life, we center our self on Buddha. We make a shift and become Buddha-centered rather than self-centered. We offer our self to Buddha. This is renunciation. With Buddha as the hub of the mandala, we are illumined from within and the six worlds become our fields of practice. This is the freedom of living by vow instead of being pulled around by karma. This is the meaning of ordination and the vow to save all beings. Even after taking our vow, we will still find our self shifting back and forth. This can only reinforce our determination for true practice.

The Three Dharma Seals

Good morning. This morning when I was offering incense, I was offering it for the victims of the Hiroshima and Nagasaki atomic bombs. Two days ago was the seventy fifth anniversary, if you want to call it that, of the atomic bombs being dropped on those two cities. I think that enthusiasm for commemorating those two events is fading. I'm sure many of us are reminded already, but I did want to remind us and to offer our condolences to those victims. And hope that this doesn't happen again. So please get out and vote.

I was talking with Ron Nestor last week about what we call the three Dharma seals of Buddhism, sometimes called the three marks of existence. And there are two versions. A Dharma seal means this is the stamp of Buddha. This is truth. So these are the three truths of our existence. When we read the Prajna Paramita Heart Sutra, it says the true mark of all dharmas is *emptiness*. I'll get back to that. But I want to remind you of what the three marks or the three Dharma seals are. The first one is "Everything changes," which is called impermanence. The second one is "There is no abiding self in anything." And the third one, in one version, is "suffering." So, 1. Everything changes. 2. There is no self in things—no abiding self or lasting self in things. And 3. Everything is suffering. That's one version. The other version is: Everything changes; There is no abiding self in things, in any thing; and the third one is Everything is living in nirvana. So take your pick. The old version is much more popular for some reason. And when you say the third Dharma seal, or the third mark, is nirvana, people raise their eyebrows. "Nirvana? No, it's suffering." So let's take a look at these three marks. These two versions are controversial—and that's good. It's good that they're controversial.

It's indisputable that everything changes. The last time I was in this room, it looked just like it does now. It doesn't look like anything's changed. But everything in this room has changed, even though I can't discern it. And the person that you see before you, do you remember that guy fifty years ago? He has changed as well, even though he's the same. Everything changes as well as it remains the same.

No self in beings is indisputable. People have various ideas about it, but when you really investigate you will see that not only does everything change, but we are not the same person exactly as we were five minutes ago, in some way, even though we relate to each other as if nothing has changed. So these two factors are somewhat indisputable—you can argue about them and present logical or illogical feelings about them, but nothing is permanent. From one moment to the next, every single moment, everything is changing. So, since everything is changing, we can't say that I am immortal, because we are all mortal, given to transformations. This is called the world of transformations. That's all there is: transformations. We try to glue everything together and wish that things were different, but that's the way it is.

So you have to take a close look at the third Dharma seal—Everything is suffering. It's not that everything is suffering. Suffering exists and is very common to all beings, but it's not permanent—it's always changing and is a psychological phenomenon. Suffering is a psychological phenomenon. Pain is pain, dislike is dislike, and so forth, but what we add to it is suffering. I can have a painful feeling, but it's not necessarily suffering, it's only suffering when I don't like it or don't want it. When we say "Please take this away, I don't want it," then it becomes suffering.

There are three kinds of suffering, or more, but one category is that suffering—you hit your thumb with a hammer and that's suffering. I mean that's a cause or condition for suffering. Or you can think of a million things that are conditions for suffering, but they don't have to be. Whereas the other two are immutable, they have to be. So there's some doubt if *suffering* is really the third Dharma seal.

Instead of suffering, we say nirvana, because nirvana is immovable, so to speak. It's always present no matter what. Nirvana is a mysterious thing. We don't talk about it very much. "Oh, nirvana, who can reach nirvana? Only a Buddha can reach nirvana." Actually, that's not so. Nirvana is the closest thing to us—closer than our hands and feet, as it says. Nirvana is our true self, which we experience every day. It's our everydayness. Just like change is our everydayness, no self, no *abiding* self, is everydayness. And nirvana is everydayness, when we allow it to appear, because things are apparent. Nirvana is our true self. But we think of reaching nirvana as some great feat. Only Buddhas can do this, and so we don't bother with it, because it's too mysterious. But it's not mysterious.

We have to "demystify" nirvana. Zazen is how we recognize nirvana. When we sit zazen we recognize nirvana—everything drops away. When everything drops away, what's left is nirvana. That's why sitting zazen is so wonderful. We let everything drop away. Things come and go. In zazen everything comes and goes—the flotsam and jetsam of our brain and our feelings and so forth. But nirvana is just our fundamental self *unbared*. It's naked, our naked self.

So nirvana is naturally the third Dharma seal because it can't be eliminated and it's constant. When we take off the coverings of our self, what's left is nirvana. It's a leftover.

I want to talk a little bit about each one of those Dharma seals. But I also want to get back to what is meant by a mark. In the Heart Sutra it says that the true mark of all dharmas is emptiness. But what a mark means is its characteristic. The characteristic of fire is heat. The characteristic of water is wetness. The characteristic of earth is solidity. And the mark of air is ether. But the true mark of all dharmas is emptiness. The true characteristic of every single thing is emptiness. And emptiness has twenty meanings, but the meaning that's most important for us is interdependence. That's because nothing has its own independent existence, even though everything exists independently. We have to be very careful because the truth is not one-sided. Whatever we encounter has a momentary existence and a total existence. That's the Buddhist understanding. And we are always falling into one side or the other, and that's what creates arguments. You can say everything is, and you can also say everything isn't. And they're both true. These are the kinds of arguments that Buddhists had during the twenty-school period, before the first century. The twenty-school period lasted for about four hundred years where the Buddhists had all these arguments about what was good. It was very good for them to discuss all this stuff. But it's all been discussed out. It's all "*dis-gusting.*" I recently read where Suzuki Roshi said, "In Buddhism everything's already been done." All you have to do is read about it.

The mark of a person is no *special* self—no abiding self, although there is a self. If we say there's no self, that's only one half. The other half is *there is a self,* otherwise who is talking about no self? The one who's talking about *no self* is the self. And the one who's talking about *self* is the nonself. So we're both self and nonself at the same time. Buddhism uses little examples, they say one thing to include everything they're talking about. So they say *no self*, but that no self has to include a self, otherwise what are we talking about? You can't talk about a hammer without a hammer being there. We didn't make this up. But our salvation is realizing that there is no abiding self in our self.

But what does that mean? How can we exist in this way? Well, we are earthlings, and all we have to do is look at nature to see how everything exists. And we are a part of nature, so our true self is the whole universe. When we realize that our true self is the whole universe, because there is no *specific* self that is abiding, then we can flow with change. We can flow—you know, we used to say go with the flow. "Oh yeah, that's just hippie stuff." Well, the hippies had it right in a lot of ways. The hippies tried to put us on the right track. Everything is constantly changing. This was one of Suzuki Roshi's main teachings. His main teaching was that everything changes. And the only thing that doesn't change is change itself.

So that is a constant. That's why it's a Dharma seal. At the same time we're growing, we're dying. We're living and dying at the same time. Being born and dying at the same time, moment by moment. That's why we can say that we are alive, because we are also dead. If we weren't dead we couldn't be alive, so why would we worry about that? We cling to life, of course. We cling because that's where we are, and we are a part of this world where so-called life is desirable and death is undesirable. But for Buddhists, birth and death are the same thing. They're just two sides of the one coin. The goal of Buddhist practice is to understand this. It's called the Great Matter, the great matter of birth and death. I don't call it life and death because life includes death and death includes life. They're not really opposites. The truer opposites are birth and death. Birth is inhalation, and death is exhalation.

Without death you can't come back to life. So we're being born and dying at the same time. If it isn't a dichotomy, it's not the truth.

We live in a dualistic world, which is one-sided like glass. We're on one side of the glass and we think it's a hemisphere, but actually it's a whole sphere because we're only looking at one side of the glass. But the glass is one whole piece. And birth and death is one whole piece. Nirvana is understanding this and living and uncovering your true nature.

So we don't have to see nirvana as a mystery, although it really is a great mysterious thing. It's the great mystery, but at the same time it's under our hands and feet. It's right there. Suzuki Roshi called it *seeing things as they are*. Nirvana is when we see things as they are instead of seeing things through our imagination. Imagination is really important for human beings. It's great. But we have to get our imagination straightened out so that it doesn't interfere with the naked truth.

If we practice zazen for a long time without trying to break through—to make it into something—nirvana will become apparent at some point, and you won't have to worry anymore. I would say nirvana is non-clinging. It's not something describable, but you can use various images to look at it. Like when everything is dropped, that's nirvana. Because there's nothing hindering its expression. But it appears in everything we do. It's kind of like salt in the ocean. It's just there, as part of the ocean. The example of the ocean is a viable example for nirvana. The waves are our activity, and nirvana is the ocean in which our waves exist. Our waves are the ocean. And the ocean is the waves. But each wave is an individual. Oh, there's John wave, there's Mary wave. None of the waves are permanent, but they all belong to the ocean. The ocean is their source. So what more could we want? When we realize that the waves are the ocean, that's nirvana.

So nirvana basically means dropping. Or "renunciation" is another term that's used. What is renunciation? It means dropping our false sense of self. When *manas* turns, it becomes the wisdom of equality, which is nirvana. So instead of talking about nirvana we usually talk about *letting go of ego* or transforming ego. Transforming ego into nirvana.

Regarding *no self*, the Diamond Sutra has a statement that says "We vow to save all beings, even though there are no living beings to be saved." That's a wonderful koan to chew on. We vow to save all living beings, even though there are no living beings to be saved. I would do you a great disservice if I took that apart and explained it.

Dealing with these three marks or three Dharma seals of existence is very deep and I think all of Buddhism, all of Buddhist understanding, comes from these three fundamental truths, and you should tear them apart if you want. If it disturbs you, you should really attack them and dig deeply in and see if you can prove them wrong. That's Buddhism. But you *can* prove that suffering is not a constant, because otherwise there would be nothing called joy. We say that joy is a constant, even though we don't always experience it as a constant. And in the same way you can say that suffering is a constant, even though we don't always experience it as a constant. Joy and suffering actually can be one thing. We always appreciate somebody who has a lot of physical problems and a lot of suffering and who can smile through their suffering. This can help other people while they're suffering. That's noble practice. We call the four truths the Four *Noble* Truths. We call Buddha the noble one, because the noble one takes in all the suffering of people and smiles. He doesn't complain and he helps other people, and suffers the suffering of all people.

Actually, without suffering we can't have any wisdom. We can't open our wisdom mind until we suffer the suffering of all beings. So in regard to the third Dharma seal you can say suffering within nirvana, and nirvana within suffering. Nirvana and suffering go together; without suffering, nirvana doesn't open up. The key to opening up nirvana is through your suffering. That's constant. Constancy.

So we could say the three marks are 1. Everything is changing. 2. There is no *abiding* self in an individual person. 3. Nirvana within suffering, and suffering within nirvana.

I want to go back to no self, no inherent self as we call it, because everything is connected to everything else and doesn't exist without everything else. You are probably familiar with Thich Nhat Hanh talking about how the table is made of elements that are not the table. Without all the other elements that are not the table, the table doesn't exist. Just like a human being. The elements that are not you *make* you into what you are, because you're just one particle of the whole being. We are all one particle of the whole being for a moment.

So even though I don't exist, please treat me as if I do.

So, do you have any questions?

Ross: Good morning, Sojun Roshi, and thank you so much for that lovely talk and the spin on nirvana and samsara.
Sojun: Yes.
Ross: So I'm thinking about the Four Noble Truths. The first truth is suffering. The second is there's an origin. The third is cessation. And the fourth is the Eightfold Path leading to cessation of suffering. Can you reword the Four Noble Truths using nirvana instead of suffering? Does it have the same resonance for us in practice, or is this from the Theravadan old way of looking at it, or original way of looking at it, and not so appropriate to reword it?
Sojun: Well, the third one as I understand it is that there is a way to deal with so-called suffering. And suffering is one term that covers the various dissatisfactions in our life. So rather than naming all the dissatisfactions in our life, the term suffering is used. But it can be anything, right? So let's take the stereotype, which is called suffering. And there's a cause, that's the Second Noble Truth. What is the cause of our unease, or what is the cause of

our delusion, or what is the cause of our misunderstandings, and what is the cause of all kinds of unwholesomeness? You can say sentient beings are *subject to* suffering. We're subject to misunderstanding. We're subject to pain and we're subject to hate and ill will and greed and so forth. And the Second Noble Truth is there's a cause for all these things. Buddha is called the physician, and so he's stating the problems that you have, and he's giving you the medicine, right?

The Four Noble Truths are divided into two and two. The first two are "This is the problem, Doc, please fix it." And then it says "Okay, here's the medicine." So the problem is delusion—that we actually are ill and not at ease for various reasons. Life is uncomfortable. The Second Truth is there's a reason for that, and these are the reasons: being with people you don't want to be with, doing stuff you don't want to do, all the stuff that you don't want or like, that causes suffering. And all the things that you do want, you don't have, and that also causes suffering. That's the stereotype. Then the Third Truth is there is a way to deal with this problem. The Fourth Truth is that way is the Noble Eightfold Path.

Ross: Well, if one could reword the Four Noble Truths, like there's the truth of suffering, can we say there's the truth of, or that we are subject to, nirvana?

Sojun: It's not that we're subject to nirvana. Nirvana is the *basis* of our life.

Ross: Okay.

Transformations

Sesshin is the practice of patience—great patience. The root of the word patience is the same as that of passion, both of which refer to painfulness and suffering. Patience is the ability to endure. To endure the painfulness in our life is an ennobling quality.

"Life is painful" is a good interpretation of Buddha's First Noble Truth. There are other interpretations of *dukkha*, but for the purpose of this talk I will use this one. The truths are "noble" because, coming from the "well-born" Buddha mind, they teach us the most basic means of dealing with the pain and the suffering that occur in our life.

The Second Noble Truth tells us that life is painful due to our delusions based on desire. Desire itself is neither good nor bad. It just gets us into trouble, mostly because we don't know how to deal with it. It gets out of hand. Suzuki Roshi used the analogy of a smoky kerosene lamp: when the wick is too high, the combination of fuel and air is unbalanced and the flame burns the chimney. We should be able to adjust the wick so that all the elements are in balance and the light is fully functioning. Our desire is a flame, and when it is out of proportion we have pain and suffering.

Pain and suffering are not the same. Pain is a feeling, and although suffering is painful, it is more of a response or an attitude. Buddha's Third Noble Truth says that there is a way to deal with or accept our suffering and not be bound by it. When we examine it, we can see that suffering is mostly attachment to pain, and if we try to escape the pain we end up with more suffering. *Sesshin* takes great patience to be present with our life as it is, without attachment to any particular state of body, mind, pleasure, or pain, and to be free from suffering. Patience is like a persimmon. If you try to eat it before it is ripe, its astringency will make your mouth pucker up in the worst way. So you have to wait until it is ripe before it gets sweet. If you try to remove the astringency, the persimmon will not get ripe. You just ruin the persimmon, because within the astringency is the element that transforms into the astonishing sweetness of a ripe persimmon.

In a similar way, if you try to cut off all your troublesome thoughts, anger, lust, criticism, all the demons, in order to have a peaceful mind, they will continue to sprout, and the process of transformation will be sidestepped because the root of the passions is the same as the root of *bodhi* [enlightenment]. This is why we must be very patient, compassionate, and understanding with our fellow practitioners. There is the saying: "Great passion, great Buddha."

The process of transformation takes place by itself along with our devotion to practice, and it can be painful. Endurance and right intention are also necessary, and these qualities bring forth joy and a sense of deep gratitude. So within joy there is pain and within pain is joy. We can't have it one way. We usually take up something because we find pleasure in it. But eventually we feel the pain. Then we look for something else. It is easy to become addicted to the pleasure principle and view the painful side as a nagging annoyance to be rid of. But one follows the other like a shadow.

The process of transformation, like electricity, does not work without both the positive and the negative. In zazen, we say over and over again to let go of aversion and grasping. Let go of discriminating judgment. Let garbage be garbage. Our mental garbage is the vital ingredient that is transformed into sweet compost, the fertile ground, from which the Bodhi Tree is nourished and grows.

Dogen Zenji

Genjokoan and the Koan of Zazen

Dogen opens his teaching of *Genjokoan* by saying, "When all dharmas are Buddha Dharma, there are enlightenment and delusion, practice, birth and death, Buddhas and creatures. And when the ten thousand dharmas are without self, there is no delusion, no enlightenment, no Buddhas, no creatures, and no birth and no death. The Buddha way transcends being and nonbeing. Therefore, there are birth and death, delusion and enlightenment, creatures and Buddhas. Nevertheless, flowers fall with our attachment, and weeds spring up with our aversion."

First, I want to clarify the word *dharmas*. It is sometimes translated as "things," but dharma has many meanings. The two meanings that we use are Dharma with a capital "D" and dharma with a small "d." Dharma with a capital "D" means Buddha's teaching, or the law of reality. Reality works according to strict laws, which we may or may not recognize. Sometimes we recognize them and sometimes we don't. Because of our limited, dualistic understanding, they may appear as a mystery to us. What is pertinent to Buddhism is the law of cause and effect, and that which pertains to the fundamental totality. Small "d" dharmas are all of the particulars of the phenomenal world. Every thing, in its broadest sense, is a dharma.

The Abhidharma schools and the Vasubandhu school categorized lists of dharmas for their own study purposes. For instance, the constituents of mentality are all dharmas, and the constituents of the body of form are dharmas. All individual things are dharmas, so Dharma is the Dharma of the dharmas. It is the teaching of the law concerning the dharmas or phenomena. This is the world of phenomena, the world of duality, the realm of cause and effect, and all dharmas are continually interacting with one another in this world of constant transformations. Buddha teaches how the parts fit together with the whole, like a box and its lid.

Dogen begins, "When all dharmas or all things are Buddha Dharma." The word "when" means at the time when you realize that all dharmas are Dharma. When we have some enlightenment or insight and realize that all dharmas are Buddha Dharma, we realize there is enlightenment and delusion, practice, birth and death, Buddhas and creatures. So these four sentences point out four different ways to look at reality. The first three go together as an expression from three different viewing points and then the fourth sentence is like a summation. The first sentence talks about dharmas from the point of view of just seeing things in the phenomenal realm; in other words, dharmas as dharmas. The second sentence, "When the ten thousand dharmas are without self," points out the side of the no-self of dharmas, or emptiness. The first sentence expresses the side of form as form, whereas the second sentence is to see from the side of emptiness as emptiness. "When the ten thousand dharmas are without self, there are no delusion, no enlightenment, no Buddhas, no creatures, no life, no death." This is like the Heart Sutra in the sense that the Heart Sutra is the sutra of *mu*. *Mu* means "no," as in Joshu's famous koan: "A monk asked, 'Does the dog have Buddha-nature?' Joshu said *"Mu."* "No." This is from the side of *mu* delusion, *mu* enlightenment, *mu* Buddhas, *mu* creatures, *mu* birth, *mu* death. When you have the koan of *mu*, everything is *mu*. You are investigating existence from the point of view of *mu* or "no," i.e., from the absolute side. Next he says that the Buddha way transcends being and non-being. Therefore, there *are* birth and death, delusion and enlightenment, creatures and Buddhas. So the third sentence is from the point of view that form is emptiness and emptiness is form; *Mu* is *U* (form), the point of view of synthesis. The Buddha way goes beyond being and nonbeing, affirmation and negation.

Dogen continues: "Therefore, there are birth and death, delusion and enlightenment, creatures and Buddhas." It is emptiness that gives rise to form, and all forms are the forms of emptiness. The Buddha way transcends form and no form. Therefore, there is form, and there is no form. Then he says, "Nevertheless, flowers fall with our attachment, and weeds spring up with our aversion." The last sentence is very interesting because it relates directly to practice. "Flowers fall with our attachment, and weeds spring up with our aversion." If we look at the two sides of our life, the two very strong aspects that we are dealing with continuously are attachment or grasping, and dislike and aversion. Attachment belongs to both of them, actually. Aversion is a kind of attachment, and grasping is a kind of attachment. We usually think of grasping as attachment or holding on to something that we want to keep or preserve, and that not wanting is the opposite of attachment. But we may become attached to what we don't want through our aversion. We are continually making discriminating choices. One of the basic aspects of Zen is that we have to face nonattachment; non-attachment to grasping, and nonattachment to aversion.

This is the *Genjokoan* of our life. *Genjokoan* is the koan that comes up continuously, moment by moment, with grasping and aversion. So every moment we have to make a choice. "Do I go this way, or do I go that way?" "Do I choose this, or do I choose that?" "Do I like this, or do I like that?" "Do I not like this, or do I not like that?" So like and dislike are coming up continuously, and we are choosing one thing over another on the basis of like and dislike, wanting and not wanting.

In the Four Noble Truths, Buddha teaches that suffering is the lot of human beings due to our inordinate desire. The Second Noble Truth is that inordinate desire creates grasping and aversion. How do we get beyond grasping and aversion in order to be free of desire? When you study Buddhism, some books say that you need to get rid of desire because desire is a hindrance. But strictly speaking, desire is not good or bad. Desire is just desire, and impossible to get rid of. You may try to get rid of desire, but you can't do it. Maybe you can, but if you do, there's not much life left.

Desire is an important aspect in our life because it motivates us. It's hard to be motivated without desire. So the problem is not so much to get rid of desire, but what to do with it. Desire is like a fire. It can either destroy us if not regulated, or light our way. "Fire seeks fire. Buddha seeks Buddha." It's the vital activity of our life. The vitality of our life is bound up with desire. When people say "Get rid of desire," it doesn't mean to put it under the cushion or sit on it. It's more a question of how do we direct it? Where does it fit? What direction does it go in so that we can find true satisfaction and freedom? Buddha said that we should direct our desire toward freeing our self and freeing others, and follow the various Dharma pathways. If you want to deal with desire, direct it toward practice. That way you don't hurt anyone and you don't hurt yourself, and you motivate yourself in the right direction, and desire, fulfilling its proper function, becomes a blessing.

All around us we see desire misdirected, confused, leaderless, and pointless. When desire has no place to go, it turns on itself and becomes destructive. When it becomes destructive and when people don't know what to do, they say you should get rid of it. But we just need to know where to direct it, and how to manage it. It's difficult.

There are a lot of channels—a lot of ways it can go. If we don't have the right outlet, then it tends to overload certain channels, and then we become obsessed in certain ways. Buddha and Dogen both taught to direct our desire to something that will give us true satisfaction, something that won't overload us or become obsessive.

We can look at these three sentences from the point of view of the ocean and waves. The ocean is like a metaphor for Dharmakaya, emptiness, Buddha-nature, or the absolute. The waves are an expression of phenomenal life, the way things arise out of emptiness. Each one of us is a wave on the ocean of emptiness, and we roll with all the other waves, and we live out our wave lives, our wave lengths, on the ground of the great ocean. It's hard for us to see where we come from when we are all just waves. It's like not being able to see the forest for the trees. We can't see the ocean for the waves. We get lost when we lose sight of the great ocean and forget that the waves are all members of the ocean people family. They are interdependent with each other and with the ocean. So when a wave thinks "I am a wave forever" or "I am a permanent wave," it gets lost, just like us. When we attach to our individuality, we get lost. So it is important to realize that waves are an expression of the ocean. Sometimes the ocean is very calm, like zazen. In zazen, the waves subside. Even though there are waves, they are on the surface, but our awareness goes all the way down to the bottom of the ocean floor. Dogen expresses it as "a fish lazily swimming by at the bottom of the ocean." In zazen, consciousness deepens and we settle on the endless bottom. The waves are still there, but they no longer bother us. It's like swimming on the surface while walking on the bottom.

When we sit, we are often concerned about the waves in our mind. When I began practicing zazen, all the time I was sitting my mind was wondering, "Is it worth it?" This is a common comment on zazen, other than "My legs hurt." "My mind is always racing. I'm making up lists while I'm sitting, and thinking about this and that, and I can't help it. Maybe I shouldn't sit zazen." The main thing is not to worry about the waves. The waves will always be there. The nature of the ocean is to have waves. If you think that you can always keep the waves still, then you have a big problem. Sometimes in Buddhist books we read, "Stop the movement of the mind"—even Dogen says that, "Stop the movement of the mind"—which is very idealistic. But stopping the movement of the mind does not mean that you don't have thoughts. Thoughts come up by themselves. It is simply the nature of the mind to create thoughts. We call it bubbling. Thoughts are bubbling up. Some teachers call it "mind excretions." The mind is relieving itself. When there is nothing to think about, the mind relieves itself of its accumulation of mental gases. So don't worry about it. Let the mind do its thing. Don't try to suppress thoughts.

As thoughts continue to bubble up in the mind, our consciousness tends to get caught up in the thoughts, and it is led astray by the thoughts. When you recognize that that is happening, just let go of the thought. You can say "Oh, excuse me, I have to go now," and you just come back. Come back to posture, come back to breathing, over and over again. Just let go and come back. This way, you keep directing desire toward maintaining the body's posture and breathing, over and over again. As soon as we realize that we are building something on the foundation of a dream, or creating a fantasy on the foundation of some wandering thought, then we let go and come back. Sometimes we build a wonderful sandcastle, and it's fascinating, and we don't want to let go of it. Well, that's okay, everybody does that, but you should still make the effort.

We may think we are supposed to have a perfect zazen with no thoughts, sitting up straight, not falling asleep, no pain, but this is not the goal of zazen. The goal of zazen is, when you wander off, to come back. If you are continually falling off, you are continually coming back, over and over, a thousand times. So it is the intention that matters the most. "I really want to do this. I really want to make an effort to do this." It is in this effort that your realization lies—not in your idea of perfection. When your effort is wholehearted, realization is there, and that's perfect. Perfection isn't necessarily what we think it is, and enlightenment doesn't match our idea.

Dogen says, "Flowers fall with our attachment, and weeds spring up with our aversion." In zazen, we are continually confronted with aversion and attachment. We want something nice—we all want something pleasant, something that feels good, a wonderful state of mind. Sometimes when we have a wonderful state of mind with no pain, we think, "This is it! This is great! This is all worth it! This is why I'm here." But as soon as we grasp onto that thought, it starts to change. It's changing anyway, whether we think so or not. We hold something and then it starts to crumble—starts to change. Then we say, "But wait a minute! Don't go away!" And it continues to change, then it starts to get painful and we are not happy—we want to hold on to that state of mind. But as soon as we hold on to it, we start to suffer. Try to be aware when you have a good feeling like that and just enjoy it. When it starts to change, just let it go. We have to accept change right away. If you are going to sit *sesshin*, you have to accept the changes immediately, without hanging on to the past moment's feeling—just accept everything as it changes, as it is. When you do that, you can sit comfortably and imperturbably, because you are open to everything. This is called samadhi.

When you are not open to everything, you suffer. Dogen said, "Flowers fall with our attachment." We want something so bad, and yet the flower falls, and weeds spring up. It is difficult. It is hard to be open to what you would ordinarily be averse to. It is counterintuitive. When we have pain or discomfort, we usually want to change it. As Suzuki Roshi said, "We are continually changing our equipment, moving around, trying to get comfortable." As soon as we get comfortable, it changes, and it becomes uncomfortable. This is how things are. The way to be comfortable, to have true comfort, is not through trying to control the world around us, but to adjust ourselves, to open ourselves from the inside. When we open ourselves from the inside, absolute and relative are transcended, subject and object are no longer a duality, and we can accept various states of body-mind without being a victim. When aversion arises, take a stand and face it, open yourself to it, and be one with it. The usual reaction is to run the other way.

Opening ourselves to what is painful is how we deal with the pain in our legs and with the pain in our mind. Actually, if we stop saying "good feelings" and "bad feelings," it's much easier. There are no good feelings and bad feelings, there are just feelings. There is no good state of mind or bad state of mind, there is "just this" state of mind. This state of mind is continually changing. There is no special state of mind which is the Zen state of mind to preserve.

In zazen, if you are open and alert and quick to accept what arises, you still have pain, you still have difficulty, but it's different—this pain and difficulty are not the same as suffering. Freedom from suffering doesn't mean to get rid of all pain. In Buddhist teaching, sometimes the phrase "free from all suffering" is used. But it doesn't mean free from all pain, because pain is a part of life. Through our pain we understand life. There is no way that we can understand life without pain. So we need to come to terms with it and accept it as a part of life, but we don't have to be a victim. This is to have freedom.

Within zazen, within the restriction of the posture, how do we find our freedom, how can we be at ease with it? As soon as we start to waver, we waver more and more, and pretty soon we lose it. So when we sit, settled in our body and mind, sitting very still, but not rigidly, there is no need to fidget as if you were defending yourself.

Just sit with good posture, good structure, very open and at ease. All the bones are aligned without being attached to each other. When we sit with single-minded effort, all the bones will line up in a harmonious way. That's why good posture is important. Don't leave anything out. Zazen is body, mind, and breath in the dynamic, harmonious activity of sitting still while completely open, and at ease.

Do you have any questions?

Question: When you talk about attachment, I find it confusing because I think in terms of getting close to people. If I get really close to somebody, I think of that as being attached to them—I care about them, I have a history with them.

Sojun: We say "The attachment of nonattachment." I have a close relationship to you, or to something, but it's not necessarily attachment. You can call it attachment, but that's just a word. Although I have a close relationship to you, you are moving and I am moving and changing. It's like when you have a close attachment to your spouse, you have a certain configuration when you get married, and then ten years later everything has changed and you wonder what happened, how did I do this? Then you have to realign the configuration. You can't be attached. Although your marriage is based on what you did in the beginning, you have to realign it to the reality of the moment. So you can't be attached to old things. Attachment can mean getting stuck in your relationship, or wanting something so much that you can't let go of it. So a reasonable relationship is desirable, but attachment is too much, too dependent, actually; through too much dependence, we have suffering on both sides. Actually, we have to renew our relationships moment by moment as well as periodically.

Question: Action without attachment to the fruit of action, is that transcendence of duality?

Sojun: Yes. Activity without attachment to the result is what we might call pure activity, because our activity at the moment is satisfying enough. In other words, we have a goal and we feel that if we arrive at the goal, we'll have satisfaction. It's all right to have a goal. But if we are attached to the result, we are easily disappointed because there is always something beyond this. So in each step of the way we should find complete satisfaction, even though there may be a goal. I would say that's nondualistic activity. When you are in the kitchen cooking, you want to get the food out, and that's the goal. But we should be experiencing the enjoyment of cutting the vegetables and washing them. Each moment's activity is a satisfactory moment. This way each step contains the whole meal. That's the attitude of the cook in the kitchen, enjoying each step. We complete each step, rather than leaving a big mess because you are so focused on the goal that you neglect the present moment. We cook and clean up as we go, and by the time we are finished, we have the product, and the kitchen is clean, everything is put away, and we have lived our life fully, moment by moment, each step of the way, and of course we have the meal. But think of how much of your life energy and time went into preparing the meal, compared to how much time you spent eating it. And in the end, where did it go?

Question: Is that another way of saying, "Following the Dharma for the sake of the Dharma?"

Sojun: Yes, it's just doing the cooking for the sake of the cooking and enjoying the eating as the eating—doing each activity for its own sake. Although there is before and after, we are not attached to before and after. We don't have to sacrifice our life now in order to reach some goal in the future. This is the same as not starting from delusion in order to finally reach enlightenment. Practice and enlightenment arise together. Thoroughness of practice on each moment is the goal.

Question: Like Blake said, "Do good in minute particulars."

Sojun: Yes. Do something small, but satisfying. A lot of people really lead miserable lives because they want something big to happen, but something small can be large if we find our satisfaction moment by moment. That's the way we need to sit zazen—moment by moment. You cannot think ahead. If you think "How can I do this for seven days," or something like that, you're already lost. All you have to think is, "How can I do this right now, in this moment, moment after moment after moment." Then we live our life moment by moment, in one big moment

Zenki

Dogen's fascicle *Zenki*, or *Total Dynamic Working*, was translated by Masao Abe and Norman Waddell with their explanatory footnotes. In the first footnote they write, "All dharmas (things) in the universe are the Buddha Dharma, and the Buddha Dharma is manifested or realized clearly in all dharmas."

Technically, according to Abhidharma teaching, a dharma (with a lowercase "d") is an aspect of experience, a feeling, emotion, thought, intention, or part of our form body. The early Buddhists put together various lists of dharmas that were most frequently encountered in human experience, which include thoughts, various feelings, and attitudes, which are wholesome, unwholesome, or neutral. Basically those are the dharmas, but actually in a wider sense, every manifestation can be called a dharma. And then in another sense, Dharma with a capital "D" refers to Buddha's teaching. When we say "the Dharma," it means the truth or reality of each of these individual dharmas, the dharmas with a small "d." The reality or the nature of our human constructs.

So, "All dharmas or things in the universe are the Buddha Dharma." There is nothing left out; everything in the universe is Buddha Dharma. There are the several universes. There is one universe that is all-encompassing and inclusive, and then there is the universe that is each one of us as an individual. Each one of us is a reflection of the whole universe, and the whole universe is contained within each one of us.

And so the question arises, where is the center of the universe? Does the universe have a center? If so, where is the center? In one sense you can say that the center of the universe is everywhere. If there is no particular center, then wherever you point can be the center. Wherever you are, wherever you stand is the center of the universe, but this doesn't mean that you alone are the center of the universe. Wherever anybody stands is also the center of the universe. So everything is standing in the center of the universe together, even though we are all in different places.

"All dharmas or things in the universe are the Buddha Dharma, and the Buddha Dharma is manifested or realized clearly in all dharmas." You can see that all dharmas are contained in the Dharma, Buddha Dharma. The Buddha Dharma is really about small, individual, particular things that have no inherent existence in themselves. For Dogen, being confirmed by all dharmas is proven by the fact of oneself in zazen. It is emancipation from all attachments. It is a breakthrough that constitutes enlightenment. For all Buddhas, that is, for all enlightened beings, there is emancipation that is shedding of ego in practice and realization, manifesting or realizing in all dharmas one's true self, a self beyond all duality. In other words, according to my understanding, what Dogen is talking about is proven or manifested in zazen. It's experiencing the unity of the oneness, as well as the diversity, of all dharmas with the universe. This is why zazen is called *zenki*, or total dynamic activity.

Two related Japanese terms are *kikan*, which is the motive force that makes each dharma's existence what it is, and *zenki*, the universal activity that exists within each dharma or each manifestation. One day a monk asked Joshu, "Does the dog have the Buddha-nature?" A great question. Joshu answered, "No." But "no" used in a nondualistic way. Another time when someone asked Joshu, "Does the dog have the Buddha-nature?" he said, "Yes," but "yes" used in a nondualistic way. In the same way, I use "life" as a nondualistic term that includes both birth and death. "No" in this case contains both yes and no. Absolute "no" has to contain its opposite. Ordinarily, we use yes and no in relative opposition. But when yes and no are considered in a nondualistic way, yes contains no and no contains yes. Birth contains death, and death contains birth.

So within each moment's activity of birth is also its death. Birth and death are happening at the same time, and in each moment. The birth of something is also the death of something, and the death of something is the birth of something. Otherwise, continuation couldn't happen. Emptiness in this sense means the space in which something can happen. Without emptiness everything would freeze as it is. In the same way if you look at birth and death in that light, death is necessary for birth or manifestation. If there was no death, there couldn't be any manifestation, and vice versa. If there was no manifestation, there couldn't be any death. So *zenki* means to live (and love) each moment in full function right now, not clinging to existence and not wishing for death. Otherwise, we have a one-sided understanding of existence that is called an upside-down view. When I studied this with Katagiri Roshi years ago, he had a picture of a little man in a circle upside down.

Dogen wrote, "'Emancipation' means that life emancipates life, and that death emancipates death. For this reason, there is deliverance from birth and death, and immersion in birth and death. Both are the great Way totally culminated. There is discarding of birth and death, and there is crossing of birth and death."

Dogen is saying, don't be attached to birth and don't be attached to death. A footnote comment on this: "Crossing birth and death and immersion in birth and death signifies entering birth and death in order to work for the salvation of all beings." For Dogen, one is totally immersed within birth and death while one is free from birth and death. But one stays within birth and death in order to help sentient beings to understand how to be free from birth and death. This is the bodhisattva ideal, the bodhisattva stays in the world of birth and death—the dualistic world of birth and death—in order to save all beings. This is what the bodhisattva vow is all about. However, all beings might not want to be saved from this problem.

Dogen continues: "When the great Way is realized, it is nothing but life's total realization, it is nothing but death's total realization." Then he writes: "This dynamic working readily brings about life and readily brings about death. At the very time that this dynamic working is thus realized, it is not necessarily large and it is not necessarily small; it is not limitless, it is not limited; it is not long or far, short or near. One's present life exists within this dynamic working: this dynamic working exists within this present life."

We don't often conceive of thinking or realizing in the realm of death, nor do we think in terms of manifestation. Dogen equated birth and death, and he set up death in a way that included manifestation. Birth and death are separate terms, but I think manifestation is good because it means existence, and death means nonexistence. So manifestation might be a better term in some ways, but he's using all three of these terms.

Usually we don't see things from death's point of view; we see things from the point of view of manifestation. Dogen said, "Since the great Way of Buddhas is beyond all dualities, including the basic duality of birth and death, from manifestation's point of view, each thing, including death, is life's total realization. And from death's point of view, each thing including manifestation is death's total realization. It is also called kikan or the eternal now. Our present manifestation exists within this dynamic working, and this dynamic working exists within this present life. Life is not a coming and it is not a going—it is not an existing and it is not a becoming. Nevertheless life is the manifestation of the total dynamic working, and death is the manifestation of the total dynamic working."

For Dogen, it is important to have what he calls a "vow of practice," i.e., living by vow rather than living by karma. Most of us live by karma without realizing the working of cause and effect and how we reap the consequences of our self-centered actions. Living by vow is living according to the Dharma. When we understand the meaning of our vow of practice, it should help us understand the nonduality of birth and death. This is what Dogen calls the Great Matter. This is why we say we are not searching for enlightenment, but when we simply sit zazen, enlightenment manifests without our seeking it. We express Buddha Dharma without trying; we are simply expressing the total reality which is *zenki*. *Zenki* is the other side of birth and death, and it includes birth and death. The side which does not discriminate but which realizes birth within death, and death within birth. It means birth emancipates birth, death emancipates death.

Another footnote explains: "This dynamic working is not something to which dualistic concepts can be applied." Dogen wrote: "This dynamic working readily brings about birth and readily brings about death. At the very time that this dynamic working is thus realized, it is not necessarily large, not necessarily small; it is not limitless, it is not limited; it is not long or far, short or near. One's present life exists within this dynamic working: this dynamic working exists within this present life." Dogen continues: "You should know that within the incalculable dharmas that are in you, there is birth and there is death. You must quietly reflect whether your present life and all the dharmas existing with this life share a common life or not. In fact, there can be nothing—not one instant of time or a single dharma—that does not share life in common. For a thing as well as for a mind, there is nothing but sharing life in common."

I would like to read footnote seven: "Each existence has its own respective dharma stage, its own 'time,' and does not intrude on any other existence. Yet that which makes each and every existence individual is also functioning equally within each and every individual. Because there is life, there is death; because there is death, there is life. Life is life and is not death, yet there cannot be life without death, and vice versa."

In Dogen's text *Genjokoan* he wrote: "It is an established Dharma teaching that life does not become death. Buddhism therefore speaks of no-life. It is an established teaching in the Buddha Dharma that death does not become life. Buddhism therefore speaks of nonextinction. Life is one stage of total time and death is one stage of total time. With winter and spring, for example, we do not say that winter becomes spring, or that spring becomes summer."

We sometimes do say this, but according to reality, it is not correct. Spring is the total time of spring, it has its before and after and its present, and the same is true for winter.

Dogen also wrote of firewood and ash. Firewood is the stage of being firewood, then when it burns, there is ash; but it is not that the firewood becomes ash. Firewood is a condition for ash. But we can't say that the firewood turns into ash—we do say that, but according to Dogen it is not correct. In the nineteenth-century Zen Master

Nishiari Bokusan's commentary on *Genjokoan*, he says: "If you asked tofu, 'Tofu, do you know that you were once beans?' Tofu would say, Are you kidding? Those round, hard things? I'm flat and smooth."

So each dharma has its own conditions for making it what it is. Indian and Buddhist philosophers say when you have a cow, you call it a cow. When it is slaughtered and you eat it, you call it meat. You don't say, "I am now eating cow." You say, "I am eating meat." Steak is in the dharma position of being steak. Steak is not the same as a steer, although the steer is a condition for the existence or the manifestation of steak.

Lectures

Section 3:
Daily Life

Daily Life

Zazen in Daily Life

In our life we all like to be comfortable. If we look and see what people are doing, mostly we are trying to find ways to be comfortable; to make our houses comfortable, make our automobiles comfortable, and trying to please ourselves. But you know, we never can get really, totally comfortable. We get comfortable for a little while, but then we become uncomfortable and have to change and get comfortable in another way, so we are always adjusting our position. Dogen's zazen is called the comfortable way, but it is not comfortable in the usual way. When you can actually accept yourself completely in all situations, you can be truly comfortable. So we say, "How do we express zazen in our daily life? How do we take our practice into our daily life?" When we know how to settle and have calm mind in zazen no matter what difficulty or discomfort we have, then, as we move in the world, we should be able to feel comfortable or have a settled mind in each situation. No matter what is happening to us, we know how to settle, we know how to reach that unconditioned place.

Often I suggest to people just to pay attention to breathing, because breathing is an activity which is somewhere between "I am doing it" and "It is doing me." In zazen breathing should be felt here, in our lower abdomen. Inhaling, it expands; exhaling, it contracts. Inhaling, it expands; exhaling, it contracts. But when we get tense or angry or frightened, our breath rises in our chest, and this is not a condition for calmness. The condition for calmness is to feel the breath down here, in your lower abdomen. If you are always breathing deeply and are aware of your breathing, you have the opportunity to establish your mind in calmness because you are used to doing that in zazen. When a problem comes up, you can establish yourself in your breath on this moment.

Otherwise, we establish ourselves on our momentum. We are all busy people, and body and mind are oriented toward accomplishing something. We are always driving somewhere, working somewhere, on the go all the time. So we easily forget about establishing ourselves on where we are. We easily forget that each one of our movements is our life; that our life is in walking and sitting and standing and lying down, in the ordinary movements. So at the same time that we are doing, we are also just being—simply existing—and this quality of pure existence is our life. Just stop for a moment, or just be aware of your body's movements while you are doing something: "I am walking from here to the store." But while I am walking from here to the store I am thinking about something, whereas one can just be aware of how the foot meets the pavement and of how one foot follows the next. How the body is being held, what the breath is like. Just being in the body. Going someplace is okay, but actually at this moment we are just where we are. So these two qualities should be flowing together at the same time—the awareness of being, as well as the awareness of doing. We may get bored, but not for long. We are open to everything, we can see things. Sometimes our vision is so concentrated on doing something that we just don't see what is around us. We don't see that we are part of our surroundings because we are only focused on our own project.

Sometimes, if you stop thinking about your project and let yourself observe what's around you, it's just incredible what you see. That way we can meet things, we can meet life.

There's a famous story about the Zen monk who was enlightened when he saw the peach blossoms in bloom. He suddenly woke up from his tunnel vision and looked up and saw a tree in blossom. He was completely blown away because his self dropped away, and he could identify with the tree as himself. When we get very busy, we get hung up in our routine and our projects, and our projects run us. It's so hard to not be run by your projects.

We come to practice for various reasons, but we don't always know what it is that we come for. I don't think I knew exactly what it was that I was coming for. But when we make a sincere effort to practice, sooner or later we realize what it is. We realize that there is nothing to "get." And this "nothing to get" has to be "found" by each one of us, by ourselves.

Lighting Up Our Own Corner of the World

We are so fortunate as human beings to be living here in Berkeley, California, in the year 2012. California is the cornucopia of the world, and Berkeley is an oasis for progressives. The spirit of tolerance and liberality here allows us more or less unrestricted freedom to explore creative solutions to universal problems, unhampered by religious or political bigotry. As we go about our normal daily activities in our relatively safe environment, we are haunted by the enormous suffering that is being inflicted on ordinary populations all over the world. When we open ourselves we can easily be overwhelmed. In order to have some mental and emotional freedom to pursue our activities, we often set up a barrier or compartmentalization in order to have some objectivity and go about our business.

Allowing ourselves to focus on the atrocities, inequalities, manipulations, deceptions, power struggles, criminal corporate control, and unemployment problems of our own country, let alone the rest of the world, day after day, leaves us with a frustrated and seemingly insurmountable feeling of helplessness.

These problems have been with us since the beginning of time, and now, because the world is becoming a smaller place, we no longer have the luxury of only dealing with our local problems. So the question is how, in the face of these overwhelming disasters that will always be with us, can we do something positive and not be drowned by so much negativity?

We can work for change by voting and adding our names to petitions for change and supporting organizations for justice and so forth. But most importantly, how, in the face of this endless process of fighting or putting out one fire only to have a new one flare up, can we maintain an attitude of equanimity and optimism, supported by wisdom and compassion? Suzuki Roshi once described our practice as "lighting up our own corner of the world." In the Diamond Sutra it says, "Although there are no sentient beings to be saved, we must save them all." What does it mean to light up our own corner of the world as well as saving all beings?

As self-creating humans, we have the capacity to influence our own house, our own environment and surroundings. Each one of us has a sphere of influence. When we do zazen in the morning, *prajna* arises in the world, radiant light arises and manifests in the world, and our activity proceeds from zazen and is sustained as compassionate action. The influence of our practice can have a positive far-reaching effect in the world. We can practice for the benefit of all beings without being attached to impossible results. This is *shikantaza*—just doing. It is *Genjokoan*, the koan of our daily life, moment by moment as it proceeds from zazen. True joy runs deep like the bottom of a river and does not depend on good and bad circumstances. It supports us through all of our suffering, and manifests through our sincere continuous practice. When we can forget our self and support those around us, the way of harmony appears unhindered. Strong confidence comes little by little through small successes.

Attitude

Extending from the Center

It seems to me that our body-mind is like a microcosm of the universe. The center of the universe within each of us is correctly called the solar plexus, while the extensions—the arms, legs, and head—are like the planetary satellites that make up our human mandala. The thinking mind, the feelings, emotions, consciousness, and breath are manifestations of this vital center. The vital center has various names, such as *ki*, which also means breath, strength, unity, peace, or happiness. It also refers to our calm, impartial mind, and the seat of our intuition. Our activity in the zendo is based on this understanding.

In zazen, all the extensions—arms, legs, breath, thoughts, etc.—take their place in a harmonious balance around the vital center. The function of the thinking mind is to think the thought of zazen without getting sidetracked, and to encourage the other limbs to maintain their function.

This attitude will then be extended to all of our activity. When we are serving food in the zendo, we learn to maintain the same harmonious balance. Our mandala, which extends from our vital center, meets and mingles with the mandala of the person who is being served. When we walk up the aisle, we are aware of doing so quietly. When we serve the food, we gently stir the goodies up from the bottom of the pot. In other words, we maintain the spirit of zazen through awareness of the harmony of body, breath, and mind, together with mindful attention to the materials we are working with. We treat the pots and pans and bowls and utensils with respect, according to their shape and function.

The *doan* learns to sound the bells without punishing them. Sounding the bell is an act of love, an offering to the sangha. Although the hand holds the striker, the impulse begins in the *hara* and extends through the arm, hand, and striker, and the resonance of the bell reflects the inspiring intention of the *doan*, which in turn inspires the chanting. The same for the *fukudo*, who maintains the beat and the rhythm while resonating with the hollow sound of the fish-shaped drum. Suzuki Roshi used to admonish us not to give the poor thing a heart attack. And the *kokyo*, who leads the chant, should find a pitch that is not too high and not too low so that everyone can feel comfortable, leading the chant without being strident. The secret is to lead and follow at the same time.

Breathing deeply, not just in zazen but continuously, is how we remain centered. When we move and our movements extend from the center, we can move with ease and grace, without restriction. As our life is transformative, we can inhale adversity and exhale love. The purpose is not to become an expert but simply to be a vehicle of light, a Buddha field for our surroundings.

Commitment

Commitment to ourselves is most important if we want to have a steady practice. Of course, sometimes we're just looking, and we come and practice for a while to see what it's like. That's fine too. But I think it's helpful to give yourself the opportunity of committing to a practice schedule for some short space of time, just to see what that's like, regardless of what your feelings are about it.

When you finally start practicing zazen, and particularly if you sit *sesshin* and your legs begin to hurt or if your back has some old problem, or if there are thoughts running through your head all the time, you'll want to get more comfortable and you may feel "Get me out of here" or "I'd rather be doing something else." But what keeps you here is your commitment. And through your commitment, you can see how feelings and thoughts arise, and how these feelings and thoughts are always trying to pull us around by the nose, one way or another. It's hard to see something all the way through, because as soon as things get a little difficult we want to escape. And when we keep trying to escape from reality, we lose ourselves. We are no longer present. We are no longer settled on ourselves.

We have to be careful that we don't sell Buddhism as "the opium of the people," or something euphoric. The fifth precept is "Don't sell liquor or intoxicants." Sometimes this is interpreted as "Don't sell Buddha Dharma as wine," or something intoxicating, as if it will take all your cares away or make you feel wonderful.

What Zen does is sit us down right in the middle of reality between pleasure and pain, between good and bad, so that we accept everything equally. We don't try to run away from our difficulty to some kind of pleasant state, or run away from some pleasant state just because it's pleasant. When something pleasant arises, it's just pleasant. When something painful arises, it's just painful. When something easy arises, it's just easy. When something difficult arises, it's just difficult.

The only way that we can really practice this is through our commitment, because otherwise, as soon as things get difficult, we will want something pleasant. Feelings are important. We should accept our feelings, but Zen is the practice of not escaping. There is no way out except to be whatever is happening. When we depend on our feelings too much, we can't experience things completely. The only way is to give up our self-centeredness.

Zen Master Dogen wrote the *Shobogenzo*, which has many essays on Zen practice. His fascicle *Genjokoan* is at the center of his writing. *Genjo* means something like "manifesting in the present" or "arising in the present." *Koan* in this case does not have the usual "Zen koan" meaning. *Ko* means leveling or completely level or sameness, and *an* means a position, like "dharma position." A "dharma" is a thing, so *Genjokoan* means something like a thing's position on level ground, manifesting in the present, like our life, moment by moment, manifesting in this phenomenal world as an expression of absolute reality, which is what zazen is. The koan of manifesting in the present, moment by moment, in reality.

In *Genjokoan*, Dogen says, "To study Buddha Dharma is to study the self. To study the self is to forget the self, or to let go of the self. To let go of the self is to be enlightened by all things, all the '10,000 dharmas.' To be enlightened by the 10,000 dharmas is to find perfect freedom for yourself and for others, and this traceless enlightenment goes on and on and on, not leaving any trace at all."

So to study the way, to study the Buddha Dharma, is to study the self. Here, "study" doesn't mean study in the sense of reading a book. The word "study" here means to do something over and over and over again, constantly doing something until it becomes part of you, until it becomes you, actually. This is to study the self, and it's like zazen. In order to practice zazen, you do it over and over until you get it through your pores, and when you get it through your pores, then you can drop the self, because you realize that all the things you need are yourself. To be enlightened by the 10,000 things is to meet everything as yourself.

Zazen is a kind of unconditioned practice, where you just exist as absolute, as an expression of reality, without discrimination. You just let everything come as it comes, and go as it goes. It's a wonderful practice, but it's not so easy. It's not easy to just sit still—it takes all of your integrity to just be able to sit without any expectation. Expectation is what gets us into trouble, and we think, "It feels very good now. This must be the enlightened state." As soon as you think that, it changes.

Then we think, "How could the enlightened state suddenly get so miserable?" We try all of the tricks in our mind to justify our feelings, but nothing works until you finally just let go. Then you can sit still. But you have to get to the point where you sit long enough so you can just sit still. It just happens by itself. This is why I say commitment is so important. You don't get to that place through your feelings; you only get to that place through your commitment to see something through.

The Problem of Self-Improvement

One morning during zazen, Suzuki Roshi gave a brief impromptu talk in which he said, "Each one of you is perfect as you are . . . and you can also use a little improvement."

He had a nice way of putting things into perspective. This was the mid-sixties, when young people were breaking out of the old societal structures and experimenting with psychedelics and mind-expansion techniques related to self-improvement. One time around the fourth day of *sesshin*, when there was enough pain and discomfort to go around, he began his talk by saying slowly, "The problems you are experiencing now"—will go away, we were sure he was going to say—"will continue for the rest of your life." The way he said it, everyone laughed. Thank goodness for laughter!

This seems like the last thing a student wants to hear from a teacher: You are doomed to be who you are for the rest of your life. Suzuki Roshi's radical statement turns our whole world back 10,000 miles. He grants us that improvement is okay, but if improvement is our goal of practice, it is easy to think that some future moment could or must be better than this present moment. After all, if we had an improved future we would have fewer problems. Wouldn't we? He liked to say: "Be careful. Solving the problems you have now might give you a bigger problem." He wasn't against solving problems, he was simply trying to help us understand that if we neglect to live fully in each moment, sacrificing this moment for a future time, we miss our life, which is only this moment with its joys and sorrows.

Our present problems are our equipment or tools for practice; gifts of our karma. Because we don't understand and appreciate what *this* is, we tend to think that there must be something better than this. Master Dogen begins his *Genjokoan*, the koan of our daily life, with the statement, "When all dharmas are Buddha Dharma . . ." That's when we can approach the world as a field of practice, responding to the ever-changing circumstances with a non-assuming, open-minded, and compassionate attitude. The way unfolds—one moment at a time.

The Fire Boy Seeks Fire

In his *Eihei Shingi*, Dogen tells stories about the Ancestors in order to encourage the monks in their practice. In one story, he gives an example of someone who, while serving as the *kansu*, clarified the Great Matter of birth and death, or *Daiji*. The term *kansu*, or *kanin*, is a little confusing because it has several meanings. In the old days in China, the *kansu* was one person in a monastery who performed the duties of the director, the treasurer, and other administrative roles. Later these jobs were divided up into three positions and *kansu*, instead of meaning all three positions, came to mean just assistant director. The name for director became *tusu*, and the name for treasurer became *fusu*.

In any case, Dogen tells the story of Master Xuanze of Baoen Monastery, who once served as *kansu* in the community of Fayen. One day Fayen asked Xuanze, "*Kansu*, how long have you been with us?"

Xuanze said, "I've been in your community for three years."

Fayen then asked, "You are a junior person in the monastery. How come you never ask questions?"

You see, one expects a student living in a monastery to come and ask questions. In *dokusan* the first question that a new person in a monastery traditionally would ask is "I am new here. Will you please teach me?" This is a very humbling attitude. It means that you are putting yourself in a proper position in relation to the teacher as well as to everyone else at the monastery, and it also shows that you are there for some reason.

So Fayen confronted Xuanze. "How come you never ask any questions? You've been here for three years and you've never said anything to me. You seem to be avoiding me, in fact."

"Well, I don't want to mislead you," Xuanze said. "I must confess, when I was with Master Qingfeng, I attained the peaceful bliss [enlightenment], so I don't feel like I need to come and talk to you."

"By what words did you enter that place?" asked Fayen.

Xuanze answered, "When I asked Qingfeng, 'What is the self of the practitioner?' he said, 'The fire boy seeks fire.'"

"Good words," Fayen retorted. "But I am afraid you misunderstood them."

So Xuanze tried to explain. "The fire boy belongs to the fire. Fire seeking fire is just like the self seeking the self."

But Fayen stopped him. "Indeed, you did not understand. If the Buddha Dharma was like that, it wouldn't have come down to this day."

Xuanze was greatly upset by this and indignantly stood up and left. He actually left the monastery. But on his way, he thought, "Fayen is the teacher of five hundred monks. He didn't approve of me, but what he said should be correct." So he turned back and approached Fayen. Bowing, he apologized. "I am very sorry I got up and left."

Fayen responded, "Well, about this question. Why didn't you ask me what I think of this question?"

"Okay," Xuanze said. "What is the self of the practitioner?"

"The fire boy seeks fire," Fayen said. And at that Xuanze experienced great awakening.

This is one of Suzuki Roshi's favorite stories. Xuanze was a good student and in a way he had some understanding. Intellectually, "The fire boy seeks fire" is not very hard to understand.

The fire boy seeks fire: Buddha-nature seeks Buddha-nature. What everyone is seeking is their true self. Of course. And it's right here, all the time. Xuanze's arrogance was a block to his understanding, but when he returned and humbled himself before the teacher, the block lifted. That was the turning point. Just at the point that he could give up his arrogance, everything started to flow very nicely.

Arrogance is one of the biggest stumbling blocks for someone who is very capable, for someone who has ability and is especially good at learning. On the other hand, for someone who is always stumbling around, arrogance is not much of a problem. And for the person who doesn't know so much and is slow and makes mistakes, it's often easier to have a good understanding.

I remember Katagiri Roshi used to say, "In Soto Zen you should be a little stupid." There were some people who didn't believe this. They had to find the hard way.

Selflessness and arrogance just don't go together. Anger, arrogance, possessiveness—these are big stumbling blocks because they are "self-builders." Ego builders.

Another point is that teachers are all different. We read about fierce teachers—Deshan with his big stick and Linji with his big shout. But the fact is that all teachers are different. And when you have some expectation about how a Zen teacher is supposed to act, that can be a stumbling block to actually picking up on a teacher.

Some teachers are very noisy, some are very extraverted, some teachers are very quiet and introverted, some teachers are very subtle, and some teachers are not so subtle. So we have the whole range of temperaments. Consequently, it is best not to have a fixed idea of what a teacher is supposed to look like or be like. A teacher who tries to fill out their role based on a stereotype is practicing the art of Zen, but not true Zen. One can act a certain way and take on various mannerisms and it might fit the picture of what Zen is supposed to look like. But a good teacher may be very plain and ordinary. Joohu never beat anyone; he always used his eloquence to teach.

When Deshan, who was proud of his knowledge of the Diamond Sutra, went to visit Lungtan up on the mountain, his intent was to destroy the Zen sect. Lungtan means "dragon pool," but when Deshan met up with Lungtan he saw just an ordinary little old man in patched-up robes. If you saw Lungtan on the street today, you might not look twice. You might even mistake him for the janitor.

So when Deshan met Lungtan he said, "I don't see any dragon pool here." Lungtan answered, "Well, this is it. You have arrived." And then the two went into Lungtan's hut and talked late into the night, discussing the Dharma. Deshan was very impressed with Lungtan. Finally, it was time to go to bed and Lungtan said to Deshan, "Well, it's dark outside, so I will give you this lamp so you can see where you are going." He lit a paper lantern and handed it to

Deshan. But as Deshan took the lantern and began to leave, Lungtan blew out the light and in the utter darkness Deshan was enlightened.

This is a very subtle teacher who leaps like a tiger. Be careful of these subtle teachers.

Purpose, Function, and Direction

I now want to talk about these three factors: purpose, function, and direction. As a leader, the abbot must never lose sight of why we are doing this. Master Dogen says over and over again that we should not pervert the practice by engaging in it for the sake of name, fame, or gain.

It's natural to want to be recognized for our efforts. We all enjoy praise. In many cultures people talk about preserving their good name. So as long as we do good work, stay out of trouble, are kind to people, and have a humble attitude, we will most likely have a good name and be admired and trusted. What I mean by humble is knowing how to find and take your correct place in any situation in a harmonious way that allows you the space to turn, and in turn to be turned, and to function in the most appropriate way; that allows the dynamics of the present situation to function in the best possible way for all concerned, even though you may not be recognized or stand out in any special way. This is beneficial action, leaving no trace.

But for one reason or another, usually because of some feeling of inadequacy, many people crave recognition, like the little kid who does crazy things to get attention. So sometimes we engage in some activity for name recognition instead of for the sake of the activity itself. Engaging in Buddhist practice in order to be famous is frowned upon. Name and fame are intertwined. Although one needs a place to be and to practice, together with food, shelter, and clothing—and, in these present circumstances, money—we should know how much is enough. Ownership is insidious. The more we get, the more we want. Expansion is the name of the game in business. This attitude promotes greed, and once it takes over, even honest people will rationalize their behavior and do unethical things. The Buddhist attitude is that there is nothing to gain and nothing to lose. It's perverse to use the Dharma as a way to collect wealth. If our practice is pure and sincere, everything we need will come.

Therefore, the teacher maintains the proper perspective and doesn't let the sangha members stray from the correct way. The teacher should know that we do the practice for the sake of practice and not let it get mixed up with other practices that offer spiritual enticements. When we have confidence in our own practice and know what we are doing, we can visit other teachers and appreciate other practices. Having confidence in your own practice means that you have touched something very deep through zazen, and that you have tasted it for yourself. Once you have tasted it, you naturally want to offer it to others.

In the late sixties Zen was beginning to become popular and San Francisco Zen Center and Tassajara were being flooded with students. Many people thought this was a good thing, but Suzuki Roshi was worried that there would be a popular Zen boom, a kind of Zen fad that might override the true spirit of practice. He also said that we should not be chauvinistic or overly partial to Zen Center; that even if we should lose Zen Center or Tassajara it would be okay. He said that Zen Center was here for the students, not the other way around. The quality of the practice comes first. When there is a big institution to support, it's easy to get focused on the institution at the expense of the practice and the members.

Relationship

Difficult Encounters

Suzuki Roshi used to say that each of us is half good and half bad. No matter how righteous we may feel, we have to reflect on this. He did not exclude himself.

First, I want to suggest that Suzuki Roshi was not infallible and that he had faults. We should be careful not to deify him. I don't think he would feel good about that. Because he was always working on his shortcomings, we didn't see them as faults. We saw them as his practice. I think it was because he could see his own faults so clearly that he was empathetic with us. There were times when Suzuki Roshi was angry and he showed it. But he said that when he was angry he would express it to make a point, but that he was not attached to the anger. "I am just giving you something to work with," he'd say.

Loving-kindness, sympathetic joy, compassion, and equanimity are aspects of love, free from self-interest. They express the Buddhist temperament. Suzuki Roshi embodied them. He worked with the most difficult people, not by rejecting or criticizing, but by understanding something about their problems and addressing them as Buddha and exercising enormous patience. He was not always successful, but the truth of his humble way continues to have a positive effect in the world today.

From time to time we have difficult encounters with people, both inside and outside the sangha. Finding a middle ground between affirmation of the person and acknowledging your differences is a wonderful practice opportunity for a Zen student. Practice involves using skillful means instead of reactivity. Reactivity brings forth defensiveness in another person, which muddies the water. Without denying our emotions and feelings, how can we rise to a place of equanimity where the solutions become obvious to everyone without carrying any defensive baggage at the bottom of the heart? Someone said to me, "I don't feel loved, but I realize that if I love everyone I will be loved in return."

The vow to awaken with all beings must be more than just lip service.

Aged Plum Tree

On cutting down the old plum tree
outside the Tassajara Monastery office

Aged Plum Tree
Venerable old monk
Pillar between heaven
And earth.
Silent partner
Offering shade and
Sweet fruit
Sometimes noticed
Sometimes not
A fixed presence
A background for our
Comings and goings.
How many times have we
Walked by
Feeling your presence
Barely aware of the subtle rustling of
Your green leaves
Dancing with
The fall breeze
Waving at the passersby for no one knows
How many years?
Now your time is up.
You will no doubt be fire

Wood turning yourself over
To ash.
Will you remember
You were once a tree?
That you were once a tiny seed?
Or that you were once our
Long-ago silent friend
On the green grass outside
The Tassajara office?
What will become of you?
What will become of us? And where?
Will we
Meet again?
In the dreamtime of our imagination
We will be sitting and swaying in
The spreading arms of your branches
Getting drunk on your delicious fruit and
Giving voice to
All the stories
You couldn't tell.
So long
Old friend.

Willow

Ever since the 1970s my wife and I have almost always had a dog
and a cat. But for me the dog was far more important. The dog is a
companion. You walk together, you train together, you share similar
emotions, you have adventures. For me the cat has been mostly in
the background. But this is the first time we have had a cat and no

dog. I always liked our cats, but I guess you could say that I was not particularly drawn to them.

Recently, my wife acquired a calico cat while I was at *sesshin*. She let me know by emailing me a photo of the new cat on the mantel! I have to admit that I was charmed, even though it had been our understanding not to bring home an animal without a prior agreement. I gave her a variance because during *sesshin* I was in a state far beyond right and wrong, form and emptiness.

Now that we are between dogs, I have this opportunity to study our cat. We are obligated to train dogs because they are responsible members of society. Dog people. Cats, on the other hand, train us. They weave in and out of society as they wish without any obligations and live according to some inner mysterious compass. Our cat mostly lives outside and comes in to eat and sometimes takes a long nap in the morning after prowling around all night. I have spotted her all over the neighborhood crossing streets.

But I have to say that she really loves us. She doesn't like to be handled, but we always greet each other with affection, bumping heads and short strokes. She often makes a little statement when she comes in to announce her arrival. She also spends time in the backyard garden, and appears seemingly from nowhere when you think she is gone. When she is around outside, she seems to know everything that is going on in the house and has an unerring sense of time and timing. She prefers to be out all night and when I get up at 4:45, we meet at the back door at exactly the same time.

I could go on about the virtues of this little creature, her intelligence, her agility, her perfect composure, and so forth. She is so well coordinated it seems like her whole being is her brain. But just one more thing. Animals are such great models for us, and have so much to teach us, including silent communication, loyalty, love, and communion. Sometime I will tell you about Doug Greiner's chickens.

Four Buddhist Views of Love

One of the topics I talked about recently was friendliness or relations between people. Because Zen puts so much emphasis on *prajna*, or wisdom, seeing the true form through the cool eye of wisdom, we tend to neglect the warm eye of compassion, without which our practice becomes unbalanced. In Buddhism there's a meditation practice that focuses on love in four different ways. It's not a formula, but it's a way of looking at love from a non-self-centered Buddhist point of view. It's something I think we need to bring up frequently and remember. They are called the four Brahmaviharas. They are four unlimited places from which we act. They are also called the Divine Abidings. They are very highly regarded in Theravada Buddhism and are considered a basis for any serious practice.

There are quite detailed meditations on each of these, but we don't have the time to go into them here. The first of the four Brahmaviharas is *metta* or love, which includes kindness. There is a Metta Sutra which we should know about. *Metta* is translated as love; it's a way of extending ourself to everyone without partiality. When we meet people or are having some interaction, our practice is to always extend *metta*. It is good will or concern with the well-being of others. Strictly speaking, it is extending love impartially without having any desire in it or any kind of ulterior motive.

We always have to look at our motives when we do something. "Why am I doing this?" If we have a motive, we may say, "Well, I'm doing this good thing now so that maybe later something good will come to me because of it." That's a kind of motive, a kind of desire. It's okay, but it's not really pure. It's okay to have a motive, and within our relationships we do have motives—if I do this for you, then you'll do this for me. But strictly speaking, pure *metta* is to extend ourselves regardless of whether or not anything comes back. So the practice of *metta* is simply to extend love in a kind way. And, of course, the enemy of love is hate or ill will. They cannot exist simultaneously. It's easy to recognize the enemy, but it's also interesting to look at the counterfeit, what's called the *near enemy*.

The near enemy is something so close it looks almost the same. Selfish affection is the near enemy of *metta*. It looks like love, but there's often so much desire in it that one's motives get mixed up easily. It's very easy to fool ourself, very easy to create an imaginary kind of love based on self-interest. So to be really clear, we should know and respect a person in many ways before we decide what kind of relationship we're going to have with them. Love, we say, hides many faults. It's easy to fall in love with someone for selfish reasons and overlook what later you will observe as faults.

This can be a big problem between men and women: how as a man can you extend love and kindness to women impartially, or as a woman, how can you extend love and kindness to men impartially? How to not let it get mixed up with our personal desire or our illusions and fantasies? It is something we have to practice in a conscious way. It's especially important in relating to members of the desired sex, where desire can easily come up, and to be able to relate from a non-possessive standpoint. That has to be at the basis of the practice so that we don't get confused in our goodwill. This is just one example. *Metta* is something that can be extended to all of our relationships. First to ourselves and to those to whom we are close, then to those we don't know, and finally, if possible, to those we don't like.

The second Brahmavihara is *karuna* or compassion. Karuna, strictly speaking, means to identify with someone's suffering or to suffer with others. We have a sympathetic understanding with people, which leads us to help them because we can identify with their suffering. Sympathy is a kind of compassion, but compassion is a little bigger than sympathy.

The near enemy of compassion is feeling sorry for people who don't get what they want in a materialistic way. If John doesn't get his Mercedes, we feel sympathy, but we don't necessarily feel compassion. But for the persecuted people in Central America and the starving people in Ethiopia, we feel compassion. And for people who don't see the underlying cause of their suffering, we feel compassion. It comes up in relation to the suffering people have because of their ignorance or because of the inability to change their lives in a wholesome way. The polar enemy of compassion is ruthlessly causing people to suffer. Anything we do that causes real suffering is the enemy of compassion.

The third Brahmavihara, *mudita*, is sometimes called gladness, but it's more usually called sympathetic joy. Sympathetic joy is being able to feel glad about another's happiness. Of course, its polar enemy would be jealousy or envy. So it's freedom from envy, freedom from competition. If something good happens to somebody, we can share that with them and rejoice in their good fortune, even if it's someone we don't like particularly. That's the hard part: even if it's somebody you don't like.

The near enemy of sympathetic joy is joy over material wealth or something that satisfies our greed. So sympathetic joy is more the happiness you feel for people's true welfare or accomplishment in a fundamental sense. If you realize your Buddha-nature, we feel sympathetic joy with you. If you make some progress for social change in the world, we rejoice in your success. I won't begrudge you your new automobile or stereo set, but strictly speaking, *mudita* applies to rejoicing in someone's success in unfolding as a human being.

The fourth Brahmavihara is *upekkha* or equanimity. Equanimity means observing things impartially, maintaining a balanced view; to be able to see every situation as it is and to be able to decide something from the point of view of impartiality. The near enemy of *upekkha* is indifference based on ignorance. *Upekkha* doesn't mean to be in-different. Rather it means not being one-sided or partial, not being influenced by resentment or approval. It's the basis for seeing clearly. In zazen meditation, impartiality is one of the major factors. But we must always be careful not to mistake indifference for impartiality or nonattachment, and to be ready to respond to each situation that confronts us, free from greed and resentment, the two enemies of equanimity.

Although these four factors are always present in our lives in some form, they become strong guiding principles when we focus on them as meditation. According to the *Visuddhimagga*, Buddhaghosa's *Path of Purification*, the near enemy is that which masquerades as the other, and the far enemy is its opposite. The far enemy is usually obvious. What one has to be careful about is the near enemy, which may not be so obvious.

If you know how to extend *metta* to everyone that you meet, you may find that people respond to your unguardedness and they in turn become unguarded. Even at some risk, this is how you can extend it in the world. Walking down the street, without any motive in mind, just to say hello to somebody. You can try some kind of greeting. Try it on someone who looks different than you do.

There are specific meditations on these four Brahmaviharas, and the meditations are very clear. The meditations are pretty much the same for all four categories, with minor differences. For *metta*, you start by extending feelings and thoughts of loving-kindness toward yourself until you feel that you can accept it. And when you can accept *metta* toward yourself, you can extend that to others.

So the first thing is to extend feelings of love and goodwill toward yourself and to be able to just settle in it. And when you've settled on that feeling, you can extend that to a friend, someone that you know and like. That's pretty easy, maybe easier than extending it to yourself. Then, when you can do that, you extend it to someone you're indifferent to, someone you don't have any particular feeling about. Then, when you can do that, try to extend *metta* to someone that you don't like, maybe someone you really can't stand. That's what's recommended: start with what is easy and work up to the difficult ones until you can completely open yourself. It's called eliminating the barriers. Then you can do the same with compassion, and with sympathetic joy, and with equanimity. After that you can extend these meditations to everyone, everywhere.

The Brahmaviharas appear in their most elaborate form in the *Visuddhimagga*, but there are other places where the meditations are more abridged. In our daily interactions they can be practiced as an outgoing expression of zazen. I myself do not say that I love everybody unequivocally. We sit down in Buddha's zazen and absorb Buddha's teaching, then get up and wander around, expressing it as unlimited selfless love.

What About Love?

From time to time the question will be asked when we give a talk: How come we never talk about love? Usually my response is that we talk about it all the time without using the term, which has been appropriated to mean many different things. It is a term that has many levels of meaning, from selfish lust to selfless universality.

Once when I was about six, I told my grandfather that I loved bananas. He got a stern look on his face and said, "You don't love bananas! You love your mother and father." That really startled me. I thought, "Gee whiz, can't I love bananas and my parents too?" Now I realize that it is not a choice. I can love bananas as well as my parents.

Let's take a look at a few categories: tainted love, true love, and pure love.

Tainted love is usually based on self-interest, infatuation, or ignorance of the laws of karma. Loneliness, fantasy, emotional hunger, and so forth create the conditions that seem to compel us to become entangled in hopeless self-seductive relationships. When these fail it can cause terrible suffering because the relationships are usually based on self-centered satisfaction, and on seeing the other as an object rather than as who they are and recognizing what is best for them. This self-love is tainted with possessiveness and attachment and turns the wheel of karma. The extreme of self-love is narcissism, but either way it's love that's really all about me and disguised as being about the other person, the object. Selfish love, of course, is using the other person for our own satisfaction, while delusional love is just not having a clue about it. It's going off emotionally in various directions, trying to find something to satisfy our imagination and not realizing what we're doing.

Other examples of tainted love: The love that demands a reward. I love you and how come you don't love me? And then there is the love/hate duality: in order for the love to be satisfying it has to include the hate, and so we have battered women and battered men. There is the wish to be loved but no wish to love back, it is a purely selfish motive. Seductive love is the need to pull someone in and captivate them in order to satisfy our needs, which is rarely satisfactory. Then there is infatuation: to feel that this person is the only person you could ever love, and then to realize that if you go around the block you could probably find one or two more you could love. There is indiscriminate love: Anyone will do. Finicky love is finding just the right person and then realizing "nah," this is not the right person, and then the next one is the right person, and you just keep going around and around.

It's like looking for a teacher. There are people who go around looking for a teacher whom they practice with for a while and they always find something wrong with this person. So then they go to the next teacher—no, there's something wrong with that one. They never settle, not realizing that it's not so much about the teacher. It's the same way with a partner. Since you can't adjust, this one is the wrong partner. And you just go from partner to partner, and it's never satisfying, because it's all about you.

Most of us go through some part of these phases in our life at one time or another, and end up looking for a way out. We are so blessed to have found our way as students of the Dharma, but even so, the strong karma of this kind of need is not so easy to let go of once we are seduced by our own cravings.

True love, as I call it, is usually associated with our positive feelings toward another person. Fortunate are those who are mutually attuned to each other in this way. Faithfulness and trust are the foundations of this kind of exclusive relationship, which is usually associated with marriage. This also applies to family intimacy, as well as to a loyalty to certain friends, lovers, and associates. These emotional and instinctive aspects of love can light up our world and extend to everyone around us. Although loyal and faithful, true love can be subject to conditions, such as attachments and the inability to let go, which can affect or destroy it through possessiveness.

Pure love is universal and unconditional, not clouded by self-interest or self-seeking. It is the pure joy of offering without expecting something. The satisfaction is in the giving without attachment to receiving. It is beyond picking and choosing, beyond likes and dislikes, beyond good feelings or bad feelings. Pure love is a foundation for pure self-expression. It is deep, like an underground stream that flows continuously and does not depend on circumstances. It is beyond attachment to me and mine.

There are many kinds of love, three of which I've mentioned:

tainted or selfish love; true or emotional and instinctive love, which can be both selfless and selfish; and pure or conscious selfless love. Mostly, we are driven by instinctive love and emotional love. So when we talk about love, that's what comes to mind.

Another, higher form of love, of course, is renunciation. In this kind of love, in which you are always giving, there is even less self. You are included, but you don't stand out in some selfish way. To realize our interconnectedness, our emptiness, is the best gift that we have. It's called *dana*. Giving up is also giving away, or helping people all the time, because the less we have the more we have and the more we can see. The wisest people are those who don't possess much. Poor people can see the state of things pretty easily. But it is intentional letting go which purifies the sage or which makes the sage complete and happy.

The highest form of love is *sunya*, or emptiness. There are several designations for *sunya*. Sometimes it's called vastness. So, what is emptiness? What is the meaning of emptiness? Nobody knows; it's empty of personal reference. There are twenty designations for the meaning of emptiness in the Dharma, ending with emptiness of emptiness. But the emptiness we are concerned with in practice as emptiness is the interdependence of all things. Emptiness here means interdependence, and the highest form of love is interdependence—realizing that everything belongs to everything, so there is no special thing. That's emptiness. Everything is part of everything else and everything is always changing and moving on in different forms. We're all forming and reforming and becoming each other, and becoming stones and sky and birds and plants. To be born as a human is very rare. In my view, love is what holds it all together. It's much deeper than me or you personally. It's impersonal and personal at the same time. The highest form of love is both personal and impersonal.

Gratitude

WHAT COMES TO MIND WHEN I REFLECT ON THE PAST FIFTY years of practice at the Berkeley Zen Center is deep gratitude. First and foremost for my late teacher, Shunryu Suzuki Roshi. His gentle but firm and nourishing example encouraged us, his disciples, to go beyond what we thought were our limitations. He once said to us, "I have nothing to offer you but my Zen spirit." He always taught by example. He had thoroughly digested the essence of Dogen's teaching and could express it in his own authentic way to make it accessible to our generation.

He was totally grounded in the Way. What he taught was self-lessness, not acting from our ego. Integrity, truthfulness, no arrogance, *shikantaza* (just doing), meeting each person right where they are with full attention. The world stops here before going on. Continuing to live our lives one moment at a time. He taught us the nature of determination and steadfastness: sit still and don't give up. And the nature of compassion: if you need to change your position, you can do so without judgment. When we can accept ourselves just as we are, both good and bad, it makes it possible to identify with others and support them. One time I told Suzuki Roshi how bad I was, and he said that was good, otherwise it would be harder to know how to help others.

He taught us what he knew: the Japanese style. His intention was not to turn us into Japanese people, but to offer what he felt was the highest virtue of his culture. He didn't have to tell us what it was. We could practice and find out for ourselves! He loved his American students because of our open-mindedness and willingness to adventure wholeheartedly into a totally foreign world. One of our virtues as Americans is our openness to accept the best that other cultures have to offer. That is what makes America great, again and again. Suzuki was not attached to Buddhism or the Soto school. That does not mean that he rejected it. His teaching of nonattachment was not based on rejection but on great respect for things in a world of constant transformation: to show respect for things and cling to nothing.

I also wish to express my gratitude to the Japanese priests who were drawn to Suzuki Roshi and our practice. Katagiri Roshi, who came in 1963, the year before me, together with Suzuki Roshi modeled the practice. Then came Kobun Chino Roshi, the "mystic," and then Yoshimura Sensei, the "friend." Then when Suzuki was too ill to come to Tassajara in 1970, Tatsugami Roshi was invited to lead and develop the monastic style, and I was the *shuso* (head monk) for the practice period.

When we opened the zendo on Dwight Way in Berkeley on February 1, 1967, I thought of our practice as a grassroots endeavor, served and maintained by the members. We had morning and evening zazen based on the San Francisco Zen Center model. Our first major work project was to refinish the splintery floor of our large, square attic to make a zendo.

When we moved to Russell Street twelve years later, the real work began. What is now the Berkeley Zen Center was two apartments set side by side, which we completely remodeled and rebuilt with the effort by both sangha members and carpenters. We raised the two-story house next to the zendo and built the ground floor under it (where my office now is). To me it felt a bit like a community barn-raising on a grand scale.

When I look back at all the dedicated work and contributions of our members that went into this entire building project over a two-year period, I am totally overwhelmed with gratitude. I doubt that we could do something like this today. All the conditions were in alignment, including my own naivete that we could do such a thing.

Last but not least, I wish to extend my gratitude to all of you who have passed through this Buddha hall and contributed time, effort, and financial support. And to everyone who has ever been a donor, a board member, a cook, a gardener, a resident, a president, a treasurer, a librarian, a coordinator, *tenzo*, dishwasher, bathroom cleaner, office manager, work leader, *sesshin* director, member of a committee, or general laborer. There is so much more that could be said, but for now please know that I honor and respect all that you do, have done, and hopefully will do to keep it all together and to continue.

Acknowledgments

SEVERAL KEY PEOPLE HAVE BEEN ENGAGED IN THE PROCESS of this book, before and after Sojun's death. For years Sojun was encouraged to write by Jack Shoemaker of Counterpoint Press. Jack's wisdom has guided this project from the beginning. Also at Counterpoint, Yukiko Tominaga, Laura Berry, Lexi Earle, Katherine Kiger, and Colin Legerton shepherded the book to print. Ron Nestor, a BZC student since 1972, was asked by Sojun to work with others, weaving the various threads together into one coherent fabric. His careful and consistent work has kept this project on track. Ron and Kika Susan Hellein (Sojun's last priest ordinee) worked closely with Sojun during the last year of his life. Together they read and edited the memoir section and dozens of lectures. When Kika left Berkeley for Tassajara early in 2021, Ron joined with Raghav Bandla, another of Sojun's lay students, to continue the editorial work and organize the lectures. I worked closely with Ron, shaping the final manuscript. Ken Knabb did his customary thorough and perceptive copy editing. Poet and Zen teacher Norman Fischer, a key resident in BZC's formative years on Dwight Way and a dharma heir of Sojun Roshi, has contributed an eloquent foreword.

Liz Horowitz, Sojun's wife, has been a perceptive reader and an earlier editor of the memoir section. Norman Fischer, Susan Moon, and Laurie Senauke were readers and advisors as the manuscript took shape. Ryushin Andrea Thach was instrumental in selecting the lectures. Other BZC members involved in selecting, transcribing, and editing include Ben Clausen, Troy DuFrene, Susan Marvin, Carol Paul, Bob Rosenbaum, Genpo Alex Senauke, Karen Sundheim, and Ellen Webb. It does take a village to accomplish such labors of love.

—HOZAN ALAN SENAUKE
Abbot, Berkeley Zen Center
April 2023

SOJUN MEL WEITSMAN grew up in Southern California. He became one of the first Americans to train with Shunryu Suzuki Roshi. In 1967, he founded a zendo in Berkeley, which, under Suzuki Roshi's guidance, became Berkeley Zen Center. As abbot of Berkeley Zen Center, he practiced and taught there for fifty-five years. Sojun died at home in January 2021, leaving more than thirty dharma heirs and hundreds of devoted students.